REDISCOVERING
GOD'S LOVE

To   Melisse

Matt 20:28
John 13:12-17

Love

Steve Stellhorn

Steve Stellhorn

ISBN 978-1-63630-326-0 (Paperback)
ISBN 978-1-63630-327-7 (Digital)

Covenant Books, Inc.
11661 Hwy 707
Murrells Inlet, SC 29576
www.covenantbooks.com

CONTENTS

Where to Start? 5
Who Is God? 8
Man's Fall 22
Cain and Abel 46
The Father of Faith 58
On the Scale of Love 86
Saul 98
King David 109
Jesus 190
Problems in the Church 229
Where Is Unity in the Bible? 244
Are We Stopping God? 251
Our Responsibility 264
Relationship Not Religion 280
Holy Spirit 284
Love Is the Answer 295

WHERE TO START?

I am not trying to reinvent the wheel. Actually, I am not coming up with anything new at all. Ecclesiastes 1:9 (NIV) says, "What has been will be again, what has been done will be done again; there is nothing new under the sun." So what I share here, I believe, is something that is old—very old, as old as the beginning of mankind. I believe that it is something that everyone knew, especially in the early centuries of the church, but got lost somehow in the growth of the church, most likely over the past two centuries. It is lost the same way that salvation by grace and not by works got lost before Martin Luther rediscovered it.

In order to be able to understand what it is that I am about to explain, the first thing that is going to have to happen is that the glasses that you have been studying the Bible through are going to have to be removed so that you can view this with an open mind.

Most people are going to say, "I don't have any glasses on. I only look at what the word says at face value." But is it possible that the way you were taught the Bible, you have always studied by, and therefore the reason that you understand it the way that you do is because of the glasses that you had on while you were being taught?

If you were a child and someone had put a set of rose-colored glasses on you and they never allowed you to take them off so that all your learning of the world is done while you looked through those glasses, then when you were taught what colors looked like, you would think that white was actually a pinkish color. If one day, someone would take the glasses off you and ask you to point to the color white, you would point to the pink color and declare it as being white. Why? Because the whole time you were learning colors, that was the way white looked to you.

Would you still be wrong when you claimed that the pink color was white? Absolutely, because it was established a long time ago what the color of white looked like. And it has no bearing on the way that you were taught or your understanding of what the color of white looks like.

So then you are going to have to take off the glasses that you have been studying the Bible through to understand where this is all coming from. You will have to come to this with an open mind and set aside the paradigm that you have been studying through to understand what was revealed to me. If in doing so you cannot see what it is that I will be showing you to be correct, then you can always put the glasses back on and continue in the direction that you are already going.

But that would leave me with the question, is the church really growing into the church that is spoken about in the Bible? If not, maybe it is because someone gave it a pair of glasses that distorted the truth so long ago that it is assumed everything to be true when it isn't. I am not saying that everything is a lie either. What if it just got distorted, the same way that the color of white gets distorted when you have on the rose-colored glasses? Isn't this what was happening before the Reformation started by Martin Luther?

The best way for us to begin would be to start at the very beginning. That is, we need to create a foundation to build on so that the information has something solid to support it. Everything that comes after the foundation is supported by the foundation. Get the foundation wrong, the rest of the information will be off also.

If I decided to build a house, and I want it to be rectangular in shape, let's say thirty feet by sixty feet. And I started my first corner, and it is out of square, let's say by one degree. So instead of a ninety-degree corner, I have an eighty-nine-degree corner. You know that at the other end of the sixty=foot wall, it will be many inches if not feet off where the corner should be. So now, the other three corners are going to have to be made out of square in order for all the walls to be connected together.

Now, can the house still be built to look like it is supposed to? Sure, it will still have four straight walls, and to the naked eye, you may not see that it is out of square, but the rest of the house—interior walls, cabinets, flooring, etc.—will have to be built by compensating for the fact that the whole house is out of square. Yet the house will be complete, and unless you helped to build it or you got out your tape measure, you would never know that it was out of square. It just looked like a nicely built house.

That is what I believe happened to the church. It somehow got its foundation slightly out of square and has been teaching its theology based on a slightly out-of-square foundation.

Now Christ is still the cornerstone, so let's not scream heresy just yet. But even if you do not place the cornerstone facing in the right direction, then the other corners will not be at the exact place that you are trying to build the building. It will be turned one direction or the other.

With all that said, let us start to build the foundation.

WHO IS GOD?

Twice John defines the description of God in verses 8 and 16 of chapter 4 of the book of 1 John. There he says that God is love. Now that to me explains it. I accept the Bible as the word of God and wouldn't have to go any further. But there is another way of looking at it also.

That would be to look at the way God operates to see if he operates out of the spirit of love. Now there is something that has to be considered before it can be determined whether or not he is love or not.

First is that the definition of love may have been skewed by our interpretations of what love should be and what love what really is. When it is said that God is love, then it would have the meaning behind it that he is the definition or has the nature of perfect love. So he himself would define what love really is.

Where it could get murky is not understanding that yes, God is perfect love, but he is also a just God, and his justice is also perfect. That said, when he serves his perfect justice, it could be interpreted as an unlovable act of God. This lack of understanding that God is both love and his love creates perfect justice could make it hard to see the forest through the trees. Later we will explain how one is of the other.

And the next question would have to be, how does God love? Both questions can be studied together.

When God operates among his people, you will be able to see that his love is portrayed in a direction of going out from him or as something that is given toward others. It is never directed toward himself; it is always directed outwardly. So simply stated, God's perfect love is a love that is given outwardly toward others.

John gave us an example on how God loves in his Gospel of John 3:16, "For God so loved the world that he gave his one and only Son, that whoever believes in him shall not perish but have eternal life." And then again in 1 John 3:16, "This is how we know what love is: Jesus Christ laid down his life for us." Since I mentioned Christ, let's look at his example.

If in your mind there is a question of "Is Jesus God?" then this is not the material that you should be reading. I am not going to debate this when there are numerous quality books to read that can explain whether Jesus is God or not. This should be determined in your mind before going any further. There are three persons of the Godhead, and he is God the son. So looking at what Jesus did or taught should also give us an indication of who God the Father is. Jesus stated in John 14:7–11,

> "If you really know me, you will know my Father as well. From now on, you do know him and have seen him." Philip said, "Lord, show us the Father and that will be enough for us." Jesus answered: "Don't you know me, Philip, even after I have been among you such a long time? Anyone who has seen me has seen the Father. How can you say, 'Show us the Father?' Don't you believe that I am in the Father, and that the Father is in me? The words I say to you I do not speak on my own authority. Rather, it is the Father, living in me, who is doing his work. Believe me when I say that I am in the Father and the Father is in me; or at least believe on the evidence of the works themselves."

So accepting that Jesus is the Son of God, we then read his statement in Mark 10:45 and Matthew 20:28, which says, "Just as the Son of Man did not come to be served, but to serve, and to give his life as a ransom for many." His whole purpose of coming to this earth was to serve or give to others, not to have others serve him. Therefore, everything that he did, he did in a way that was not self-serving.

He was born as a man, but when he came into this world, he did it in the most humble way. He actually was born in a stable, and his bed was a feed trough or manger as they called it. He didn't even give himself a hotel room. Now I realize that this is in fulfillment of prophecy, but wouldn't it have been just as prophetic to have it say that he will be born on the corner of main and donkey trail in a hotel with the red roof called the Red Roof Inn Room 777?

After he started his ministry, he had no place to call home. Matthew 8:20 states, "Jesus replied, 'Foxes have dens and birds have nests, but the Son of Man has no place to lay his head.'" Wouldn't you at least have a semi-nice house? He owns the cattle on a thousand hills or, in other words, everything is his.

When riding into Jerusalem, he could have ridden on a horse, like a king should have. Instead he rode on a colt of a donkey. Wouldn't it have been just as prophetic to have it say that he will ride on a horse of a certain color with a particular marking?

But the thing that seems to stand out to me more than anything is the fact that when Jesus did get angry; it was never for the things that the world did to him. It was for things like the Pharisees for their hypocrisies and the hardness of their heart or the money changers for turning his father's house into a den of thieves. Yet when he was being brutally beaten and accused, he didn't retaliate, he didn't even open his mouth, especially knowing what he could have done. He says in Matthew 26:53, "Do you think I cannot call on my Father, and he will at once put at my disposal more than twelve legions of angels?" He had the ability to defend himself, yet he chose not to.

Think about it. Jesus knows everything, period—all the lies, all the issues behind the lies, where this whole thing is headed, absolutely everything. Wouldn't you have wanted to have at least justified yourself before them in a way that after it was over, it would have been so obvious that they were in the wrong? I mean, come on, at the very minimum, wouldn't you have wanted to play major mind games with them or something to get back at them? But the most he did was to give them the truth and then take their abuse and then in the end ask for the guilty parties' forgiveness.

In the earlier New International Version of the Bible, there is a statement that I think explains the last night of Jesus's life up to the moment of the cross. It is John 13:1 (emphasis added), "It was just before the Passover Feast. Jesus knew that the time had come for him to leave this world and go to the Father. Having loved his own who were in the world, *he now showed them the full extent of his love.*"

I think that from the eve of the last Passover supper to the ascension into heaven, he was showing them the full extent of his love. I'll explain what I mean.

Starting at the Passover supper in John 13:2–17:

> The evening meal was in progress, and the devil had already prompted Judas, the son of Simon Iscariot, to betray Jesus. Jesus knew that the Father had put all things under his power, and that he had come from God and was returning to God; so he got up from the meal, took off his outer clothing, and wrapped a towel around his waist. After that, he poured water into a basin and began to wash his disciples' feet, drying them with the towel that was wrapped around him.
>
> He came to Simon Peter, who said to him, "Lord, are you going to wash my feet?"
>
> Jesus replied, "You do not realize now what I am doing, but later you will understand."
>
> "No," said Peter, "you shall never wash my feet."
>
> Jesus answered, "Unless I wash you, you have no part with me."
>
> "Then, Lord," Simon Peter replied, "not just my feet but my hands and my head as well!"
>
> Jesus answered, "Those who have had a bath need only to wash their feet; their whole body is clean. And you are clean, though not every one of you." [11] For he knew who was going to betray him, and that was why he said not everyone was clean.

11

When he had finished washing their feet, he put on his clothes and returned to his place. "Do you understand what I have done for you?" he asked them. "You call me 'Teacher' and 'Lord,' and rightly so, for that is what I am. Now that I, your Lord and Teacher, have washed your feet, you also should wash one another's feet. I have set you an example that you should do as I have done for you. Very truly I tell you, no servant is greater than his master, nor is a messenger greater than the one who sent him. Now that you know these things, you will be blessed if you do them.

Look at what Matthew Henry (1662–1714), an English commentator on the Bible and Presbyterian minister, who published his *Complete Commentary* in 1706, had this to say about this verse:

Christ washed his disciples' feet that he might give an instance of his own wonderful humility, and show how lowly and condescending he was, and let all the world know how low he could stoop in love to his own. This is intimated, John 13:3–5. Jesus knowing, and now actually considering, and perhaps discoursing of, his honours as Mediator, and telling his friends that the Father had given all things into his hand, rises from supper and, to the great surprise of the company, who wondered what he was going to do, washed his disciples' feet.

1. Here is the rightful advancement of the Lord Jesus. Glorious things are here said of Christ as Mediator.

(1.) The Father had given all things into his hands; had given him a propriety in all, and a power over all, as possessor of heaven and earth, in pursuance of the great designs of his undertaking; see Matt. 11:27. The accommodation and arbitration of all matters in variance between God and man were committed into his hands as the great umpire and referee; and the administration of the kingdom of God among men, in all the branches of it, was committed to him; so that all acts, both of government and judgment, were to pass through his hands; he is heir of all things.

(2.) He came from God. This implies that he was in the beginning with God, and had a being and glory, not only before he was born into this world, but before the world itself was born; and that when he came into the world he came as God's ambassador, with a commission from him. He came from God as the son of God, and the sent of God. The Old-Testament prophets were raised up and employed for God, but Christ came directly from him.

(3.) He went to God, to be glorified with him with the same glory which he had with God from eternity. That which comes from God shall go to God; those that are born from heaven are bound for heaven. As Christ came from God to be an agent for him on earth, so he went to God to be an agent for us in heaven; and it is a comfort to us to think how welcome he was there: he was brought near to the Ancient of days, Dan. 7:13. And it was said to him, Sit thou at my right hand, Ps. 110:1.

(4.) He knew all this; was not like a prince in the cradle, that knows nothing of the honour he is born to, or like Moses, who wist not that his face shone; no, he had a full view of all the honours of his exalted state, and yet stooped thus low. But how does this come in here?

[1.] As an inducement to him now quickly to leave what lessons and legacies he had to leave to his disciples, because his hour was now come when he must take his leave of them, and be exalted above that familiar converse which he now had with them, John 13:1.

[2.] It may come in as that which supported him under his sufferings, and carried him cheerfully through this sharp encounter. Judas was now betraying him, and he knew it, and knew what would be the consequence of it; yet, knowing also that he came from God and went to God, he did not draw back, but went on cheerfully.

[3.] It seems to come in as a foil to his condescension, to make it the more admirable. The reasons of divine grace are sometimes represented in scripture as strange and surprising (as Isa. 57:17, 18; Hos. 2:13, 14); so here, that is given as an inducement to Christ to stoop which should rather have been a reason for his taking state; for God's thoughts are not as ours. Compare with this those passages which preface the most signal instances of condescending grace with the displays of divine glory, as Ps. 68:4, 5; Isa. 57:15; 66:1, 2.

2. Here is the voluntary abasement of our Lord Jesus notwithstanding this. Jesus knowing his own glory as God, and his own authority and power as Mediator, one would think it should follow, He rises from supper, lays aside his ordinary garments, calls for robes, bids them keep their distance, and do him homage; but no, quite the contrary, when he considered this he gave the greatest instance of humility. Note, a well-grounded assur-

ance of heaven and happiness, instead of puffing a man up with pride, will make and keep him very humble. Those that would be found conformable to Christ, and partakers of his Spirit, must study to keep their minds low in the midst of the greatest advancements. Now that which Christ humbled himself to was to wash his disciples' feet.

(1.) The action itself was mean and servile, and that which servants of the lowest rank were employed in. Let thine handmaid (saith Abigail) be a servant to wash the feet of the servants of my lord; let me be in the meanest employment, 1 Sam. 25:41. If he had washed their hands or faces, it had been great condescension (Elisha poured water on the hands of Elijah, 2 Kgs. 3:11); but for Christ to stoop to such a piece of drudgery as this may well excite our admiration. Thus he would teach us to think nothing below us wherein we may be serviceable to God's glory and the good of our brethren.

(2.) The condescension was so much the greater that he did this for his own disciples, who in themselves were of a low and despicable condition, not curious about their bodies; their feet, it is likely, were seldom washed, and therefore very dirty. In relation to him, they were his scholars, his servants, and such as should have washed his feet, whose dependence was upon him, and their expectations from him. Many of great spirits otherwise will do a mean thing to curry favour with their superiors; they rise by stooping, and climb by cringing; but for Christ to do this to his disciples could be no act of policy nor complaisance, but pure humility.

(3.) He rose from supper to do it. Though we translate it (John 13:2) supper being ended, it might be better read, there being a supper made, or he being at supper, for he sat down again (John 13:12), and we find him dipping a sop (John 13:26), so that he did it in the midst of his meal, and thereby taught us,

[1.] Not to reckon it a disturbance, nor any just cause of uneasiness, to be called from our meal to do God or our brother any real service, esteeming the discharge of our duty more than our necessary food, John 4:34. Christ would not leave his preaching to oblige his nearest relations (Mark 3:33), but would leave his supper to show his love to his disciples.

[2.] Not to be over nice about our meat. It would have turned many a squeamish stomach to wash dirty feet at supper-time; but Christ did it, not that we might learn to be rude and slovenly (cleanliness and godliness will do well together), but to teach us not to be curious, not to indulge, but mortify, the delicacy of the appetite, giving good manners their due place, and no more.

(4.) He put himself into the garb of a servant, to do it: he laid aside his loose and upper garments, that he might apply himself to this service the more expedite. We must address ourselves to duty as those that are resolved not to take state, but to take pains; we must divest ourselves of everything that would either feed our pride or hang in our way and hinder us in what we have to do, must gird up the loins of our mind, as those that in earnest buckle to business.

(5.) He did it with all the humble ceremony that could be, went through all the parts of the service distinctly, and passed by none of them; he did it as if he had been used thus to serve; did it himself alone, and had none to minister to him in it. He girded himself with the towel, as servants throw a napkin on their arm, or put an apron before them; he poured water into the basin out of the water-pots that stood by (John 2:6), and then washed their feet; and, to complete the service, wiped them. Some think that he did not wash the feet of them all, but only four or five of them, that being thought sufficient to answer the end; but I see nothing to countenance this conjecture, for in other places where he did make a difference it is taken notice of; and his washing the feet of them all, without exception, teaches us a catholic and extensive charity to all Christ's disciples, even the least.

(6.) Nothing appears to the contrary but that he washed the feet of Judas among the rest, for he was present, John 13:26. It is the character of a widow indeed that she had washed the saints' feet (1 Tim. 5:10), and there is some comfort in this; but the blessed Jesus here washed the feet of a sinner, the worst of sinners, the worst to him, who was at this time contriving to betray him.

Many interpreters consider Christ's washing his disciples' feet as a representation of his whole undertaking. He knew that he was equal with God and all things were his, yet he rose from his table in glory, laid aside his robes of light, girded himself with our nature, took upon him the form of a servant, came not to be ministered to but to minister, poured out his blood, poured out his soul unto death, and thereby prepared a laver to wash us from our sins (Revelation 1:5).

So in short, this is not to be taken lightly. In the days of Jesus, the lowest slave or servant of the household was the one who washed the feet of those who entered the house. This was a most menial task of the servants. So when the master or teacher, which is of the highest regard, is to wash your feet, then it is a lesson of the utmost importance. Why else would Peter not want Jesus to wash his feet? He was like "No way, you are the teacher, the king, the Christ. You will never stoop so low as to wash my feet." But when Jesus told him that he had to in order for him to be a part of Jesus, then he was like, "Well then, wash all of me." It wasn't the washing of the feet that was the important part, it was the point of being served by the master. Why? Because the love of God is a love that is of giving or going out toward others.

The next thing is the way that he gave up his life. Remember, no one took it from him; he gave it up. Look at what he said in John 10:11, "I am the good shepherd. The good shepherd lays down his life for the sheep." Again in John 10:15, "Just as the Father knows me and I know the Father—and I lay down my life for the sheep." And again in John 10:17, "The reason my Father loves me is that I lay down my life—only to take it up again."

But the thing that stands out to me is the way he chose to lay down his life. In the past when there was a sacrifice that was offered, nowhere did it say in the laws that the offered animal or lamb was to die a death as cruel as possible. It was just the opposite. The death happened as quick as possible and then the sprinkling of blood on the altar.

So then wouldn't it have been just as sacrificial of a death if Jesus would have died by the sword or any other death that would had been quick and less painless? Yet he chose to lay down his life in the most cruel manner that has been ever invented since the existence of man. There has not been found a more cruel way to be executed. Wouldn't it seem that if I am going to choose to lay down my life, when I did nothing to deserve it, I would choose the easiest way possible to carry it out? The wages of sin is death, but it didn't specify that it had to be a death by the cruelest manner possible.

Yet that is only half the point. He didn't only die on the cross, which by itself was cruel enough. First, he was flogged, which, by what I understand, was so bad in itself that many people didn't live through the flogging. So all that had to happen was for Jesus to have been flogged a little longer, and he would have been just as dead, and it would have been for the sin of the world. And it would have also been a horrible way to die.

Instead he not only gets flogged, which was cruel all by itself, but he dies in the cruelest manner possible. Why? I believe that the purpose of this was that there is no way that you or I or anyone else for that matter could say that in any way, when Jesus died for us, he was self-serving in the process.

Think about it. Who, on this earth, would think to use the most horrible way to die possible when the penalty is just death? Wouldn't we think, isn't my life enough?

Something else to observe is that after Jesus dies this horrible death and he has now resurrected from the dead and has proven to the apostles that he is the Christ, then comes this story:

> Afterward Jesus appeared again to his disciples, by the Sea of Galilee. It happened this way: Simon Peter, Thomas (also known as Didymus), Nathanael from Cana in Galilee, the sons of Zebedee, and two other disciples were together. "I'm going out to fish," Simon Peter told them, and they said, "We'll go with you." So they went out and got into the boat, but that night they caught nothing.
>
> Early in the morning, Jesus stood on the shore, but the disciples did not realize that it was Jesus.
>
> He called out to them, "Friends, haven't you any fish?"
>
> "No," they answered.
>
> He said, "Throw your net on the right side of the boat and you will find some." When they

did, they were unable to haul the net in because of the large number of fish.

Then the disciple whom Jesus loved said to Peter, "It is the Lord!" As soon as Simon Peter heard him say, "It is the Lord," he wrapped his outer garment around him (for he had taken it off) and jumped into the water. The other disciples followed in the boat, towing the net full of fish, for they were not far from shore, about a hundred yards. When they landed, they saw a fire of burning coals there with fish on it, and some bread.

Jesus said to them, "Bring some of the fish you have just caught." So Simon Peter climbed back into the boat and dragged the net ashore. It was full of large fish, 153, but even with so many the net was not torn. Jesus said to them, "Come and have breakfast." None of the disciples dared ask him, "Who are you?" They knew it was the Lord. Jesus came, took the bread and gave it to them, and did the same with the fish. This was now the third time Jesus appeared to his disciples after he was raised from the dead. (John 21:1–14)

Think about it. After all Jesus has went through, he has done more than anyone possibly could. He appeared to them, and what did he do? He cooked them breakfast! I am sure that cooking for him was not as cumbersome as it is for us. What did he do? Say "Fish, come here" and they jumped into the skillet? I mean every April 15, I am wondering how I can pay my taxes like Jesus did by going fishing, better yet by sending someone else to fish for you. But my point is, wouldn't just showing up have been more than enough for the apostles? It would have been for me, but instead, he also cooked them breakfast.

Now I hear people say that God is generous or that he is a giving God. Like one of the characteristics of God is that he is loving, another is that he is giving or generous. I think that the two are one and the same. I believe the definition of God is love, and his love is characterized by his giving.

Look at the definition of love in 1 Corinthians 13:4–7,

> Love is patient, love is kind. It does not envy, it does not boast, it is not proud. It does not dishonor others, it is not self-seeking, it is not easily angered, it keeps no record of wrongs. Love does not delight in evil but rejoices with the truth. It always protects, always trusts, always hopes, always perseveres.

Isn't godly love in the Bible always described as something that we do toward others? Why? Because the definition of God's love is a love that goes outward; that is, a love for the benefit of others.

MAN'S FALL

So God is love, and from studying the Scriptures, we know that God is one essence that is made up of three different beings. There is the Father, the Son, and the Holy Spirit that make up the one God. And since the love of God is directed outward, then there has to be a love relationship between all of them. I say this because of what Jesus tells us in John 17:24, "Father, I want those you have given me to be with me where I am, and to see my glory, the glory you have given me because you loved me before the creation of the world."

Now there is no real way of knowing how this came about, but it would seem that it is possible that God decided that it would be a good idea to be able to create other beings that they would be able to give this love too outside of the Trinity, and so they created the heavens and everything in it, including all the angels. And then he created the universe, which included the planet Earth. On the planet Earth, he created all the living things.

What we do have is a record of a conversation between them, which went as follows. Genesis 1:26, "Then God said, 'Let us make mankind in our image, in our likeness, so that they may rule over the fish in the sea and the birds in the sky, over the livestock and all the wild animals, and over all the creatures that move along the ground.'"

And that was what he did.

> So God created mankind in his own image,
> in the image of God he created them; male and
> female he created them.
>
> God blessed them and said to them, "Be
> fruitful and increase in number; fill the earth and
> subdue it. Rule over the fish in the sea and the

birds in the sky and over every living creature that moves on the ground."

Then God said, "I give you every seed-bearing plant on the face of the whole earth and every tree that has fruit with seed in it. They will be yours for food. And to all the beasts of the earth and all the birds in the sky and all the creatures that move along the ground—everything that has the breath of life in it—I give every green plant for food." And it was so. (Genesis 1:27–30 NIV)

I realize that we have always taught that the way we are like God is that we have three parts—the mind, the body, and the spirit—and I'm not here to argue with that. But if God created man in his own image and God is love, then wouldn't it be logical that God would have created man *to be love* also?

In other versions, just like the AMP, it says in verse 1:26, "God said, 'Let Us [Father, Son, and Holy Spirit] make mankind *in Our image, after Our likeness*, and let them have complete authority over the fish of the sea, the birds of the air, the [tame] beasts, and over all of the earth, and over everything that creeps upon the earth." They are using two different words to describe that we are to be like God. The definition of these two words from Dictionary.com are *image*, "1) a representation or likeness of a person or thing, especially in sculpture; 2) a person or thing that resembles another closely; double or copy," and *likeness*, "1) the condition of being alike; similarity; 2) an imitative appearance; semblance."

I have not studied enough in Greek and Hebrew to interpret the meaning of the original words used with authority. Even if it can be seen in the translation of the word, I believe that as we go along in this study, scriptures will prove this point also.

Just think about the nature of man. Can it not be said that man is always loving something? Wouldn't it be safe to say that man is either loving himself or that he is loving others and that all actions and motives are based on man loving himself or loving someone else? Isn't all that man accomplishes or his passions, etc., driven by a love of something? And isn't the base root of that love on him, or what is his, or on others? Don't we usually describe someone by their love of God, family, money, justice, power, etc.? We describe you by what you love, whether it is for the good or the bad. I believe that was the way we were created; we were created to be love, just like God is love.

So if a man is created in the image of God and God is love and God's love goes outward or away from himself toward others, then man should be love, and his love should be directed toward others also.

So what happened? Someone or something had to change the heart of man and how he loved. This someone is known by one of his names which is Satan.

Here are two stories that are credited as the story of Satan. The first in Ezekiel and then in Isaiah.

> Son of man, take up a lamentation over the king of Tyre and say to him, "Thus says the Lord GOD,
> 'You had the seal of perfection,
> Full of wisdom and perfect in beauty.
> 'You were in Eden, the garden of God;
> Every precious stone was your covering:
> The ruby, the topaz and the diamond;
> The beryl, the onyx and the jasper;
> The lapis lazuli, the turquoise and the emerald;
> And the gold, the workmanship of your settings and sockets,
> Was in you.
> On the day that you were created
> They were prepared.
> 'You were the anointed cherub who covers,
> And I placed you there
> You were on the holy mountain of God;
> You walked in the midst of the stones of fire.
> 'You were blameless in your ways
> From the day you were created
> *Until unrighteousness was found in you.*

'By the abundance of your trade
You were internally filled with violence,
And you sinned;
Therefore I have cast you as profane
From the mountain of God.
And I have destroyed you, O covering cherub,
From the midst of the stones of fire.
'Your heart was lifted up because of you beauty;
You corrupted your wisdom by reason of your splendor
I cast you to the ground;
I put you before kings,
That they may see you.'" (Ezekiel 28:12–17 NAS) (emphasis added)
And in Isaiah:
How you have fallen from heaven,
morning star, son of the dawn!
You have been cast down to the earth,
you who once laid low the nations!
You said in your heart,
"I will ascend to the heavens;
I will raise my throne
above the stars of God;
I will sit enthroned on the mount of assembly,
on the utmost heights of Mount Zaphon.
I will ascend above the tops of the clouds;
I will make myself like the Most High."
But you are brought down to the realm of the dead,
to the depths of the pit. (Isaiah 14:12–15 NAS)

So as you can see, Satan was God's most beautiful creation. He was one of the best when it came to angels. The angels are created to worship God also. That can be seen throughout Scriptures and when the angels were worshiping the birth of Christ. But that wasn't good enough for Satan. He had to be just like God. So he decided he was going to create his own kingdom. Naturally, there is only one God, and there can be no other, so God had him thrown out of heaven. And as we all know, it was his pride, or better defined as *his love of himself,* that was the problem, which I will call sin.

So how does he get revenge? It's not like he could go back and try to wage war again to get back in. Once you get kicked out of heaven, that's it—you're kicked out of heaven, period, end of discussion.

So Satan wants revenge, and how can he get it? If I wanted to hurt someone, in this case God, but I can't touch him or the ones he loves, how could I do it? Wouldn't it hurt God the most if I was able to get the ones he loves to turn their attention or their love away from him?

How could you possibly do that? What is the easiest thing that they could love instead of God? How about if you get the ones God loves to love themselves instead, the same thing that got Satan himself thrown out of heaven. Isn't this what happened to Adam and Eve?

> Then the LORD God formed man of dust from the ground, and breathed into his nostrils the breath of life; and man became a living being.
>
> The LORD God planted a garden toward the east, in Eden; and there He placed the man whom He had formed.
>
> Out of the ground the LORD God caused to grow every tree that is pleasing to the sight and good for food; the tree of life also in the midst of the garden, and the tree of the knowledge of good and evil.
>
> Now a river flowed out of Eden to water the garden; and from there it divided and became four rivers.
>
> The name of the first is Pishon; it flows around the whole land of Havilah, where there is gold.
>
> The gold of that land is good; the bdellium and the onyx stone are there.
>
> The name of the second river is Gihon; it flows around the whole land of Cush.

The name of the third river is Tigris; it flows east of Assyria. And the fourth river is the Euphrates.

Then the LORD God took the man and put him into the garden of Eden to cultivate it and keep it.

The LORD God commanded the man, saying, "From any tree of the garden you may eat freely; but from the tree of the knowledge of good and evil you shall not eat, for in the day that you eat from it you will surely die."

Then the LORD God said, "It is not good for the man to be alone; I will make him a helper suitable for him."

Out of the ground the LORD God formed every beast of the field and every bird of the sky, and brought them to the man to see what he would call them; and whatever the man called a living creature, that was its name.

The man gave names to all the cattle, and to the birds of the sky, and to every beast of the field, but for Adam there was not found a helper suitable for him.

So the LORD God caused a deep sleep to fall upon the man, and he slept; then He took one of his ribs and closed up the flesh at that place.

The LORD God fashioned into a woman the rib which He had taken from the man, and brought her to the man.

The man said,
"This is now bone of my bones,
And flesh of my flesh;
She shall be called Woman,
Because she was taken out of Man."

> For this reason a man shall leave his father
> and his mother, and be joined to his wife; and
> they shall become one flesh.
>
> And the man and his wife were both naked
> and were not ashamed. (Genesis 2:7–25)

So God has created man and woman and has given them a garden to supply all their needs. For this argument and because we're told that they were created in God's image, then we are going to assume, if that's the case, that they only knew how to love outwardly the way that God loves.

Why would we assume this? Well, why would God create us in a way that he clearly states throughout the rest of the Bible, and especially through the teachings of Jesus, how not to love or, for that matter, live? Could God be considered just or fair if he created us to be one way and then chastises us for being that way?

But we also know that they had the ability or the choice of whether or not they would love the way God loves. God has given us all the choice of whether or not we're going to love outwardly (his way) or we're going to love ourselves, just as he gave Satan the same choice. Let's read on.

> Now the serpent was more crafty than any
> beast of the field which the LORD God had
> made. And he said to the woman, "Indeed, has
> God said, 'You shall not eat from any tree of the
> garden?'"
>
> The woman said to the serpent, "From the
> fruit of the trees of the garden we may eat; but
> from the fruit of the tree which is in the middle
> of the garden, God has said, 'You shall not eat
> from it or touch it, or you will die.'"
>
> The serpent said to the woman, "You surely
> will not die! For God knows that in the day you
> eat from it your eyes will be opened, and you will
> be like God, knowing good and evil."

When the woman saw that the tree was good for food, and that it was a delight to the eyes, and that the tree was desirable to make one wise, she took from its fruit and ate; and she gave also to her husband with her, and he ate.

Then the eyes of both of them were opened, and they knew that they were naked; and they sewed fig leaves together and made themselves loin coverings. (Genesis 3:1–7 NAS)

So now we see that they have sinned. The question I have is, was the sin the disobedience of the eating of the apple, or was the sin the decision of wanting to be like God by being self-sufficient, which boils down to the love of self (inwardly)?

I believe that we will see as we go along that the sin was the actual loving of oneself, rather than the disobedience of a law, which I will call a transgression. Whenever I hear someone talking about sinning, they're always talking in the sense of disobedience, or as in missing the mark. I believe that as we go along in this study, you will see that disobedience is not sinning but that sin actually creates disobedience. Or in other words, disobedience or transgression is a result of sin, not that disobedience is sin.

Isn't that the sinful nature? Take a small child, say the age of one or two. Place a spoon on the table and then say "mine" and watch what happens. Even though the spoon is not his, he will immediately want the spoon as if it was his. Or watch while he is playing with another child. The minute the other child starts to play with a certain toy, that same toy will be the toy that he will want even though he did not know it was there before the other child started to play with it. Isn't this what we're trying to overcome all our lives?

Take a look at what Paul is explaining in 1 Corinthians. He starts to explain about the Holy Spirit and the gifts that the Holy Spirit gives to us so that we can operate in the body of Christ. Apparently, there must've been some comparison going on between the members of the church in Corinth on which of the gifts were the most important. Members with one gift were envying members with another gift. So Paul goes into an explanation of how one part of the body is not any more important than any of the other parts of the body. Each part plays a vital part in the functioning of the body. And that one part should not envy any of the other parts. Also the parts that were considered the least important were actually of the utmost importance. And then he says at the very end of it all, "Let me show you a most excellent way."

Have you ever asked the question "Most excellent way of what?" How about serving the body of Christ through love?

Then he starts explaining that it doesn't matter what gifts you have; if you do not use it in love, then it is useless. The gifts are supposed to be used to benefit the body of Christ, which would coincide with the definition of God's love. Then he explains the definition of a love.

> Love is patient, love is kind. It does not envy, it does not boast, it is not proud. It does not dishonor others, it is not self-seeking, it is not easily angered, it keeps no record of wrongs. Love does not delight in evil but rejoices with the truth. It always protects, always trusts, always hopes, always perseveres.
>
> Love never fails. But where there are prophecies, they will cease; where there are tongues, they will be stilled; where there is knowledge, it will pass away. For we know in part and we prophesy in part, but when completeness comes, what is in part disappears. (1 Corinthians 13:4–9 NIV)

Listen to Matthew Henry's in-depth description of love he refers to as charity:

> The apostle gives us in these verses some of the properties and effects of charity, both to describe and commend it, that we may know whether we have this grace and that if we have not we may fall in love with what is so exceed-

ingly amiable, and not rest till we have obtained it. It is an excellent grace, and has a world of good properties belonging to it, as:

1. It is long-suffering—makrothymei. It can endure evil, injury, and provocation, without being filled with resentment, indignation, or revenge. It makes the mind firm, gives it power over the angry passions, and furnishes it with a persevering patience, that shall rather wait and wish for the reformation of a brother than fly out in resentment of his conduct. It will put up with many slights and neglects from the person it loves, and wait long to see the kindly effects of such patience on him.

2. It is kind—chresteuetai. It is benign, bountiful; it is courteous and obliging. The law of kindness is in her lips; her heart is large, and her hand open. She is ready to show favours and to do good. She seeks to be useful; and not only seizes on opportunities of doing good, but searches for them. This is her general character. She is patient under injuries, and apt and inclined to do all the good offices in her power. And under these two generals all the particulars of the character may be reduced.

3. Charity suppresses envy: It envieth not; it is not grieved at the good of others; neither at their gifts nor at their good qualities, their honours not their estates. If we love our neighbour we shall be so far from envying his welfare, or being displeased with it, that we shall share in it and rejoice at it. His bliss and sanctification will be an addition to ours, instead of impairing or lessening

it. This is the proper effect of kindness and benevolence: envy is the effect of ill-will. The prosperity of those to whom we wish well can never grieve us; and the mind which is bent on doing good to all can never with ill to any.

4. Charity subdues pride and vain-glory; It vaunteth not itself, is not puffed up, is not bloated with self-conceit, does not swell upon its acquisitions, nor arrogate to itself that honour, or power, or respect, which does not belong to it. It is not insolent, apt to despise others, or trample on them, or treat them with contempt and scorn. Those who are animated with a principle of true brotherly love will in honour prefer one another, Rom. 12:10. They will do nothing out of a spirit of contention or vain-glory, but in lowliness of mind will esteem others better than themselves, Phil. 2:3. True love will give us an esteem of our brethren, and raise our value for them; and this will limit our esteem of ourselves, and prevent the tumours of self-conceit and arrogance. These ill qualities can never grow out of tender affection for the brethren, nor a diffusive benevolence. The word rendered in our translation vaunteth itself bears other significations; nor is the proper meaning, as I can find, settled; but in every sense and meaning true charity stands in opposition to it. The Syriac renders it, non tumultuatur—does not raise tumults and disturbances. Charity calms the angry passions, instead of raising them. Others render it, Non perperàm et perversè agit—It does

not act insidiously with any, seek to ensnare them, nor tease them with needless importunities and addresses. It is not forward, nor stubborn and intractable, nor apt to be cross and contradictory. Some understand it of dissembling and flattery, when a fair face is put on, and fine words are said, without any regard to truth, or intention of good. Charity abhors such falsehood and flattery. Nothing is commonly more pernicious, nor more apt to cross the purposes of true love and good will.

5.   Charity is careful not to pass the bounds of decency; ouk aschemonei—it behaveth not unseemly; it does nothing indecorous, nothing that in the common account of men is base or vile. It does nothing out of place or time; but behaves towards all men as becomes their rank and ours, with reverence and respect to superiors, with kindness and condescension to inferiors, with courtesy and good-will towards all men. It is not for breaking order, confounding ranks bringing all men on a level; but for keeping up the distinction God has made between men, and acting decently in its own station, and minding its own business, without taking upon it to mend, or censure, or despise, the conduct of others. Charity will do nothing that misbecomes it.

6.   Charity is an utter enemy to selfishness: Seeketh not its own, does not inordinately desire nor seek its own praise, or honour, or profit, or pleasure. Indeed self-love, in some degree, is natural to all men, enters into their very constitution. And a reason-

able love of self is by our Saviour made the measure of our love to others, that charity which is here described, Thou shalt love thy neighbour as thyself. The apostle does not mean that charity destroys all regard to self; he does not mean that the charitable man should never challenge what is his own, but utterly neglect himself and all his interests. Charity must then root up that principle which is wrought into our nature. But charity never seeks its own to the hurt of others, or with the neglect of others. It often neglects its own for the sake of others; prefers their welfare, and satisfaction, and advantage, to its own; and it ever prefers the weal of the public, of the community, whether civil or ecclesiastical, to its private advantage. It would not advance, nor aggrandize, nor enrich, nor gratify itself, at the cost and damage of the public.

7. It tempers and restrains the passions. Ou paroxynetai—is not exasperated. It corrects a sharpness of temper, sweetens and softens the mind, so that it does not suddenly conceive, nor long continue, a vehement passion. Where the fire of love is kept in, the flames of wrath will not easily kindle, nor long keep burning. Charity will never be angry without a cause, and will endeavour to confine the passions within proper limits, that they may not exceed the measure that is just, either in degree or duration. Anger cannot rest in the bosom where love reigns. It is hard to be angry with those we love, but very easy to drop our resentments and be reconciled.

8. Charity thinks no evil. It cherishes no malice, nor gives way to revenge: so some understand it. It is not soon, nor long, angry; it is never mischievous, nor inclined to revenge; it does not suspect evil of others, ou logizetai to kakon—it does not reason out evil, charge guilt upon them by inference and innuendo, when nothing of this sort appears open. True love is not apt to be jealous and suspicious; it will hide faults that appear, and draw a veil over them, instead of hunting and raking out those that lie covered and concealed: it will never indulge suspicion without proofs, but will rather incline to darken and disbelieve evidence against the person it affects. It will hardly give into an ill opinion of another, and it will do it with regret and reluctance when the evidence cannot be resisted; hence it will never be forward to suspect ill, and reason itself into a bad opinion upon mere appearances, nor give way to suspicion without any. It will not make the worst construction of things, but put the best face that it can on circumstances that have no good appearance.

9. The matter of its joy and pleasure is here suggested: 1. Negatively: It rejoiceth not in iniquity. It takes no pleasure in doing injury or hurt to any. It thinks not evil of any, without very clear proof. It wishes ill to none, much less will it hurt or wrong any, and least of all make this matter of its delight, rejoice in doing harm and mischief. Nor will it rejoice at the faults and failings of others, and triumph over them, either out of pride or ill-will, because it will set

off its own excellences or gratify its spite.
The sins of others are rather the grief of a
charitable spirit than its sport or delight;
they will touch it to the quick, and stir all its
compassion, but give it no entertainment.
It is the very height of malice to take pleasure in the misery of a fellow-creature. And
is not falling into sin the greatest calamity
that can befal one? How inconsistent is it
with Christian charity, to rejoice at such fall!
2. Affirmatively: It rejoiceth in the truth, is
glad of the success of the gospel, commonly
called the truth, by way of emphasis, in the
New Testament; and rejoices to see men
moulded into an evangelical temper by it,
and made good. It takes no pleasure in their
sins, but is highly delighted to see them do
well, to approve themselves men of probity
and integrity. It gives it much satisfaction
to see truth and justice prevail among men,
innocency cleared, and mutual faith and
trust established, and to see piety and true
religion flourish.

10. It beareth all things, it endureth all things,
panta stegei, panta hypomenei. Some read
the first, covers all things. So the original
also signifies. Charity will cover a multi-
tude of sins, 1 Pet. 4:8. It will draw a veil
over them, as far as it can consistently with
duty. It is not for blazing nor publishing
the faults of a brother, till duty manifestly
demands it. Necessity only can extort this
from the charitable mind. Though such a
man be free to tell his brother his faults in
private, he is very unwilling to expose him
by making them public. Thus we do by our

own faults, and thus charity would teach us to do by the faults of others; not publish them to their shame and reproach, but cover them from public notice as long as we can, and be faithful to God and to others. Or, it beareth all things—will pass by and put up with injuries, without indulging anger or cherishing revenge, will be patient upon provocation, and long patient, panta hypomenei—holds firm, though it be much shocked, and borne hard upon; sustains all manner of injury and ill usage, and bears up under it, such as curses, contumacies, slanders, prison, exile, bonds, torments, and death itself, for the sake of the injurious, and of others; and perseveres in this firmness. Note, What a fortitude and firmness fervent love will give the mind! What cannot a lover endure for the beloved and for his sake! How many slights and injuries will he put up with! How many hazards will he run and how many difficulties encounter!

11. Charity believes and hopes well of others: Believeth all things; hopeth all things. Indeed charity does by no means destroy prudence, and, out of mere simplicity and silliness, believe every word, Prov. 14:15. Wisdom may dwell with love, and charity be cautious. But it is apt to believe well of all, to entertain a good opinion of them when there is no appearance to the contrary; nay, to believe well when there may be some dark appearances, if the evidence of ill be not clear. All charity is full of candour, apt to make the best of everything, and put on it the best face and appearance?

It will judge well, and believe well, as far
as it can with any reason, and will rather
stretch its faith beyond appearances for the
support of a kind opinion; but it will go
into a bad one with the upmost reluctance,
and fence against it as much as it fairly and
honestly can. And when, in spite of incli-
nation, it cannot believe well of others, it
will yet hope well, and continue to hope
as long as there is any ground for it. It will
not presently conclude a case desperate,
but wishes the amendment of the worst
of men, and is very apt to hope for what
it wishes. How well-natured and amiable
a thing is Christian charity? How lovely a
mind is that which is tinctured throughout
with such benevolence, and has it diffused
over its whole frame! Happy the man who
has this heavenly fire glowing in his heart,
flowing out of his mouth, and diffusing
its warmth over all with whom he has to
do! How lovely a thing would Christianity
appear to the world, if those who profess it
were more actuated and animated by this
divine principle, and paid a due regard to a
command on which its blessed author laid
a chief stress! A new commandment give I
to you, that you love one another, as I have
loved you, that you also love one another,
John 13:34. By this shall all men know that
you are my disciples, John 13:35. Blessed
Jesus! How few of thy professed disciples are
to be distinguished and marked out by this
characteristic!

And then it seemed like Paul switches gears. He continues in verse 11, "When I was a child, I talked like a child, I thought like a child, I reasoned like a child. When I became a man, I put the ways of childhood behind me." Isn't this what he was referring to? He was putting away his childish ways of acting, or in other words, he was setting aside his sinful nature of loving himself.

Think about it, in all the different types of sin that are listed or that we are taught are considered sin, doesn't all of them have a bases of love of self? Isn't the motive that happens before the actual occurrence based on the love of self, and the actual occurrence the result of the motive? So then sin is the motive of why we do what we're going to do (loving ourselves), and the transgression would be the actual occurrence. So if we are loving others as we were taught to do or as God does himself, would we even commit the transgression?

Look at what Jesus taught us in Matthew 5:27–28, "You have heard that it was said, 'You shall not commit adultery.' But I say that anyone who looks at a woman lustfully has already committed adultery with her in his heart." Isn't the reason why adultery is committed is the self-gratification of the two people involved, regardless of the harm that it does to others? But isn't *self-gratification* created first in the heart and acted out on later?

Yet we always hear the occurrence called sin. Or we lump transgressions, trespass, iniquity, and sin as the same thing. But it is not found that way in other passages in the Old and New Testaments.

To illustrate the point, look at these passages:

> Of David. A maskil.
> *Blessed is the one*
> *whose transgressions* [H6588] *are forgiven,*
> *whose sins* [H2403] *are covered.*
> Blessed is the one
> whose sin the LORD does not count against them
> and in whose spirit is no deceit.
> When I kept silent,
> my bones wasted away

through my groaning all day long.
For day and night
your hand was heavy on me;
my strength was sapped
as in the heat of summer.
Then I acknowledged my sin [H2403] *to you*
and did not cover up my iniquity [H5771].
I said, "*I will confess*
my transgressions [H6588] *to the LORD.*"
And you forgave
the guilt [H5771] *of my sin* [H2403]*.*
Therefore let all the faithful pray to you
while you may be found;
surely the rising of the mighty waters
will not reach them.
You are my hiding place;
you will protect me from trouble
and surround me with songs of deliverance.
I will instruct you and teach you in the way
you should go;
I will counsel you with my loving eye on you.
Do not be like the horse or the mule,
which have no understanding
but must be controlled by bit and bridle
or they will not come to you.
Many are the woes of the wicked,
but the LORD's unfailing love
surrounds the one who trusts in him.
Rejoice in the LORD and be glad, you
righteous;
sing, all you who are upright in heart! (Psalm
32:1–11) (emphasis added)
I confess my iniquity [H5771]; I am troubled by my sin [H2403]. (Psalm 38:18)
Wash away all my iniquity [H5771] and cleanse me from my sin [H2403]. (Psalm 51:2)

Hide your face from my sins [H2399] and blot out all my iniquity [H5771]. (Psalm 51:9)

You forgave the iniquity [H5771] of your people and covered all their sins [H2403]. (Psalm 85:2)

I will punish their sin [H6588] with the rod, their iniquity [H5771] with flogging; (Psalm 89:32)

May the iniquity [H5771] of his fathers be remembered before the LORD; may the sin [H2403] of his mother never be blotted out. (Psalm 109:14)

Ephraim boasts, "I am very rich; I have become wealthy. With all my wealth they will not find in me any iniquity [H5771] or sin [H2399]." (Hosea 12:8)

For I know my transgressions [H6588], and my sin [H2403] is always before me. (Psalm 51:3)

When we were overwhelmed by sins [H1697–H5771], you forgave our transgressions [H6588]. (Psalm 65:3)

But he was pierced for our transgressions [H6588], he was crushed for our iniquities [H5771]; the punishment that brought us peace was on him, and by his wounds we are healed. (Isaiah 53:5)

You who live in Lachish, harness fast horses to the chariot. You are where the sin [H2403] of Daughter Zion began, for the transgressions [H6588] of Israel were found in you. (Micah 1:13)

The law was brought in so that the trespass [G3900] might increase. But where sin [G266] increased, grace increased all the more. (Romans 5:20)

> [*Made Alive in Christ*] As for you, you were
> dead in your transgressions [G3900] and sins
> [G266]. (Ephesians 2:1)

I am not going to get into the meaning of each word because different interpreters interpreted the words differently. What I want to point out is, there are always the different words used together, which shows the writer is differentiating between different meanings. Sometimes the same English words are used for the different Hebrew and Greek words. So there has to be a difference between the three.

Let's continue with the story.

> They heard the sound of the LORD God walking in the garden in the cool of the day, and the man and his wife hid themselves from the presence of the LORD God among the trees of the garden.
>
> Then the LORD God called to the man, and said to him, "Where are you?"
>
> He said, "I heard the sound of You in the garden, and I was afraid because I was naked; so I hid myself."
>
> And He said, "Who told you that you were naked? Have you eaten from the tree of which I commanded you not to eat?"
>
> The man said, "The woman whom You gave to be with me, she gave me from the tree, and I ate."
>
> Then the LORD God said to the woman, "What is this you have done?" And the woman said, "The serpent deceived me, and I ate." (Genesis 3:8–13)

Now we have self-preservation going on or, in laymen terms, the oldest game of passing the buck. Isn't this the way that it always goes? First, we have the motive or the love of self, which we will define as sin, and then we act out on the occurrence, which I'll call the trespass, which leads to someone being injured, which is the iniquity. The combination of the occurrence and the injury will be the transgression. Because of this transgression, we feel ashamed because of our conscience or because we get caught. Even if we don't get caught, we still have to find a way to justify our actions in our minds so that it doesn't destroy us literally (the wages of sin is death). If we do get caught, then we have to find a way to shift the blame off us and onto something or someone else.

Isn't this what Adam did? Adam was loving the way he was created to love; he loved God and had a relationship with him, and he also loved Eve. But the minute he started to love himself, he throws Eve under the bus. "The woman you gave me, she gave it to me to eat. It wasn't my fault." How is this honoring or protecting her?

Isn't this what happens in today's marriages? One or both parties in the marriage forget what the vows were all about? "[Groom's name], do you take [bride's name] to be your wedded wife to live together in marriage? *Do you promise to love, comfort, honor, and keep her* for better or worse, for richer or poorer, in sickness and in health, and forsaking all others, be faithful only to her so long as you both shall live?" But then, they start focusing on themselves and what they are not getting or how they are not being fulfilled, or better yet, they start to feel like "I don't love her anymore," so they start thinking they are better off without the other or they search for a different person. Don't we agree that love is an action toward one another and rather than just a feeling? Better yet, the feeling of love is the result of the action of love. So the giving of love is the way that you will end up feeling love for that person. This would coincide with the way that God loves us and the way he designed us to live.

Look at what Jesus said about divorce in Matthew 19:3–9 (NIV):

> Some Pharisees came to him to test him. They asked, "Is it lawful for a man to divorce his wife for any and every reason?"
>
> "Haven't you read," he replied, "that at the beginning the Creator 'made them male and female,' and said, 'For this reason a man will

> leave his father and mother and be united to his
> wife, and the two will become one flesh?' So they
> are no longer two, but one flesh. Therefore what
> God has joined together, let no one separate."
>
> "Why then," they asked, "did Moses com-
> mand that a man give his wife a certificate of
> divorce and send her away?"
>
> Jesus replied, "Moses permitted you to
> divorce your wives *because your hearts were hard.*
> But it was not this way from the beginning. I tell
> you that anyone who divorces his wife, except for
> sexual immorality, and marries another woman
> commits adultery." (emphasis added)

Isn't a hard heart the condition of loving oneself? What they were doing was giving a certificate of divorce whenever they didn't feel like loving their wives anymore. Of course, their excuse was that they didn't love their wife any more, as if love is just a feeling. Or actually it was even worse than that. If the wife did something that ticked them off, like cooked the eggs wrong or they didn't like the new color of her hair, then it was time for her to go. It could have even been that a hotter model came strutting through town that had better options, so the old model had to go. Is that much different than what is going on today? Especially since now we have no fault divorce decrees. I'm not talking about those outside of the church, but those that are in the church.

Think about this. What is irreconcilable differences when you're supposed to be living in love? Isn't that a part of the definition of love? Wouldn't it be more honest to say that I refuse to love her or him? Or better yet, I'm in love with myself; therefore, I cannot love you. It is just amazing the way mankind can justify his sinful nature, just like Adam.

Another thing to consider is why did Jesus allow divorce in the matter of sexual immorality? Is this based on the consideration of trust? When a man and a woman marries, isn't he saying to her and she saying to him that I am giving you a commitment or, better yet, my word that there will be no other people in my life that I will be intimate with other than you? Yet if the love that I have is focused on me and my wants, what good is my word? Isn't that what got Adam kicked out of the garden?

There was the tree of good and evil, and then there was also a tree of life. Can you imagine God saying to Adam, "All right, guy, you blew it the first time. You see what happened when you didn't listen to me. Now I'm going to give you another chance. You can stay in the garden, but don't eat from the tree of life." What do you think would happen the first time he's seen the tree of life? Would not the devil be standing right there beside him saying something like this? "Look, Adam, who would have known that eating from the tree of good and evil would have created such a result? But think about it, do you want to die? Don't you want to live forever, just like God?" And that would be about all that it would take. Why? He can't be trusted for his word.

Isn't that what the issue is? When we're focused on loving ourselves, aren't we putting other people or even God in second place? How can you trust someone who is always concerned about their welfare without consideration of others? God had no other choice but to kick Adam and Eve out of the garden because they couldn't be trusted.

CAIN AND ABEL

Let us look at the story of Cain and Abel.

At least Adam didn't divorced Eve, and we see that they started a family. In Genesis 4:1–16 (NIV) (emphasis added), we read,

> Adam made love to his wife Eve, and she became pregnant and gave birth to Cain. She said, "With the help of the LORD I have brought forth a man." Later she gave birth to his brother Abel.
>
> Now Abel kept flocks, and Cain worked the soil. In the course of time Cain brought *some of the fruits of the soil* as an offering to the LORD. And Abel also brought an offering—*fat portions* from some of the firstborn of his flock. The LORD looked with favor on Abel and his offering, but on Cain and his offering he did not look with favor. So Cain was very angry, and his face was downcast.
>
> Then the LORD said to Cain, "Why are you angry? Why is your face downcast? If you do what is right, will you not be accepted? But if you do not do what is right, *sin is crouching at your door; it desires to have you, but you must rule over it.*"
>
> Now Cain said to his brother Abel, "Let's go out to the field." While they were in the field, Cain attacked his brother Abel and killed him.
>
> Then the LORD said to Cain, "Where is your brother Abel?"

"I don't know," he replied. "Am I my brother's keeper?"

The LORD said, "What have you done? Listen! Your brother's blood cries out to me from the ground. Now you are under a curse and driven from the ground, which opened its mouth to receive your brother's blood from your hand. When you work the ground, it will no longer yield its crops for you. You will be a restless wanderer on the earth."

Cain said to the LORD, "My punishment is more than I can bear. Today you are driving me from the land, and I will be hidden from your presence; I will be a restless wanderer on the earth, and whoever finds me will kill me."

But the LORD said to him, "Not so; anyone who kills Cain will suffer vengeance seven times over." Then the LORD put a mark on Cain so that no one who found him would kill him. So Cain went out from the LORD's presence and lived in the land of Nod, east of Eden.

So the way that this has been explained is that Cain basically tries to do things his own way. When God does not accept it, then he gets angry. Even if this explanation is true, isn't the root of his anger based on love of self? Just like the little child that doesn't get what he wants, he gets angry and throws a fit, or in the case of Cain, he kills his brother.

But what this is really showing us is the condition of both of their hearts. Abel brought fat portions to the Lord. Cain brought some of his fruits to the Lord. It appears that Abel's heart was more generous than that of Cain's. Probably indicating more thanksgiving and love toward the Lord than Cain, who was more focused on himself.

Up until this time, there is no written law that there had to be an offering of blood, even though God did offer up the life of one of his loved animals to cover up Adam and Eve. It is said that this set the precedence of having a blood offering, and that may be true. But there is another way of looking at it also. God provided a better way of covering up the two of them than they could do for themselves. No different than God offering us a superior sacrifice than we are able to offer up for ourselves. Besides, no one had ever killed an animal before, so how could they even know that it was okay to do so? The only thing that we are shown is that Adam named the animals. Animals weren't used for food until after the time of the flood. (Now you know why Noah wasn't tempted to make steaks out of the cows on board.) So whether or not the point was that Cain's came from the land or not, there was still the fact of the difference of the heart of the giver.

There's an old saying that says, "If you want to have the biggest building in the city, you can do one of two things. Build the biggest building in the city or tear the biggest building in the city down." Either way, isn't the sin in wanting to have the biggest building or needing to have the biggest building for the purpose of pride? There is nothing wrong in building the biggest building, but only if you are doing so for the right reason, as in need. But when you have to tear the other person down to build yourself up, isn't that the love of self by having to be first or the biggest or whatever it may be? Why didn't Cain just do what was right rather than have to destroy someone who is doing right? Ever hear of someone being called a brown nose or teacher's pet? Isn't it because the one that is doing the name-calling does not want to do the right thing, so instead of him doing right, he will tear down the one that is? When you get to the basic root of the problem, doesn't it go back to the love of self or self-preservation?

Do you know how to keep a crab in a bucket? Put in another crab. The minute that one crab tries to climb out, the other crab will pull it back down with him. Isn't this the way that human beings can be also? When one person is doing the right thing, this in turn shines a light on the other person that isn't. You wouldn't believe how many people tell me that they wish they could quit drinking or ask me to have just one drink when they find out that I quit more than twenty-nine years ago. It's almost like there is a level of guilt that is imposed on them when they find out that I quit. There is nothing that I impose on them; they take it upon themselves, which leads to the question, why do we need any laws? Aren't they put in place to make us obey? So then, isn't obedience still the definition of sin?

Okay, if everyone was loving outwardly, not themselves, would there be a need for a law or any laws? Wouldn't everyone be looking out for each other's welfare? There would be no need for police, armies, rulers, etc. Why? No one would be trying to take from someone else in order that they would have more. Actually, they would probably have more already, because it would be given freely by others. So wouldn't that eliminate jealousy, envy, and murder?

Jesus taught us in Matthew 22:34–40 the greatest commandments:

> Hearing that Jesus had silenced the Sadducees, the Pharisees got together. One of them, an expert in the law, tested him with this question: "Teacher, which is the greatest commandment in the Law?"
>
> Jesus replied: "'Love the Lord your God with all your heart and with all your soul and with all your mind.' This is the first and greatest commandment. And the second is like it: 'Love your neighbor as yourself.' All the Law and the Prophets hang on these two commandments."

Look at what Matthew Henry had to say:

> All the law is fulfilled in one word, and that is, love. See Rom. 13:10. All obedience begins in the affections, and nothing in religion is done right, that is not done there first. Love is the leading affection, which gives law, and gives ground, to the rest; and therefore that, as the main fort, is to be first secured and garrisoned for God. Man is a creature cut out for love; thus therefore is the law written in the heart, that it is a law of love. Love is a short and sweet word; and, if that be the fulfilling of the law, surely the yoke of the com-

mand is very easy. Love is the rest and satisfaction of the soul; if we walk in this good old way, we shall find rest.

The *love of God* is the first and great commandment of all, and the summary of all the commands of the first table. The proper act of love being complacency, good is the proper object of it. Now God, being good infinitely, originally, and eternally, is to be loved in the first place, and nothing loved beside him, but what is loved for him. *Love* is the first and great thing that God demands from us, and therefore the first and great thing that we should devote to him.

So Jesus claiming that all the laws and the prophets hang on that basis of loving God and others would be an indication that when they broke any of the laws, they were acting out of a love for self and not love for others or God. That seems to me then that sin is not the act of disobedience, but the act of loving oneself. For if disobedience is sin, how could all the law and prophets be covered by the act of loving God and your neighbor?

Look at the parable of the sheep and goats that Jesus taught us in Matthew 25:31–46:

"When the Son of Man comes in his glory, and all the angels with him, he will sit on his glorious throne. All the nations will be gathered before him, and he will separate the people one from another as a shepherd separates the sheep from the goats. He will put the sheep on his right and the goats on his left.

"Then the King will say to those on his right, 'Come, you who are blessed by my Father; take your inheritance, the kingdom prepared for you since the creation of the world. For I was hungry and you gave me something to eat, I was thirsty and you gave me something to drink, I was a stranger and you invited me in, I needed clothes and you clothed me, I was sick and you looked after me, I was in prison and you came to visit me.'

"Then the righteous will answer him, 'Lord, when did we see you hungry and feed you, or thirsty and give you something to drink? When did we see you a stranger and invite you in, or needing clothes and clothe you? When did we see you sick or in prison and go to visit you?'

"The King will reply, 'Truly I tell you, whatever you did for one of the least of these brothers and sisters of mine, you did for me.'

"Then he will say to those on his left, 'Depart from me, you who are cursed, into the eternal fire prepared for the devil and his angels. For I was hungry and you gave me nothing to eat, I was thirsty and you gave me nothing to drink, I was a stranger and you did not invite me in, I needed clothes and you did not clothe me, I was sick and in prison and you did not look after me.'

"They also will answer, 'Lord, when did we see you hungry or thirsty or a stranger or needing clothes or sick or in prison, and did not help you?'

"He will reply, 'Truly I tell you, whatever you did not do for one of the least of these, you did not do for me.'

"Then they will go away to eternal punishment, but the righteous to eternal life."

Was this an act of love, or was it being obedient? I think you could say it was both. But the question I have is, was Jesus showing us an example of being obedient or was he showing us the condition of our hearts?

Yes, we are loving God by our obedience, but isn't obedience the result of love and not the other way around? Forced obedience does not create love. For there are many situations in which people are forced to be obedient, and that forcing of obedience creates resentment against those that force it and even disobedience in the end. I believe we can use the seat belt law as an example. I still believe it should be my choice whether I will wear a seat belt or not. Forcing me to wear the seat belt doesn't make me want to love the law or the people that created the law. Even if I had an accident and the seat belt saved my life, I may love the seat belt for what it did, I may even appreciate the law that enforced me to use it, but I wouldn't love the fact that I didn't have the choice of wearing in or not.

Look at what Jesus had to say to the Pharisees in Matthew 23:1–32 (emphasis added):

> Then Jesus said to the crowds and to his disciples: "The teachers of the law and the Pharisees sit in Moses' seat. So you must be careful to do everything they tell you. But do not do what they do, for they do not practice what they preach. They tie up heavy, cumbersome loads and put them on other people's shoulders, but they themselves are not willing to lift a finger to move them.
>
> *"Everything they do is done for people to see:* They make their phylacteries wide and the tassels on their garments long; they love the place of honor at banquets and the most important seats in the synagogues; they love to be greeted with respect in the marketplaces and to be called 'Rabbi' by others.
>
> "But you are not to be called 'Rabbi,' for you have one Teacher, and you are all brothers. And do not call anyone on earth 'father,' for you have one Father, and he is in heaven. Nor are you to be called instructors, for you have one Instructor, the Messiah. The greatest among you will be your servant. For those who exalt them-

selves will be humbled, and those who humble themselves will be exalted.

"Woe to you, teachers of the law and Pharisees, you hypocrites! You shut the door of the kingdom of heaven in people's faces. You yourselves do not enter, nor will you let those enter who are trying to.

"Woe to you, teachers of the law and Pharisees, you hypocrites! You travel over land and sea to win a single convert, and when you have succeeded, you make them twice as much a child of hell as you are.

"Woe to you, blind guides! You say, 'If anyone swears by the temple, it means nothing; but anyone who swears by the gold of the temple is bound by that oath.' You blind fools! Which is greater: the gold, or the temple that makes the gold sacred? You also say, 'If anyone swears by the altar, it means nothing; but anyone who swears by the gift on the altar is bound by that oath.' You blind men! Which is greater: the gift, or the altar that makes the gift sacred? Therefore, anyone who swears by the altar swears by it and by everything on it. And anyone who swears by the temple swears by it and by the one who dwells in it. And anyone who swears by heaven swears by God's throne and by the one who sits on it.

"Woe to you, teachers of the law and Pharisees, you hypocrites! You give a tenth of your spices—mint, dill and cumin. But you have neglected the more important matters of the law—justice, mercy and faithfulness. You should have practiced the latter, without neglecting the former. You blind guides! You strain out a gnat but swallow a camel.

"Woe to you, teachers of the law and Pharisees, you hypocrites! You clean the outside of the cup and dish, but inside they are full of greed and self-indulgence. Blind Pharisee! First clean the inside of the cup and dish, and then the outside also will be clean.

"Woe to you, teachers of the law and Pharisees, you hypocrites! You are like whitewashed tombs, which look beautiful on the outside but on the inside are full of the bones of the dead and everything unclean. In the same way, on the outside you appear to people as righteous but on the inside you are full of hypocrisy and wickedness.

"Woe to you, teachers of the law and Pharisees, you hypocrites! You build tombs for the prophets and decorate the graves of the righteous. And you say, 'If we had lived in the days of our ancestors, we would not have taken part with them in shedding the blood of the prophets.' So you testify against yourselves that you are the descendants of those who murdered the prophets. Go ahead, then, and complete what your ancestors started!

Think about it, they were following the law. They had laws on top of the laws that God had given them to make sure they didn't break the laws. Jesus wasn't talking to them about breaking the law, but about their heart and not loving. He said that they cleaned the cup on the outside, but inside, they were full of greed and self-indulgence. Isn't that saying they are loving themselves. He also said that they are tithing correctly by the law, yet they are neglecting more important things like justice, mercy, and faithfulness. Isn't that a way of loving others?

Hear we see God's love in action through his justice and mercy.

The LORD said, "What have you done? Listen! Your brother's blood cries out to me from the ground. Now you are under a curse and driven from the ground, which opened its mouth to receive your brother's blood from your hand. When you work the ground, it will no longer yield its crops for you. You will be a restless wanderer on the earth."

Cain said to the LORD, "My punishment is more than I can bear. Today you are driving me from the land, and I will be hidden from your presence; I will be a restless wanderer on the earth, and whoever finds me will kill me."

But the LORD said to him, "Not so; anyone who kills Cain will suffer vengeance seven times over." Then the LORD put a mark on Cain so that no one who found him would kill him. So Cain went out from the LORD's presence and lived in the land of Nod, east of Eden. (Genesis 4:10–16 NIV)

Speaking of justice and mercy, we say that God is just and merciful or that he uses perfect justice and mercy, and this is true. But isn't his justice and mercy just another expression of his love? Also would he need to be just and merciful toward us if we were acting in love the way we were created to?

Imagine you and your family are driving home from the movies. Also driving in the opposite direction is a man going home from a birthday party. He's not an evil man; he just has been at the party all day, and because he wasn't paying attention, he had too much to drink and should never have been operating a vehicle.

You and your family are driving along having fun discussing the movie you just enjoyed, not too concerned with what's going on around you. Out of nowhere, a set of headlights are right in front of you, and the next thing you know, you're waking up in the hospital wondering what just happened. You find out that you have been in the hospital for several days and that your family was killed in a car accident, except for one of your children.

Fast-forward, you are in a court room watching the drunk driver being convicted. He is found guilty of involuntary manslaughter, and the judge is now going to sentence him. The judge claims that the just sentence for this crime is death.

Being the kindhearted person that you are, you ask the judge to approach the bench. You tell the judge you appreciate his just sentence, but you are going to appeal to the mercy of the court. You ask that his sentence be lowered to a sentence less than death.

The judge understands your concern but explains that the penalty of this is nothing less than death. But he will give you an option to spare the man's life. If you will offer your child that has survived to be put to death in his place, he can spare the man's life and set him free.

Would you do it?

I explain this situation to people when I share the gospel with them, and the answer I get is always the same: "No, absolutely not. That man deserves his punishment!" Then I explain to them that we are all the drunk driver and that God the Father is the one who gave up his son so that we could live.

As it says in John 3:16, "For God so loved the world that he gave his one and only Son, that whoever believes in him shall not perish but have eternal life."

Another thing to consider is what sin did Cain commit if sin is being disobedient? There was no law that said "Thou shall not kill." Paul tells us in Romans 5:13–14,

> To be sure, sin was in the world before the law was given, but sin is not charged against anyone's account where there is no law. Nevertheless, death reigned from the time of Adam to the time of Moses, even over those who did not sin by breaking a command, as did Adam, who is a pattern of the one to come.

Yet Cain still sinned. If sin is disobedience, and the law of "Thou shall not kill" hadn't been written yet, what law did he break?

Read Genesis 4:6–7 again:

> Then the LORD said to Cain, "Why are you angry? Why is your face downcast? If you do what is right, will you not be accepted? But if you do not do what is right, sin is crouching at your door; it desires to have you, but you must rule over it."

Let's read the last verse but replace *sin* with *self-love*.

> Then the LORD said to Cain, "Why are you angry? Why is your face downcast? If you do what is right, will you not be accepted? But if you do not do what is right, self-love is crouching at your door; it desires to have you, but you must rule over it."

It makes sense, for it was self-love that made him angry.

Since the wages of sin is death, God could have killed Cain on the spot. But instead, God gives him a just punishment and then, out of God's mercy, puts a hedge of protection around him to keep him safe. And then the worst thing that could ever happen to anyone happened: he left the Lord's presence.

THE FATHER OF FAITH

There was another man that God spoke to on a regular basis. Though he was not perfect, I believe for the most part he had the right heart. I believe this can be proven in several ways.

Consider the story of Abram. A brief summary of what happened is, Lot's father died, and when Abram, later to be known as Abraham, was told to leave his country, he took Lot, his nephew, with him. The Lord was greatly blessing them, and they both prospered.

> So Abram went up from Egypt to the Negev, with his wife and everything he had, and Lot went with him. Abram had become very wealthy in livestock and in silver and gold.
>
> From the Negev he went from place to place until he came to Bethel, to the place between Bethel and Ai where his tent had been earlier and where he had first built an altar. There Abram called on the name of the LORD.
>
> Now Lot, who was moving about with Abram, also had flocks and herds and tents. But the land could not support them while they stayed together, for their possessions were so great that they were not able to stay together. And quarreling arose between Abram's herders and Lot's. The Canaanites and Perizzites were also living in the land at that time.
>
> So Abram said to Lot, "Let's not have any quarreling between you and me, or between your herders and mine, for we are close relatives. Is not

the whole land before you? Let's part company. If you go to the left, I'll go to the right; if you go to the right, I'll go to the left."

Lot looked around and saw that the whole plain of the Jordan toward Zoar was well watered, like the garden of the LORD, like the land of Egypt. [This was before the LORD destroyed Sodom and Gomorrah.] So Lot chose for himself the whole plain of the Jordan and set out toward the east. The two men parted company: Abram lived in the land of Canaan, while Lot lived among the cities of the plain and pitched his tents near Sodom. Now the people of Sodom were wicked and were sinning greatly against the LORD.

The LORD said to Abram after Lot had parted from him, "Look around from where you are, to the north and south, to the east and west. All the land that you see I will give to you and your offspring forever. I will make your offspring like the dust of the earth, so that if anyone could count the dust, then your offspring could be counted. Go, walk through the length and breadth of the land, for I am giving it to you."

So Abram went to live near the great trees of Mamre at Hebron, where he pitched his tents. There he built an altar to the LORD. (Genesis 13:1–18)

So let's put this in perspective. Abraham, who is the uncle, brings along Lot, not only prospers himself but prospers Lot as well. Now the two of them are growing so fast that the land can't hold the two of them. And there is starting to be a ruckus between the two different herds and their workers. So they have to separate the herds somehow. Abraham has the option on what he wants to do. But what he does is give the option to Lot.

Under normal circumstances, wouldn't it seem like the normal thing that would happen would be that Abraham would decide which way he was going to go and then Lot would go the opposite direction? But instead, Abraham does just the opposite. Now that Abraham makes a loving decision, God the Father gives Abraham all the land that he can see.

Now I hear in some churches that this would be called the law of reciprocity. The purpose of giving to God is to get from God, or the reciprocating result of your giving is that God will give back. But I don't think that is what this shows. I believe what it shows is the condition of Abraham's heart and love of God. Here's what I mean.

Abraham had no indication that God would give him this land; he gave it out of the kindness of his heart. I believe too that God did the same thing. If Abraham had given the land to Lot for the purpose of getting something from God, wouldn't he have been giving it for the purpose of his personal gain and not just from the heart? I'm not feeling the love in that.

They use verse 38 in Luke 6 where Jesus says, "Give, and it will be given to you. A good measure, pressed down, shaken together and running over, will be poured into your lap. For with the measure you use, it will be measured to you." But the context that Jesus was using it in was when he was talking about judgment not everything.

What Jesus told us to do in Matthew 7 was to ask.

> Ask and it will be given to you; seek and you will find; knock and the door will be opened to you. For everyone who asks receives; the one who seeks finds; and to the one who knocks, the door will be opened.
>
> Which of you, if your son asks for bread, will give him a stone? Or if he asks for a fish, will give him a snake? If you, then, though you are evil, know how to give good gifts to your children, how much more will your Father in heaven give good gifts to those who ask him! (Matthew 7:7–11 NIV)

We are to be asking God for what we need, and he gives it to us in the way that we need it.

What if God doesn't give it to us? Then it is probably for a good reason. It could be we don't need it or shouldn't have it, which shows us his love. How you say? Think about it. You have a little boy who comes to you and asks if he can play out in the street. You know that it is a busy street and that the chances of him getting hit by a car are almost certain. Would the loving thing to do be to give him what he wants so that he can have his way, that way he feels like you love him? Or would the loving thing to do be to not give him what he wants, because you are protecting him from the dangers that he doesn't understand?

What if the child kicks and screams and tells you he hates you, etc., are you going to give in? If you do, are you loving him? If God did, would he be loving you? Doesn't this apply when you are walking past the candy aisle and your child wants a candy bar and you say no?

You may think that this is an extreme comparison, but doesn't it apply here just the same? We live in a world of instant gratification. I want it when I want it and I want it now. If you give him the candy bar when he is kicking and screaming, because you want him to feel like you love him, are you really loving him? Are you not giving in to his uncontrollable hunger of instant gratification that can never be satisfied? Therefore, he never learns how to practice self-discipline. I believe this can be shown best by looking at our current credit crisis both in the government and in our personal lives.

Isn't this what James was referring to in his letter in chapter 4, verse 3, "When you ask, you do not receive, because you ask with wrong motives, that you may spend what you get on your pleasures." Or another way of saying it is, you're in love with yourself, and what you are asking for is for you.

I don't believe Abraham gave to get what he wanted, or to receive from God because of his giving or expected anything other than God taking care of his needs. I believe he gave out of the heart and wasn't concerned with what he was going to do or how he was going to get by, because he knew the heart of God and that God's love was a love of giving. He knew that God would take care of him in all situations. That was the basis of Abraham's faith.

Look at what Jesus taught us in Matthew 6:19–34 (NIV):

> Do not store up for yourselves treasures on earth, where moths and vermin destroy, and where thieves break in and steal. But store up for yourselves treasures in heaven, where moths and vermin do not destroy, and where thieves do not break in and steal. For where your treasure is, there your heart will be also.
>
> The eye is the lamp of the body. If your eyes are healthy, your whole body will be full of light. But if your eyes are unhealthy, your whole body will be full of darkness. If then the light within you is darkness, how great is that darkness!
>
> No one can serve two masters. Either you will hate the one and love the other, or you will be devoted to the one and despise the other. You cannot serve both God and money.
>
> Therefore I tell you, do not worry about your life, what you will eat or drink; or about your body, what you will wear. Is not life more than food, and the body more than clothes? Look at the birds of the air; they do not sow or reap or store away in barns, and yet your heavenly Father feeds them. Are you not much more valuable than they? Can any one of you by worrying add a single hour to your life?
>
> And why do you worry about clothes? See how the flowers of the field grow. They do not labor or spin. Yet I tell you that not even Solomon in all his splendor was dressed like one of these. If that is how God clothes the grass of the field, which is here today and tomorrow is thrown into the fire, will he not much more clothe you—

you of little faith? So do not worry, saying, "What shall we eat?" or "What shall we drink?" or "What shall we wear?" For the pagans run after all these things, and your heavenly Father knows that you need them. But seek first his kingdom and his righteousness, and all these things will be given to you as well. Therefore do not worry about tomorrow, for tomorrow will worry about itself. Each day has enough trouble of its own.

The writer of Hebrews 11:6 tells us "And without faith it is impossible to please God, because anyone who comes to him must believe that he exists and that he rewards those who earnestly seek him." I have seen teaching that tells us that when we believe God for the new Cadillac, or in my case a new Harley, we are pleasing God by trusting in him for it. Is that what this really means? Come on, isn't this nothing more than self-gratification in a religious form?

Abraham wasn't worried about Lot choosing the best ground for his herd because he knew that God would provide for all his needs? And this is what Jesus was trying to teach us also. Isn't having the faith that God's nature of loving is outwardly and includes me and is going to take care of my every need, what is really pleasing to him?

Consider this: You are a parent and you have a small child that you have been taking care of without any issues of want, according to need. Every night when he goes to bed, after you have left the room, you hear him crying. So you go into the room and ask him what's wrong. He tells you that he's worried that you won't feed him tomorrow or take care of his basic needs. You reassure him that you will, and he goes to sleep. This continues every night. After the first couple of nights, wouldn't it start to get on your nerves? It's like "Come on, haven't I been taking care of you all this time? Why wouldn't I take care of you now?" Wouldn't it be frustrating?

Thankfully God understands our nature and is forgiving. So wouldn't that be a better understanding of what Hebrews 11:6 means?

Let's look at how Abraham operated in faith in Genesis 12:1–9 (NIV):

> The LORD had said to Abram, "Go from your country, your people and your father's household to the land I will show you.
>
> "I will make you into a great nation,
> and I will bless you;
> I will make your name great,
> and you will be a blessing.
> I will bless those who bless you,
> and whoever curses you I will curse;
> and all peoples on earth
> will be blessed through you."
>
> So Abram went, as the LORD had told him; and Lot went with him. Abram was seventy-five years old when he set out from Harran. He took his wife Sarai, his nephew Lot, all the possessions they had accumulated and the people they had acquired in Harran, and they set out for the land of Canaan, and they arrived there.

It is one thing for God to tell us to go somewhere like to the mission field or a ministry or something similar to that. But could you imagine God just telling you to go without a destination at all? Wouldn't you have to totally trust someone, this someone being God, to be able to do this? How could you totally trust someone that much unless you understood how much that person loves you? Isn't giving someone that much trust in them paying them a huge compliment to their character?

Think of it this way. Let's say that you knew of a need or was trying to start a ministry that would fill a need. You also have a friend or an acquaintance that had been prosperous in his life. So you go to ask him if he could help you fund this project. But before you can even get the explanation out of your mouth, he stops you and asks how much. You try to continue, but he won't let you. He then states,

"Look, I trust you, how much do you need?" Isn't this the ultimate compliment to or glorifying your character?

Understanding this, I believe it makes it easier to understand why our faith in God is pleasing to him. Hebrew 11:6 tells us that "without faith it is impossible to please God, because anyone who comes to him must believe that he exists and that he rewards those who earnestly seek him." For when we totally trust him or have faith in him, aren't we glorifying his character? When we glorify his character, isn't it the same as worshiping him for whom he is?

Let's consider another story of Abraham. In Genesis 14, we read of the story of Abraham rescuing Lot.

> At the time when Amraphel was king of Shinar, Arioch king of Ellasar, Kedorlaomer king of Elam and Tidal king of Goyim, these kings went to war against Bera king of Sodom, Birsha king of Gomorrah, Shinab king of Admah, Shemeber king of Zeboyim, and the king of Bela (that is, Zoar). All these latter kings joined forces in the Valley of Siddim (that is, the Dead Sea Valley). For twelve years they had been subject to Kedorlaomer, but in the thirteenth year they rebelled.
>
> In the fourteenth year, Kedorlaomer and the kings allied with him went out and defeated the Rephaites in Ashteroth Karnaim, the Zuzites in Ham, the Emites in Shaveh Kiriathaim and the Horites in the hill country of Seir, as far as El Paran near the desert. Then they turned back and went to En Mishpat (that is, Kadesh), and they conquered the whole territory of the Amalekites, as well as the Amorites who were living in Hazezon Tamar.
>
> Then the king of Sodom, the king of Gomorrah, the king of Admah, the king of Zeboyim and the king of Bela (that is, Zoar) marched out and drew up their battle lines in

the Valley of Siddim against Kedorlaomer king of Elam, Tidal king of Goyim, Amraphel king of Shinar and Arioch king of Ellasar—four kings against five. Now the Valley of Siddim was full of tar pits, and when the kings of Sodom and Gomorrah fled, some of the men fell into them and the rest fled to the hills. The four kings seized all the goods of Sodom and Gomorrah and all their food; then they went away. They also carried off Abram's nephew Lot and his possessions, since he was living in Sodom.

A man who had escaped came and reported this to Abram the Hebrew. Now Abram was living near the great trees of Mamre the Amorite, a brother of Eshkol and Aner, all of whom were allied with Abram. When Abram heard that his relative had been taken captive, he called out the 318 trained men born in his household and went in pursuit as far as Dan. During the night Abram divided his men to attack them and he routed them, pursuing them as far as Hobah, north of Damascus. He recovered all the goods and brought back his relative Lot and his possessions, together with the women and the other people.

After Abram returned from defeating Kedorlaomer and the kings allied with him, the king of Sodom came out to meet him in the Valley of Shaveh (that is, the King's Valley).

Then Melchizedek king of Salem brought out bread and wine. He was priest of God Most High, and he blessed Abram, saying,

"Blessed be Abram by God Most High,
Creator of heaven and earth.
And praise be to God Most High,
who delivered your enemies into your hand."
Then Abram gave him a tenth of everything.

The king of Sodom said to Abram, "Give me the people and keep the goods for yourself."

But Abram said to the king of Sodom, "With raised hand I have sworn an oath to the LORD, God Most High, Creator of heaven and earth, that I will accept nothing belonging to you, not even a thread or the strap of a sandal, so that you will never be able to say, 'I made Abram rich.' I will accept nothing but what my men have eaten and the share that belongs to the men who went with me—to Aner, Eshkol and Mamre. Let them have their share." (Genesis 14:1–24 NIV)

Now I realize that everyone focuses on the fact that Abraham gave a tenth of everything to the high priest Melchizedek. And rightfully so, they show the fact that Abraham gives this before there was ever a law to do so and that this was done out of the condition of Abraham's heart. This is all very true, but it's not the whole story.

What also needs to be considered is the fact that Abraham didn't keep any of the spoils. He didn't want anybody to be able to say that they made him rich. He wanted to make sure that nobody could get the credit for his prospering other than God himself. In order for him to operate out of that type of faith, he would have to trust that God can and will take care of him. He was able to do this because he understood how God loves.

Again we see Abraham operating out of his love for others, particularly referring to Lot, when the Lord told Abraham about his plans to destroy Sodom and Gomorrah. He pleaded with God for the salvation of those who were to be found righteous.

Do you know what their sin was? Most people believe that it was their sexual practices, namely homosexuality, that was the cause of their destruction. This is because of the story of Lot's attempt to save the angels that came to destroy the town. But Ezekiel gives us a different reason. Ezekiel 16:49 (AMP) says, "Now this was the sin of your sister Sodom: She and her daughters were arrogant, overfed and unconcerned; they did not help the poor and needy." Isn't this a detailed way of saying they were loving themselves?

Yet even with Abraham's understanding of God's love, his enormous amount of faith in God, and his love for others, God still tested him.

We see in Genesis 15:1–6 God giving Abraham the promise he has always wanted.

> After this, the word of the LORD came to Abram in a vision:
> "Do not be afraid, Abram.
> I am your shield,
> your very great reward."
> But Abram said, "Sovereign LORD, what can you give me since I remain childless and the one who will inherit my estate is Eliezer of Damascus?" And Abram said, "You have given me no children; so a servant in my household will be my heir."
> Then the word of the LORD came to him: "This man will not be your heir, but a son who is your own flesh and blood will be your heir." He took him outside and said, "Look up at the sky and count the stars—if indeed you can count them." Then he said to him, "So shall your offspring be."
> Abram believed the LORD, and he credited it to him as righteousness. (Genesis 15:1–6)

We always use this passage to show that because Abraham believe the Lord about having a son from his own flesh and blood, it was credited to him as righteousness. But Abraham has been believing God to keep *all* his promises. I believe this why he could be considered the father of faith. But something in this story changes.

Now Sarai, Abram's wife, had borne him no children. But she had an Egyptian slave named Hagar; so she said to Abram, "The LORD has kept me from having children. Go, sleep with my slave; perhaps I can build a family through her."

Abram agreed to what Sarai said. So after Abram had been living in Canaan ten years, Sarai his wife took her Egyptian slave Hagar and gave her to her husband to be his wife. He slept with Hagar, and she conceived.

When she knew she was pregnant, she began to despise her mistress. Then Sarai said to Abram, "You are responsible for the wrong I am suffering. I put my slave in your arms, and now that she knows she is pregnant, she despises me. May the LORD judge between you and me."

"Your slave is in your hands," Abram said. "Do with her whatever you think best." Then Sarai mistreated Hagar; so she fled from her.

The angel of the LORD found Hagar near a spring in the desert; it was the spring that is beside the road to Shur. And he said, "Hagar, slave of Sarai, where have you come from, and where are you going?"

"I'm running away from my mistress Sarai," she answered.

Then the angel of the LORD told her, "Go back to your mistress and submit to her." The angel added, "I will increase your descendants so much that they will be too numerous to count."

The angel of the LORD also said to her:
"You are now pregnant
and you will give birth to a son.
You shall name him Ishmael,
for the LORD has heard of your misery.
He will be a wild donkey of a man;

his hand will be against everyone
and everyone's hand against him,
and he will live in hostility
toward all his brothers."
She gave this name to the LORD who spoke
to her: "You are the God who sees me," for she
said, "I have now seen the One who sees me."
That is why the well was called Beer Lahai Roi; it
is still there, between Kadesh and Bered.
So Hagar bore Abram a son, and Abram
gave the name Ishmael to the son she had borne.
Abram was eighty-six years old when Hagar bore
him Ishmael. (Genesis 16:1–16)

Whether this is right or not, I have heard it many times that the time between Abraham was promised a son and the time that he had Isaac was twenty years. So this would mean that Ishmael was thirteen or fourteen years old when Isaac was born. This means that Abraham and Sarah had waited six or seven years for the promise to come about. So by no means can we accuse this couple of acting on instant gratification. At the same time, they did act outside of God's timing and outside of God's plan.

This is something I understand in my own life. As of the time that I am writing this, I have yet to be married. Not that I don't want to, but I have been waiting for God to put her in my life. It has been almost twenty years since I had asked him for my wife. So I can totally understand getting impatient and wanting to move the ball yourself. Even though, I believe what this shows us is that by moving the ball yourself, you only create your own problems. Though I have not picked up the ball and ran with it myself, I will admit that I have blown on it, try to get other people to move it, even tilt the surface that it was sitting on in order to get the ball to move. So I have nothing but understanding for their situation.

Couldn't that have been considered a lack of faith? I guess it could have. But I understand the amount of head games that goes along with this in the terms of "Did I miss hearing him?" or "Am I not doing something right?" Yet verse 6 says, "Abram believed the LORD, and he credited it to him as righteousness." So even though he didn't know how God was going to do it, or when he was going to, he still believed he was going to. Thank God he overlooks our impatience and is still good for his promises. Because of this, he gave Abraham his son Isaac through Sarah.

Now the ultimate test comes.

> Some time later God tested Abraham. He said to him, "Abraham!"
>
> "Here I am," he replied.
>
> Then God said, "Take your son, your only son, whom you love—Isaac—and go to the region of Moriah. Sacrifice him there as a burnt offering on a mountain I will show you."
>
> Early the next morning Abraham got up and loaded his donkey. He took with him two of his servants and his son Isaac. When he had cut enough wood for the burnt offering, he set out for the place God had told him about. On the third day Abraham looked up and saw the place in the distance. He said to his servants, "Stay here with the donkey while I and the boy go over there. We will worship and then we will come back to you."
>
> Abraham took the wood for the burnt offering and placed it on his son Isaac, and he himself carried the fire and the knife. As the two of them went on together, Isaac spoke up and said to his father Abraham, "Father?"
>
> "Yes, my son?" Abraham replied.
>
> "The fire and wood are here," Isaac said, "but where is the lamb for the burnt offering?"
>
> Abraham answered, "God himself will provide the lamb for the burnt offering, my son." And the two of them went on together.

When they reached the place God had told him about, Abraham built an altar there and arranged the wood on it. He bound his son Isaac and laid him on the altar, on top of the wood. Then he reached out his hand and took the knife to slay his son. But the angel of the LORD called out to him from heaven, "Abraham! Abraham!"

"Here I am," he replied.

"Do not lay a hand on the boy," he said. "Do not do anything to him. Now I know that you fear God, because you have not withheld from me your son, your only son."

Abraham looked up and there in a thicket he saw a ram caught by its horns. He went over and took the ram and sacrificed it as a burnt offering instead of his son. So Abraham called that place The LORD Will Provide. And to this day it is said, "On the mountain of the LORD it will be provided."

The angel of the LORD called to Abraham from heaven a second time and said, "I swear by myself, declares the LORD, that because you have done this and have not withheld your son, your only son, I will surely bless you and make your descendants as numerous as the stars in the sky and as the sand on the seashore. Your descendants will take possession of the cities of their enemies, and through your offspring all nations on earth will be blessed, because you have obeyed me." (Genesis 22:1–18)

I realize that this passage shows us the strength of his faith. There's no doubt that Abraham was operating in his faith based on his knowledge of what he knew about the character of God. He knew that when God gave a promise, because of his character, that promise would come to pass.

I also realize that this is a precursor to what God is going to do with his son, except this time there will be no stopping—the sacrifice will be completed through his son. But there's something else that is worth looking at. It's the purpose of sacrifices and offerings.

Hebrews 11:17–19 says,

> By faith Abraham, when God tested him, offered Isaac as a sacrifice. He who had embraced the promises was about to sacrifice his one and only son, even though God had said to him, "It is through Isaac that your offspring will be reckoned." Abraham reasoned that God could even raise the dead, and so in a manner of speaking he did receive Isaac back from death.

The passage of Genesis 22:1 starts out with "God tested Abraham," and then again we see Hebrews 11:17 stating when God tested him. With the understanding that the wages of sin is death and the requirement of the shedding of the blood for the atonement of sin, is there another purpose for the sacrifice and the offering?

Go back to the situation in the courtroom, where we established that you are the drunk driver and that the penalty is death. Would it be considered justice for the judge to order you to offer up your own son's life to pay for your crime? Ezekiel 18:20 says,

> The one who sins is the one who will die. The child will not share the guilt of the parent, nor will the parent share the guilt of the child. The righteousness of the righteous will be credited to them, and the wickedness of the wicked will be charged against them.

It is explained that when they gave a burnt offering, it was supposed to be without a defect, and this was a representation of the perfect sacrifice of Jesus Christ given to us from God the Father. There were all kinds of different offerings, like food offerings, guilt offerings, first offerings, grain offerings, and then there was the tithe and firstfruits. All of these offerings were to be of the finest quality to be acceptable to God. Why is that?

Think of it this way. God loves outwardly or as an act of giving love to others. If sin is actually loving ourselves, or loving inwardly rather than outwardly, was the sacrifice and offering a way for us to give a portion of ourselves to God or maybe even a way to reveal our love for him and not for the restitution of our wrongdoings?

Isaac was everything to Abraham. He was his deepest earthly desire. Yet God was testing him on who he loved more, his desire or God. When he showed that his love for God was stronger, then God provided him with a different sacrifice.

Isn't that what God did to show us his love? John 3:16 says, "For God so loved the world that he gave his one and only Son." He gave Jesus his only begotten son to be our sacrifice.

God the Father loved us so much that he gave us God the Son to be our sacrifice, because even when we did sacrifice the things we loved, we went back to loving ourselves.

Yet if you think about it, didn't God provide all the sacrifices?

> Listen, my people, and I will speak; I will testify against you, Israel: I am God, your God. I bring no charges against you concerning your sacrifices or concerning your burnt offerings, which are ever before me. I have no need of a bull from your stall or of goats from your pens, for every animal of the forest is mine, and the cattle on a thousand hills. I know every bird in the mountains, and the insects in the fields are mine. If I were hungry I would not tell you, for the world is mine, and all that is in it. Do I eat the flesh of bulls or drink the blood of goats? Sacrifice thank offerings to God, fulfill your vows to the Most High, and call on me in the day of trouble; I will deliver you, and you will honor me. (Psalm 50:7–15)

If he provided everything for us, then all that we are sacrificing is what was already given to us. Would it not seem that the sacrifice and the offering was more of a test to see if we are more in love with our provisions, which would be an indication of love for ourselves, rather than the provider?

If we then are not willing to give up the best of what we are already provided with, then are we not saying that we are more in love with ourselves or the things that we are entrusted with? Doesn't this revert back to the original problem that Adam and Eve had in the garden? They had everything in the garden given to them to provide them with all of their needs. There was only one tree that God didn't allow them to partake of, and their focus of love turned toward themselves overcame their love for the Father who provided it all to them in the first place.

Here is the thing: They were being disobedient, but the disobedience was due to their heart being in the wrong place. It seems possible that the reason for sacrifice and offerings were to keep our hearts in check by letting go of the things that had been provided to us and now had a hold on us. The problem that arose was it soon was done out of obedience and not out of love. Eventually anything done out of obedience rather than out of the love of the heart is done with as little effort that is needed to be considered obedient. Due to human nature or sin (loving of self), eventually we will become disobedient not only because if we are not totally obedient, we are automatically disobedient, but because we ignore something that we have no heart in. We won't be able to live with the guilt of disobedience, especially to God, so then we have to justify our actions to alleviate the guilt.

Think about Malachi 1.

> The burden or oracle (the thing to be lifted up) of the word of the Lord to Israel by Malachi [My messenger].
>
> I have loved you, says the Lord. Yet you say, How and in what way have You loved us? Was not Esau Jacob's brother? says the Lord; yet I loved Jacob (Israel),

But [in comparison with the degree of love I have for Jacob] I have hated Esau [Edom] and have laid waste his mountains, and his heritage I have given to the jackals of the wilderness.

Though [impoverished] Edom should say, We are beaten down, but we will return and build the waste places—thus says the Lord of hosts: They may build, but I will tear and throw down; and men will call them the Wicked Country, the people against whom the Lord has indignation forever.

Your own eyes shall see this and you shall say, The Lord is great and will be magnified over and beyond the border of Israel!

A son honors his father, and a servant his master. If then I am a Father, where is My honor? And if I am a Master, where is the [reverent] fear due Me? says the Lord of hosts to you, O priests, who despise My name. You say, How and in what way have we despised Your name?

By offering polluted food upon My altar. And you ask, How have we polluted it and profaned You? By thinking that the table of the Lord is contemptible and may be despised.

When you [priests] offer blind [animals] for sacrifice, is it not evil? And when you offer the lame and the sick, is it not evil? Present such a thing [a blind or lame or sick animal] now to your governor [in payment of your taxes, and see what will happen]. Will he be pleased with you? Or will he receive you graciously? says the Lord of hosts.

Now then, I [Malachi] beg [you priests], entreat God [earnestly] that He will be gracious to us. With such a gift from your hand [as a defective animal for sacrifice], will He accept it or show favor to any of you? says the Lord of hosts.

Oh, that there were even one among you [whose duty it is to minister to Me] who would shut the doors, that you might not kindle fire on My altar to no purpose [an empty, futile, fruitless pretense]! I have no pleasure in you, says the Lord of hosts, nor will I accept an offering from your hand.

For from the rising of the sun to its setting My name shall be great among the nations, and in every place incense shall be offered to My name, and indeed a pure offering; for My name shall be great among the nations, says the Lord of hosts.

But you [priests] profane it when [by your actions] you say, The table of the Lord is polluted, and the fruit of it, its food, is contemptible and may be despised.

You say also, Behold, what a drudgery and weariness this is! And you have sniffed at it, says the Lord of hosts. And you have brought that which was taken by violence, or the lame or the sick; this you bring as an offering! Shall I accept this from your hand? says the Lord.

But cursed is the [cheating] deceiver who has a male in his flock and vows to offer it, yet sacrifices to the [sovereign] Lord a blemished or diseased thing! For I am a great King, says the Lord of hosts, and My name is terrible and to be [reverently] feared among the nations. (Malachi 1:1–14 AMP)

Was God stating all of this for the fact that they were being disobedient, or was it because of the condition of their hearts? They were disobedient because in their act of obedience, they went through the motions of the sacrifice halfhearted at best. God was addressing the condition of the heart.

Look at what Jesus told the Pharisees twice in Matthew 9:13, "But go and learn what this means: 'I desire mercy, not sacrifice.' For I have not come to call the righteous, but sinners." And then again in Matthew 12:7, "If you had known what these words mean, 'I desire mercy, not sacrifice,' you would not have condemned the innocent." He was referring back to Hosea 6:6, "For I desire mercy, not sacrifice, and acknowledgment of God rather than burnt offerings." God was telling Israel that he wanted their love not their empty rituals. Jesus refers to this to remind the Pharisees of the same thing. They were more worried about their righteous images and rituals than the condition of the people that needed to have the love of God in their hearts.

Here is Matthew Henry's take on this:

> The displeasure of the Pharisees at this, Matt. 9:11. They cavilled at it; why eateth your Master with publicans and sinners? Here observe,
> 1. That Christ was quarreled with. It was not the least of his sufferings, that he endured the contradiction of sinners against himself. None was more quarreled with by men, than he that came to take up the great quarrel between God and man. Thus he denied himself the honour due to an incarnate Deity, which was to be justified in what he spake, and to have all he said readily subscribed to: for though he never spoke or did anything amiss, everything he said and did was found fault with. Thus he taught us to expect and prepare for reproach, and to bear it patiently.
> 2. They that quarreled with him were the Pharisees; a proud generation of men, conceited of themselves, and censorious of oth-

ers; of the same temper with those in the prophet's time, who said, Stand by thyself, come not near me; I am holier than thou: they were very strict in avoiding sinners, but not in avoiding sin; none greater zealots than they for the form of godliness, nor greater enemies to the power of it. They were for keeping up the traditions of the elders to a nicety, and so propagating the same spirit that they were themselves governed by.

3. They brought their cavil, not to Christ himself; they had not the courage to face him with it, but to his disciples. The disciples were in the same company, but the quarrel is with the Master: for they would not have done it, if he had not; and they thought it worse in him who was a prophet, than in them; his dignity, they thought, should set him at a greater distance from such company than others. Being offended at the Master, they quarrel with the disciples. Note, It concerns Christians to be able to vindicate and justify Christ, and his doctrines and laws, and to be ready always to give an answer to those that ask them a reason of the hope that is in them, 1 Pet. 3:15. While he is an Advocate for us in heaven, let us be advocates for him on earth, and make his reproach our own.

4. The complaint was his eating with publicans and sinners: to be intimate with wicked people is against the law of God (Ps. 119:115; Ps. 1:1); and perhaps by accusing Christ of this to his disciples, they hoped to tempt them from him, to put them out of conceit with him, and so to bring them over

to themselves to be their disciples, who kept better company; for they compassed sea and land to make proselytes. To be intimate with publicans was against the tradition of the elders, and, therefore, they looked upon it as a heinous thing. They were angry with Christ for this,

1.) Because they wished ill to him, and sought occasion to misrepresent him. Note, it is an easy and very common thing to put the worst constructions upon the best words and actions.

2.) Because they wished no good to publicans and sinners, but envied Christ's favour to them, and were grieved to see them brought to repentance. Note, It may justly be suspected, that they have not the grace of God themselves, who grudge others a share in that grace, who are not pleased with it.

IV. The defence that Christ made for himself and his disciples, in justification of their converse with publicans and sinners. The disciples, it should seem, being yet weak, had to seek for an answer to the Pharisees' cavil, and, therefore, bring it to Christ, and he heard it (Matt. 9:12), or perhaps overheard them whispering it to his disciples. Let him alone to vindicate himself and to plead his own cause, to answer for himself and for us too. Two things he urges in his defence,

1. The necessity and exigency of the case of the publicans, which called aloud for his help, and therefore justified him in conversing with them for their good. It was the extreme necessity of poor, lost sinners, that brought

Christ from the pure regions above, to these impure ones; and the same was it, that brought him into this company which was thought impure. Now,

1.) He proves the necessity of the case of the publicans: they that be whole need not a physician, but they that are sick. The publicans are sick, and they need one to help and heal them, which the Pharisees think they do not. Note,

[1.] Sin is the sickness of the soul; sinners are spiritually sick. Original corruptions are the diseases of the soul, actual transgressions are its wounds, or the eruptions of the disease. It is deforming, weakening, disquieting, wasting, killing, but, blessed be God, not incurable.

[2.] Jesus Christ is the great Physician of souls. His curing of bodily diseases signified this, that he arose with healing under his wings. He is a skilful, faithful, compassionate Physician, and it is his office and business to heal the sick. Wise and good men should be as physicians to all about them; Christ was so. Hunc affectum versus omnes habet sapiens, quem versus aegros suos medicus—A wise man cherishes towards all around him the feelings of a physician for his patient. Seneca Deut. Const.

[3.] Sin-sick souls have need of this Physician, for their disease is dangerous; nature will not help itself;

no man can help us; such need have we of Christ, that we are undone, eternally undone, without him. Sensible sinners see their need, and apply themselves to him accordingly.

[4.] There are multitudes who fancy themselves to be sound and whole, who think they have no need of Christ, but that they can shift for themselves well enough without him, as Laodicea, Rev. 3:17. Thus the Pharisees desired not the knowledge of Christ's word and ways, not because they had no need of him, but because they thought they had none. See John 9:40, 41.

2.) He proves, that their necessity did sufficiently justify his conduct, in conversing familiarly with them, and that he ought not to be blamed for it; for that necessity made it an act of charity, which ought always to be preferred before the formalities of a religious profession, in which beneficence and munificence are far better than magnificence, as much as substance is better than shows or shadows. Those duties, which are of moral and natural obligation, are to take place even of those divine laws which are positive and ritual, much more of those impositions of men, and traditions of the elders, which make God's law stricter than he has made it. This he proves (Matt. 9:13) by a passage quoted out of Hos. 6:6; I will have mercy and not sacrifice. That morose separation from the society of publicans, which the Pharisees enjoined, was less than sacrifice; but Christ's conversing with them was more than an act of common mercy, and therefore to be preferred before it. If to do well ourselves is better than sacrifice, as Samuel shows (1 Sam. 15:22, 23), much more to do good to others. Christ's conversing with sinners is here called mercy: to promote the conversion of souls is the greatest act of mercy imaginable; it is saving a soul from death, Jas. 5:20. Observe how Christ quotes this, Go ye and learn what that meaneth. Note, It is not enough to be acquainted with the letter of scripture, but we must learn to understand the meaning of it. And they have best learned the meaning of the scriptures, that have learned how to apply them as a reproof to their own faults, and a rule for their own practice. This scripture which Christ quoted, served not only to vindicate him, but,

[1.] To show wherein true religion consists; not in external observances: not in meats and drinks and shows of sanctity, not in little particular opinions and doubtful disputations, but in doing all the good we can to the bodies and souls of others; in righteousness and peace; in visiting the fatherless and widows.

[2.] To condemn the Pharisaical hypocrisy of those who place religion in rituals, more than in morals, Matt. 23:23. They espouse those forms of godliness which may be made consistent with, and perhaps subservient to, their pride, covetousness, ambition, and malice, while they hate that power of it which is mortifying to those lusts.

2. He urges the nature and end of his own commission. He must keep to his orders, and prosecute that for which he was appointed to be the great Teacher; now, says he, "I am not come to call the righteous, but sinners to repentance, and therefore must converse with publicans." Observe,

1.) What his errand was; it was to call to repentance. This was his first text (Matt. 4:17), and it was the tendency of all his sermons. Note, The gospel call is a call to repentance; a call to us to change our mind and to change our way.

2.) With whom his errand lay; not with the righteous, but with sinners. That is,

[1.] If the children of men had not been sinners, there had been no occasion for Christ's coming among them. He is the Saviour, not of man as man, but of man as fallen. Had the first Adam continued in his original righteousness, we had not needed a second Adam.

[2.] Therefore his greatest business lies with the greatest sinners; the more dangerous the sick man's case is, the more occasion there is for the physician's help. Christ came into the world to save sinners, but especially the chief (1 Tim. 1:15); to call not those so much, who, though sinners, are comparatively righteous, but the worst of sinners. [3.] The more sensible any sinners are of their sinfulness, the more welcome will Christ and his gospel be to them; and every one chooses to go where his company is desired, not to those who would rather have his room. Christ came not with an expectation of succeeding among the righteous, those who conceit themselves so, and therefore will sooner be sick of their Saviour, than sick of their sins, but among the convinced humble sinners; to them Christ will come, for to them he will be welcome.

Can the same thing be said to us today? Don't we get more focused on our Christian obligations than we do about helping others to understand the love of God? Isn't that what salvation was all about (John 3:16)? How many people make sure that they show up at church, usher, or serve in whatever capacity needed yet have no compassion in the leading of others to the Lord or the understanding of his love, like someone had led them? No different than the Pharisees point their boney finger at the disciples for picking wheat on the Sabbath or the Lord eating with sinners. There are those who refuse to associate with those who are not Christian because they are afraid that the influences of the world will wear off on them. I am not referring to new Christians that need to protect themselves, but those that are supposed to be mature Christians. Wow, isn't their love for the Lord strong enough to sustain them to be light and salt in the world and not be a sponge instead?

ON THE SCALE OF LOVE

I went to school for heating and cooling. One of the first things I learned was that there was no such thing as cold; there is only the absence of heat. The word *cold* is used to describe the absence of the heat.

On one end of the spectrum is absolute zero, which is the absence of all heat, and at the other end of the spectrum is infinity, for who really knows what the hottest thing is or ever will be. At the temperature of 32°F or 0°C, pure water particles begin to turn to ice.

What if love worked in a similar way? On the one end of the spectrum is the absence of godly love in which one would be in total love of self, and on the other end of the spectrum is God, for God is love and he is infinite. Sin would be the point where we are loving ourselves more than or rather than God or others. The point where we are putting ourselves first over God or others.

Isaiah 59:2 tells us, "But your iniquities have separated you from your God; your sins have hidden his face from you, so that he will not hear." This makes sense, because if sin is the loving of self and transgression are the results of sin, then the farther we go down the scale or the more that we focused on our love of ourselves, then the farther away that we go from God or from loving God.

In John 14:21, we hear Jesus tell the apostle, "Whoever has my commands and keeps them is the one who loves me. The one who loves me will be loved by my Father, and I too will love them and show myself to them." Jesus then gave us a new command in John 15:12 (NASB): "This is My commandment, that you love one another, just as I have loved you."

So then, we are loving God when we are loving others and our doing for others is like we are doing it for God. Going back to Matthew 25:31–46 with the sheep and the goats, Jesus says that those of you who did it for the least of my brothers and sisters did it for me. So the way that we love God is that we do for others as if we are doing it for the Lord.

How do we define somebody that is always doing things for others and for the Lord? Don't we say that they are "on fire for God"? Don't we refer to people that are only concerned with themselves as being cold?

It works the same with light and darkness. Darkness is the absence of light. Darkness never overcomes light, but light always overcomes darkness. The closer we move up the scale toward God, the lighter the path is.

Think about those who are dealing with depression and suicidal thoughts. Their focus is only on themselves and on what is happening to them. Even if it is about someone else, there is still a focus on how it affected them. I had a close friend that killed himself because of something that happened to his mother, but he was so focused on the fact that he could have prevented it that he couldn't deal with the pain. I too have dealt with depression and suicidal thoughts for the greater part of my earlier life. I know what it is like to walk around with tunnel vision and not be able to see anything due to the darkness around you. What is sad but true is that I was focused on nothing else but myself.

Here is the thing: everyone born into this world have sin or love of self on them. This is the result of Adam and Eve's sin. God used sacrifice and offering to break the pattern of sin. The problem was that it was a short-term fix at best.

John the Baptist proclaimed in John 1:29, "Look, the Lamb of God, who takes away the sin of the world!" What is interesting is the fact that in all the different versions of the Bible that I looked this verse up in, all the interpreters use the term "sin" in a singular pretense. Yet the Greek word could have been used either way and is used both ways throughout the New Testament. I think this is an accurate way to use it. Because if sin is the love of self, then it is an ongoing condition of the heart and not different reoccurring actions.

God sent his son Jesus to offer up his life to be the one and only sacrifice for the forgiveness of sin and become a permanent solution to break the pattern of sin. Jesus came into a cold and dark world to gives us a path to the light and warmth of God the Father. John 8:12 says, "When Jesus spoke again to the people, he said, 'I am the light of the world. Whoever follows me will never walk in darkness, but will have the light of life.'" Now we have the ability and the choice of which direction we will focus our love to. We can still choose to focus our love on ourselves, or we can choose to focus our love toward others. The difference today is that when we choose Jesus as our Lord and Savior, we have the Holy Spirit residing in us, so we have the ability to make a choice, where before we were slaves to our human nature (Romans 8).

But it is not like a light switch where it is just one or the other, on or off. The more we move up the scale toward God or directing more attention toward others, then the less we think of ourselves. Jesus, through the Holy Spirit, gives us the power or ability to stop the process of loving ourselves and move up the scale toward loving God through others, which we were unable to do before.

Now there is one who totally loves himself, he has no love for God, and we find him on the other end of the scale. His name is Satan. So the more we are focused on ourselves, then the farther down the scale we go, and the more we become like the devil. Look at what Jesus told the Pharisees in John 8:31–47:

> To the Jews who had believed him, Jesus said, "If you hold to my teaching, you are really my disciples. Then you will know the truth, and the truth will set you free."
>
> They answered him, "We are Abraham's descendants and have never been slaves of any-one. How can you say that we shall be set free?"
>
> Jesus replied, "Very truly I tell you, every-one who sins is a slave to sin. Now a slave has no permanent place in the family, but a son belongs to it forever. So if the Son sets you free, you will be free indeed. I know that you are Abraham's descendants. Yet you are looking for a way to kill

me, because you have no room for my word. I am telling you what I have seen in the Father's presence, and you are doing what you have heard from your father."

"Abraham is our father," they answered.

"If you were Abraham's children," said Jesus, "then you would do what Abraham did. As it is, you are looking for a way to kill me, a man who has told you the truth that I heard from God. Abraham did not do such things. You are doing the works of your own father."

"We are not illegitimate children," they protested. "The only Father we have is God himself."

Jesus said to them, "If God were your Father, you would love me, for I have come here from God. I have not come on my own; God sent me. Why is my language not clear to you? Because you are unable to hear what I say. You belong to your father, the devil, and you want to carry out your father's desires. He was a murderer from the beginning, not holding to the truth, for there is no truth in him. When he lies, he speaks his native language, for he is a liar and the father of lies. Yet because I tell the truth, you do not believe me! Can any of you prove me guilty of sin? If I am telling the truth, why don't you believe me? Whoever belongs to God hears what God says. The reason you do not hear is that you do not belong to God."

So the farther we go up the scale or, in other terms, the more we are loving God through others, then the more we are free of sin or the more we are free of loving ourselves.

Now think about this. Are we ever totally loving others or totally loving ourselves? Can't we be loving others and still be loving ourselves through our own motives? Or can we be focused on loving ourselves and still show some love for others?

I use this as an example, not for any particular story, but I have a friend who was a missionary for twenty years in Africa, and we were discussing this very issue. There are people who become missionaries not for the love of the calling of being a missionary for Christ. They become one so that they can escape or recover from the realities of their own life. I'm not saying this is totally wrong. What I am pointing out is that they could love the people they are helping and doing great things for the work of Christ and still be doing it for themselves.

We could be doing what we feel is right or what may even be right yet not loving others while we are doing it. Look at what Paul was saying in Romans 14.

> Accept the one whose faith is weak, without quarreling over disputable matters. One person's faith allows them to eat anything, but another, whose faith is weak, eats only vegetables. The one who eats everything must not treat with contempt the one who does not, and the one who does not eat everything must not judge the one who does, for God has accepted them. Who are you to judge someone else's servant? To their own master, servants stand or fall. And they will stand, for the Lord is able to make them stand.

> One person considers one day more sacred than another; another considers every day alike. Each of them should be fully convinced in their own mind. Whoever regards one day as special does so to the Lord. Whoever eats meat does so to the Lord, for they give thanks to God; and whoever abstains does so to the Lord and gives thanks to God. For none of us lives for ourselves alone, and none of us dies for ourselves alone. If we live, we live for the Lord; and if we die, we die for the Lord. So, whether we live or die, we

belong to the Lord. For this very reason, Christ died and returned to life so that he might be the Lord of both the dead and the living.

You, then, why do you judge your brother or sister? Or why do you treat them with contempt? For we will all stand before God's judgment seat. It is written:

"'As surely as I live,' says the Lord,
'every knee will bow before me;
every tongue will acknowledge God.'"

So then, each of us will give an account of ourselves to God.

Therefore let us stop passing judgment on one another. Instead, make up your mind not to put any stumbling block or obstacle in the way of a brother or sister. I am convinced, being fully persuaded in the Lord Jesus, that nothing is unclean in itself. But if anyone regards something as unclean, then for that person it is unclean. *If your brother or sister is distressed because of what you eat, you are no longer acting in love.* Do not by your eating destroy someone for whom Christ died. Therefore do not let what you know is good be spoken of as evil. For the kingdom of God is not a matter of eating and drinking, but of righteousness, peace and joy in the Holy Spirit, because anyone who serves Christ in this way is pleasing to God and receives human approval.

Let us therefore make every effort to do what leads to peace and to mutual edification. Do not destroy the work of God for the sake of food. All food is clean, but it is wrong for a person to eat anything that causes someone else to stumble. It is better not to eat meat or drink wine or to do anything else that will cause your brother or sister to fall.

So whatever you believe about these things keep between yourself and God. Blessed is the one who does not condemn himself by what he approves. *But whoever has doubts is condemned if they eat, because their eating is not from faith; and everything that does not come from faith is sin.* (Romans 14:1–23) (emphasis added)

Here Paul is saying you could do what is right according to your beliefs and faith, and technically, you wouldn't be doing anything wrong. Except you would be doing something wrong if whatever you are doing is harmful to someone else's faith or beliefs. And it can be as simple as what you are eating.

Now was he talking about operating in a godly love or about being disobedient?

If he was talking about disobedience, then it seems to me that the line of disobedience just got smudged a little. Instead of a straight line of right or wrong, there now seems to be a smudged or crooked line defining right or wrong. Right or wrong is now defined by our convictions.

What happens when we learn the art of justification? Can't we trump our convictions with justifications? We have a conviction of where the line of right and wrong are, and we use justification to move the line far enough so that our actions are now not considered wrong. This can be seen over and over in our daily lives.

To give an example, let's start by looking at Matthew 19:4–6:

"Haven't you read," he replied, "that at the beginning the Creator 'made them male and female,' and said, 'For this reason a man will leave his father and mother and be united to his wife, and the two will become one flesh?' So they are no longer two, but one flesh. Therefore what God has joined together, let no one separate."

And then in 1 Corinthians 6:9–20, Paul explains:

> Or do you not know that wrongdoers will not inherit the kingdom of God? Do not be deceived: Neither the sexually immoral nor idolaters nor adulterers nor men who have sex with men nor thieves nor the greedy nor drunkards nor slanderers nor swindlers will inherit the kingdom of God. And that is what some of you were. But you were washed, you were sanctified, you were justified in the name of the Lord Jesus Christ and by the Spirit of our God.
>
> "I have the right to do anything," you say— but not everything is beneficial. "I have the right to do anything"—but I will not be mastered by anything. You say, "Food for the stomach and the stomach for food, and God will destroy them both." The body, however, is not meant for sexual immorality but for the Lord, and the Lord for the body. By his power God raised the Lord from the dead, and he will raise us also. Do you not know that your bodies are members of Christ himself? Shall I then take the members of Christ and unite them with a prostitute? Never! Do you not know that he who unites himself with a prostitute is one with her in body? For it is said, "The two will become one flesh." But whoever is united with the Lord is one with him in spirit.
>
> Flee from sexual immorality. All other sins a person commits are outside the body, but whoever sins sexually, sins against their own body. Do you not know that your bodies are temples of the Holy Spirit, who is in you, whom you have received from God? You are not your own; you were bought at a price. Therefore honor God with your bodies.

By this, we can see in these two passages that both divorce and sex outside the bonds of marriage are against the will of God. Yet even in the church today, it is as common place as it is outside the church. How can this be? It clearly states what is right and what is wrong, so how can this still be going on? Don't people have to justify their actions in some way in order to believe or feel that what they are doing is okay?

So let's say in this example, we have a young couple named John and Mary (totally fictitious). They are your average young adults who have a relatively good lifestyle in regard to the Christian community. They fall in love with each other and enjoy the time they have together so much that they want to be together on a daily basis. In order to do this, they have to make a commitment to get married. Problem is they have seen so many marriages fail they are afraid to make such a serious commitment. They don't want to become another statistic.

Using their best logic, they decide that the best way to handle this is that they both move in together and see if they are compatible. What's wrong with just living together? They love each other, and that's the way everybody is doing it today. So they've moved in together and are living the life of a married couple, minus the commitment of a married couple. It's kind of like getting to eat chocolate without having to consume the calories.

After a couple of months of this lifestyle, nature takes its course when natural processes occur. The next thing they know Mary is pregnant. The problem is that the two of them are just starting their careers, and they barely had time to get to know each other and see if they can handle living with each other. They know that is wrong to have an abortion according to the church. But the rest of the world does say that it's okay because it's her body and she has the choice. "We haven't made a commitment to each other yet, and realistically, we can't afford to have a child right now. If we brought a baby into this world, we would be doing it more harm than good. So a baby right now is out of the question. There's only one logical way to fix this, and that is to have an abortion," they say, which is what they do.

With this decision comes a level of guilt that they both have to deal with. They know why they did what they did, but did they cross the line? It just seems so murky right now. Naturally the guilt starts to eat at them, and then the other pressures of life continue to come at them at the normal pace that life usually sends them. Guilt can lead to depression or anger, and now they are not getting along as well as they used to. This is not the way they envisioned it, and they come to the conclusion that their experiment is not working out, and they need to part ways and get on with their lives.

So the power of justification moved or distorted the lines and destroyed the possibility of this young couple living a married life together that could've been possibly the most beautiful thing in their lives had they followed God's plan for unity.

But it goes even farther than that. Now in today's society, we don't need justification; it has been taken to a whole new level. If I decide it is right for me, then it is. I am the definer of what is right and what is wrong. Where does that logic end? Since there is no way to satisfy the lust of the flesh, then the individual's definition of right and wrong will continue to change in order to get the desired result. This is not just a sexual lust, but a lust of all sorts, such as money, power, and success, etc.

What if the couple had asked the question "Are my decisions about loving me and getting my desires, or is it about loving others?" For example, what if John had asked that question? Would he have found out that if he really loved Mary he would be willing to give her the commitment that she deserves? If Mary wasn't ready to make that commitment then if he loved her, he would be willing to wait for her to be able to? Or if she wasn't willing to wait until they were both ready to make a commitment and gave him the ultimatum of "now or never" that the loving thing for him to do would be to let her go so she did not make that mistake? Also would they have been able to get an abortion if their love was directed outwardly to the other person or, in this case, the unborn child affected by this decision and not just themselves?

What if Mary had left and then John had been without her, how is that helping John? Well, he wouldn't have had all the heartache, guilt, and problems that came with the decision that he made.

This may have fictitious characters, but this is not a fictitious story. This story is played out over and over every day in real life.

Then you have the fact that people want to live by their feelings and not by the truth. A pastor decides to run off with another woman and leaves his wife and family behind because "it feels so right," when the fact of the matter is that the Word of God says it is so wrong. How many people destroy their lives because "it feels so right"? Isn't that feeling based on love of self?

What if our decisions were filtered through the question of "Is this loving others or is this loving myself?" and not through the filter of disobedience? Wouldn't this change the outcome of many of our decisions and dealings with other people? Would this change our relationship with God?

Think about all of the things in our lives like careers, bank accounts, toys in the garage, etc. that we put all our energy into because of what it does for our personal gratification. I'm not saying that they are all bad, but do we give them more focus then we ought to? So if we ask the question of who are we loving, first, wouldn't it direct our thoughts toward others rather than just satisfying ourselves or the things that are gratifying to us?

I know from experience this is harder than it sounds, which makes me think this is what Paul meant when he told us in Romans 12:1–2 (NIV),

> Therefore, I urge you, brothers and sisters, in view of God's mercy, to offer your bodies as a living sacrifice, holy and pleasing to God—this is your true and proper worship. Do not conform to the pattern of this world, but be transformed by the renewing of your mind. Then you will be able to test and approve what God's will is—his good, pleasing and perfect will.

Offering up our bodies as a sacrifice would be the same as thinking of others first. The pattern of this world tends to do what is best for themselves in the form of self-fulfillment, etc., contrary to God's perfect will is to focus on others and not ourselves.

And this was God's test for Abraham. God told Abraham he would be the father of many nations. This was what Abraham wanted so bad that he took the advice of his wife, Sarah, rather than question her motive and waited for the one who gave him the promise. So Isaac was his world when God asked him the same question: Who do you love?

SAUL

Let's look at another man in the Old Testament.

When Samuel grew old, he appointed his sons as Israel's leaders. The name of his firstborn was Joel and the name of his second was Abijah, and they served at Beersheba. But his sons did not follow his ways. They turned aside after dishonest gain and accepted bribes and perverted justice.

So all the elders of Israel gathered together and came to Samuel at Ramah. They said to him, "You are old, and your sons do not follow your ways; now appoint a king to lead us, such as all the other nations have."

But when they said, "Give us a king to lead us," this displeased Samuel; so he prayed to the LORD. And the LORD told him: "Listen to all that the people are saying to you; it is not you they have rejected, but they have rejected me as their king. As they have done from the day I brought them up out of Egypt until this day, forsaking me and serving other gods, so they are doing to you. Now listen to them; but warn them solemnly and let them know what the king who will reign over them will claim as his rights."

Samuel told all the words of the LORD to the people who were asking him for a king. He said, "This is what the king who will reign over you will claim as his rights: He will take your sons and make them serve with his chariots and horses, and they will run in front of his chariots. Some he will assign to be commanders of thousands and commanders of fifties, and others to plow his ground and reap his harvest, and still others to make weapons of war and equipment for his chariots. He will take your daughters to be perfumers and cooks and bakers. He will take the best of your fields and vineyards and olive groves and give them to his attendants. He will take a tenth of your grain and of your vintage and give it to his officials and attendants. Your male and female servants and the best of your cattle and donkeys he will take for his own use. He will take a tenth of your flocks, and you yourselves will become his slaves. When that day comes, you will cry out for relief from the king you have chosen, but the LORD will not answer you in that day."

But the people refused to listen to Samuel. "No!" they said. "We want a king over us. Then we will be like all the other nations, with a king to lead us and to go out before us and fight our battles."

When Samuel heard all that the people said, he repeated it before the LORD. The LORD answered, "Listen to them and give them a king."

Then Samuel said to the Israelites, "Everyone go back to your own town." (1 Samuel 8:1–22 NIV)

It is kind of funny when you sit back and think about this. They had no king to rule over them, but what they had was God the creator of the whole world leading them. They looked at what the other nations had, and so they wanted one too. Sounds just like a little kid, doesn't it? They have a king; we want a king. Why do they want this king? To lead them and to go out for them and fight their battles.

God has been leading them and fighting their battles for about four hundred years from the time of Moses. And the funny thing is I don't think there is a general today that would not want to win a war the way God does. Yet they want a human king to lead them rather than God.

God was telling them that they didn't need a king. He wanted to be their king. He warns them of what would happen if they did have a king. He tells them about all the things this king will take from them, yet they still wouldn't listen and demanded that they have a king.

There is as big push going on today from people who want to change America's government from a *republic* to a socialistic type of government. What doesn't make sense is just like the Israelites having several hundred years of history to understand how well God ruled, these people have several hundred years to look at how well the socialistic types of governments don't work. Yet they still want one because they think the theory will work.

The socialistic government theory would be a great thing if man's sinful nature would not be involved. Everyone would do their best, and we all share in the fruits all of our labor. But the problem comes when the one man doesn't do his share, so the next man doesn't, and then the next wonders, "Why should I do my best if they get to live the same way I do and not do their share of the work?" Paul tells us in 2 Thessalonians 3:10, "For even when we were with you, we gave you this rule: 'The one who is unwilling to work shall not eat.'" And then the whole system breaks down. The person who doesn't do his share is not considering the result of his action concerning others; he's only thinking of himself.

Besides, just like God warned the Israelites of what a king will do, we can look at the rulers of other socialistic governments and see how their rulers rule. Why is it that the rulers of these governments live such lavish lifestyles yet their people are usually dirt poor? If they think that everybody should live at the same level, why don't they? Or do they feel that they're so much better than the people they govern?

And why do the people who want to push for a socialistic government and make millions of dollars each year, not giving it to other people who don't? Wouldn't it make sense that they continue to make millions of dollars each year, take a determined amount, say $50,000, to live off, and give the rest of it to as many people as they can who don't make $50,000 a year? That way more people will have the lifestyle they have. Or is the problem that they talk a good game while they are focused on keeping theirs? Who do you think they love?

So God gave them a king. His name was Saul.

From the reading of scriptures in 1 Samuel, it appears that Saul was a humble man. When Samuel came to tell Saul that he is going to be that king, look at Saul's response in 1 Samuel 9:21, "Saul answered, 'But am I not a Benjamite, from the smallest tribe of Israel, and is not my clan the least of all the clans of the tribe of Benjamin? Why do you say such a thing to me?'" Then on the day Samuel announces to the nation of Israel who the king will be, look at where Saul was in 1 Samuel 10:20–27 (NIV):

> When Samuel had all Israel come forward by tribes, the tribe of Benjamin was taken by lot. Then he brought forward the tribe of Benjamin, clan by clan, and Matri's clan was taken. Finally Saul son of Kish was taken. But when they looked for him, he was not to be found. So they inquired further of the LORD, "Has the man come here yet?"
>
> And the LORD said, "Yes, he has hidden himself among the supplies."
>
> They ran and brought him out, and as he stood among the people he was a head taller than any of the others. Samuel said to all the people, "Do you see the man the LORD has chosen? There is no one like him among all the people."
>
> Then the people shouted, "Long live the king!"
>
> Samuel explained to the people the rights and duties of kingship. He wrote them down on a scroll

and deposited it before the LORD. Then Samuel dismissed the people to go to their own homes.

Saul also went to his home in Gibeah, accompanied by valiant men whose hearts God had touched. [27] But some scoundrels said, "How can this fellow save us?" They despised him and brought him no gifts. But Saul kept silent.

He was hiding because he was scared to be king. Most people would jump at the chance, but he was hiding from it. Then read what happened.

Nahash the Ammonite went up and besieged Jabesh Gilead. And all the men of Jabesh said to him, "Make a treaty with us, and we will be subject to you."

But Nahash the Ammonite replied, "I will make a treaty with you only on the condition that I gouge out the right eye of every one of you and so bring disgrace on all Israel."

The elders of Jabesh said to him, "Give us seven days so we can send messengers throughout Israel; if no one comes to rescue us, we will surrender to you."

When the messengers came to Gibeah of Saul and reported these terms to the people, they all wept aloud. Just then Saul was returning from the fields, behind his oxen, and he asked, "What is wrong with everyone? Why are they weeping?" Then they repeated to him what the men of Jabesh had said.

When Saul heard their words, the Spirit of God came powerfully upon him, and he burned with anger. He took a pair of oxen, cut them into pieces, and sent the pieces by messengers throughout Israel, proclaiming, "This is what will be done to the oxen of anyone who does not follow Saul and Samuel." Then the terror of the LORD fell on the people, and they came out together as one. When Saul mustered them at Bezek, the men of Israel numbered three hundred thousand and those of Judah thirty thousand.

They told the messengers who had come, "Say to the men of Jabesh Gilead, 'By the time the sun is hot tomorrow, you will be rescued.'" When the messengers went and reported this to the men of Jabesh, they were elated. They said to the Ammonites, "Tomorrow we will surrender to you, and you can do to us whatever you like."

The next day Saul separated his men into three divisions; during the last watch of the night they broke into the camp of the Ammonites and slaughtered them until the heat of the day. Those who survived were scattered, so that no two of them were left together.

The people then said to Samuel, "Who was it that asked, 'Shall Saul reign over us?' Turn these men over to us so that we may put them to death."

But Saul said, "No one will be put to death today, for this day the LORD has rescued Israel."

Then Samuel said to the people, "Come, let us go to Gilgal and there renew the kingship." So all the people went to Gilgal and made Saul king in the presence of the LORD. There they sacrificed fellowship offerings before the LORD, and Saul and all the Israelites held a great celebration. (1 Samuel 11:1–15)

The next thing he did was he went home and started plowing the fields. Who after being anointed king would then go home and start plowing the field? This doesn't even follow human nature. And then last but not least, the people wanted to kill the men who questioned his being king, and he wouldn't let them.

I believe it is fairly easy to see that he was a humble man. But what happened?

Saul reigned for forty-two years, so this didn't happen overnight. There was a point in the beginning of his reign we see in 1 Samuel 13, where he was to wait for Samuel, and because his men started to scatter, he got nervous and made the sacrifice that Samuel was supposed to make. Samuel showed up right after he finished sacrificing, and it was at this time that Samuel told Saul that his kingdom would not reign forever and that it would be given to someone that was "a man after God's own heart."

But the last straw happened in 1 Samuel 15.

> Samuel said to Saul, "I am the one the LORD sent to anoint you king over his people Israel; so listen now to the message from the LORD. This is what the LORD Almighty says: 'I will punish the Amalekites for what they did to Israel when they waylaid them as they came up from Egypt. [3] Now go, attack the Amalekites and totally destroy all that belongs to them. Do not spare them; put to death men and women, children and infants, cattle and sheep, camels and donkeys.'"
>
> So Saul summoned the men and mustered them at Telaim—two hundred thousand foot soldiers and ten thousand from Judah. Saul went to the city of Amalek and set an ambush in the ravine. Then he said to the Kenites, "Go away, leave the Amalekites so that I do not destroy you along with them; for you showed kindness to all the Israelites when they came up out of Egypt." So the Kenites moved away from the Amalekites.
>
> Then Saul attacked the Amalekites all the way from Havilah to Shur, near the eastern border of Egypt. He took Agag king of the Amalekites

alive, and all his people he totally destroyed with the sword. But Saul and the army spared Agag and the best of the sheep and cattle, the fat calves and lambs—everything that was good. These they were unwilling to destroy completely, but everything that was despised and weak they totally destroyed.

Then the word of the LORD came to Samuel: "I regret that I have made Saul king, because he has turned away from me and has not carried out my instructions." Samuel was angry, and he cried out to the LORD all that night.

Early in the morning Samuel got up and went to meet Saul, but he was told, "Saul has gone to Carmel. There he has set up a monument in his own honor and has turned and gone on down to Gilgal."

When Samuel reached him, Saul said, "The LORD bless you! I have carried out the LORD's instructions."

But Samuel said, "What then is this bleating of sheep in my ears? What is this lowing of cattle that I hear?"

Saul answered, "The soldiers brought them from the Amalekites; they spared the best of the sheep and cattle to sacrifice to the LORD your God, but we totally destroyed the rest."

"Enough!" Samuel said to Saul. "Let me tell you what the LORD said to me last night."

"Tell me," Saul replied.

Samuel said, "Although you were once small in your own eyes, did you not become the head of the tribes of Israel? The LORD anointed you king over Israel. And he sent you on a mission, saying, 'Go and completely destroy those wicked people, the Amalekites; wage war against them until you have wiped them out.' Why did you not obey the LORD? Why did you pounce on the plunder and do evil in the eyes of the LORD?"

"But I did obey the LORD," Saul said. "I went on the mission the LORD assigned me. I completely destroyed the Amalekites and brought back Agag their king. The soldiers took sheep and cattle from the plunder, the best of what was devoted to God, in order to sacrifice them to the LORD your God at Gilgal."

But Samuel replied:

"Does the LORD delight in burnt offerings and sacrifices as much as in obeying the LORD? To obey is better than sacrifice, and to heed is better than the fat of rams. For rebellion is like the sin of divination, and arrogance like the evil of idolatry. Because you have rejected the word of the LORD, he has rejected you as king."

Then Saul said to Samuel, "I have sinned. I violated the LORD's command and your instructions. I was afraid of the men and so I gave in to them. Now I beg you, forgive my sin and come back with me, so that I may worship the LORD."

But Samuel said to him, "I will not go back with you. You have rejected the word of the LORD, and the LORD has rejected you as king over Israel!"

As Samuel turned to leave, Saul caught hold of the hem of his robe, and it tore. Samuel said to him, "The LORD has torn the kingdom of Israel from you today and has given it to one of your neighbors—to one better than you. He who is the Glory of Israel does not lie or change his mind; for he is not a human being, that he should change his mind."

Saul replied, "I have sinned. But please honor me before the elders of my people and before Israel; come back with me, so that I may worship the LORD your God." So Samuel went back with Saul, and Saul worshiped the LORD.

Then Samuel said, "Bring me Agag king of the Amalekites."

Agag came to him in chains. And he thought, "Surely the bitterness of death is past."

But Samuel said,

"As your sword has made women childless, so will your mother be childless among women."

And Samuel put Agag to death before the LORD at Gilgal.

Then Samuel left for Ramah, but Saul went up to his home in Gibeah of Saul. Until the day Samuel died, he did not go to see Saul again, though Samuel mourned for him. And the LORD regretted that he had made Saul king over Israel. (1 Samuel 15:1–35 NIV)

So here we see Saul justifying his disobedience, just as we talked about before. But the thing I want to point out is what happened in verse 12. He erected a monument in his own honor. You have to be really full of yourself or in love with yourself in order to erect a monument of yourself.

Think about this. If there was no such thing as man's sinful nature or man loving himself, would we erect monuments for great men? Why would we need to? We erect monuments for men that do great things, and these great things are for the benefit of others. Wouldn't everyone do great things for others in proportion to their God-given ability? So all things that men did would be considered great or they would be considered average because everyone would be doing their best for others. Maybe there wouldn't be anything such as great or average; there would just be men. So there would be no need to erect monuments for great men; we would only want to worship our great God.

Saul's story continues on, but we will be looking at it through another man whom God considered a man after his own heart.

KING DAVID

I had a problem understanding how David was considered a man after God's own heart. He was a warrior, he murdered someone, had an adulterous relationship, and so on and so forth. But when you look at it deeper, you realize how much his heart is just like God's heart. I'll show you what I mean.

First off, we see God ordered Samuel to go to the house of Jesse of Bethlehem and anoint the one God appoints to be the new king. When he gets there, he goes to all of Jesse's sons who were in the house to get God's approval. Samuel thought it was going to be the eldest son, and here's what the Lord told him in 1 Samuel 16:7, "Do not consider his appearance or his height, for I have rejected him. The LORD does not look at the things people look at. People look at the outward appearance, but the LORD looks at the heart."

We too can look at the heart. We do that by watching a person's actions. James tells us in James 2:14–26 (NIV):

> What good is it, my brothers and sisters, if someone claims to have faith but has no deeds? Can such faith save them? Suppose a brother or a sister is without clothes and daily food. If one of you says to them, "Go in peace; keep warm and well fed," but does nothing about their physical needs, what good is it? In the same way, faith by itself, if it is not accompanied by action, is dead.
>
> But someone will say, "You have faith; I have deeds."
>
> Show me your faith without deeds, and I will show you my faith by my deeds. You believe

that there is one God. Good! Even the demons believe that—and shudder.

You foolish person, do you want evidence that faith without deeds is useless? Was not our father Abraham considered righteous for what he did when he offered his son Isaac on the altar? You see that his faith and his actions were working together, and his faith was made complete by what he did. And the scripture was fulfilled that says, "Abraham believed God, and it was credited to him as righteousness," and he was called God's friend. You see that a person is considered righteous by what they do and not by faith alone.

In the same way, was not even Rahab the prostitute considered righteous for what she did when she gave lodging to the spies and sent them off in a different direction? As the body without the spirit is dead, so faith without deeds is dead.

Isn't this the same way with love or, better yet, loving others? We can talk about how we love others, but can it be seen? Before Jesus died on the cross, he left us with the command, which says in John 15:12–13 (NIV), "My command is this: Love each other as I have loved you. Greater love has no one than this: to lay down one's life for one's friends." How can you lay down your life for a friend without an action? Isn't this what James was referring to?

Look at what Jesus told the Pharisees in Luke 10:25–37:

On one occasion an expert in the law stood up to test Jesus. "Teacher," he asked, "what must I do to inherit eternal life?"

"What is written in the Law?" he replied. "How do you read it?"

He answered, "'Love the Lord your God with all your heart and with all your soul and with all your strength and with all your mind'; and, 'Love your neighbor as yourself.'

"You have answered correctly," Jesus replied. "Do this and you will live."

But he wanted to justify himself, so he asked Jesus, "And who is my neighbor?"

In reply Jesus said: "A man was going down from Jerusalem to Jericho, when he was attacked by robbers. They stripped him of his clothes, beat him and went away, leaving him half dead. A priest happened to be going down the same road, and when he saw the man, he passed by on the other side. So too, a Levite, when he came to the place and saw him, passed by on the other side. But a Samaritan, as he traveled, came where the man was; and when he saw him, he took pity on him. He went to him and bandaged his wounds, pouring on oil and wine. Then he put the man on his own donkey, brought him to an inn and took care of him. The next day he took out two denarii and gave them to the innkeeper. 'Look after him,' he said, 'and when I return, I will reimburse you for any extra expense you may have.'

"Which of these three do you think was a neighbor to the man who fell into the hands of robbers?"

The expert in the law replied, "The one who had mercy on him."

Jesus told him, "Go and do likewise."

Matthew Henry explains it this way:

How he was slighted by those who should have been his friends, who were not only men of his own nation and religion, but one a priest and the other a Levite, men of a public charac-

111

ter and station; nay, they were men of professed sanctity, whose offices obliged them to tenderness and compassion (Heb. 5:2), who ought to have taught others their duty in such a case as this, which was to deliver them that were drawn unto death; yet they would not themselves do it. Dr. Lightfoot tells us that many of the courses of the priests had their residence in Jericho, and thence came up to Jerusalem, when it was their turn to officiate there, and so back again, which occasioned abundance of passing and repassing of priests that way, and Levites their attendants. They came this way, and saw the poor wounded man. It is probable that they heard his groans, and could not but perceive that if he were not helped he must quickly perish. The Levite not only saw him, but came and looked on him Luke 10:32. But they passed by on the other side; when they saw his case, they got as far off him as ever they could, as if they would have had a pretense to say, Behold, we knew it not. It is sad when those who should be examples of charity are prodigies of cruelty, and when those who should by displaying the mercies of God, open the bowels of compassion in others, shut up their own.

How he was succoured and relieved by a stranger, a certain Samaritan, of that nation which of all others the Jews most despised and detested and would have no dealings with. This man had some humanity in him, Luke 10:33. The priest had his heart hardened against one of his own people, but the Samaritan had his opened towards one of another people. When he saw him he had compassion on him, and never took into consideration what country he was of. Though he was a Jew, he was a man, and a man in misery, and the Samaritan has learned to honour all men; he knows not how soon this poor man's case may be his own, and therefore pities him, as he himself would desire and expect to be pitied in the like case. That such great love should be found in a Samaritan was perhaps thought as wonderful as that great faith which Christ admired in a Roman, and in a woman of Canaan; but really it was not so, for pity is the work of a man, but faith is the work of divine grace. The compassion of this Samaritan was not an idle compassion; he did not think it enough to say, "Be healed, be helped" (Jas. 2:16); but, when he drew out his soul, he reached forth his hand also to this poor needy creature, Isa. 58:7; Prov. 31:20. See how friendly this good Samaritan was. First, He went to the poor man, whom the priest and Levite kept at a distance from; he enquired, no doubt, how he came into this deplorable condition, and condoled with him. Secondly, He did the surgeon's part, for want of a better. He bound up his wounds, making use of his own linen, it is likely, for that purpose; and poured in oil and wine, which perhaps he had with him; wine to wash the wound, and oil to mollify it, and close it up. He did all he could to ease the pain, and prevent the peril, of his wounds, as one whose heart bled with him. Thirdly, He set him on his own beast, and went on foot himself, and brought him to an inn. A great mercy it is to have inns upon the road, where we may be furnished for our money with all the conveniences for food and rest. Perhaps the Samaritan, if he had not met with this hindrance, would have got that night to his journey's end; but, in compassion to that poor man, he takes up short at an inn. Some think that the priest and Levite pretended they could not stay to help the poor man, because they were in haste to go and attend the temple-service at Jerusalem. We suppose the Samaritan went upon business; but he understood that both his own business and God's sacrifice too must give place to such an act of mercy as this. Fourthly, He took care of him in the inn, got him to bed, had food for him that was proper, and due attendance, and, it may be, prayed with him. Nay, Fifthly, As if he had been his own child, or one he was obliged to look after, when he left him next morning, he left money with the landlord, to be laid out for his use, and passed his word for what he should spend more. Two pence of their money was about fifteen pence of ours, which, according to the rate of things then, would go a great way; however, here it was an earnest of satisfaction to the full of all demands. All this was kind and generous, and as much as one could have expected from a friend or a brother; and yet here it is done by a stranger and foreigner.

Now this parable is applicable to another purpose than that for which it was intended; and does excellently set forth the kindness and love of God our Saviour towards sinful miserable man. We were like this poor distressed traveller. Satan, our enemy, had robbed us, stripped us, wounded us; such is the mischief that sin had done us. We were by nature more than half dead, twice dead, in trespasses and sins; utterly unable to help ourselves, for we were without strength. The law of Moses, like the priest and Levite, the ministers of the law, looks upon us, but has no compassion on us, gives us no relief, passes by on the other side, as having neither pity nor power to help us; but then comes the blessed Jesus, that good Samaritan (and they said of him, by way of reproach, he is a Samaritan), he has compassion on us, he binds up our bleeding wounds (Ps. 147:3; Isa. 61:1), pours in, not oil and wine, but that which is infinitely more precious, his own blood. He takes care of us, and bids us put all the expenses of our cure upon his account; and all this though he was none of us, till he was pleased by his voluntary condescension to make himself so, but infinitely above us. This magnifies the riches of his love, and obliges us all to say, "How much are we indebted, and what shall we render?"

    1.) The application of the parable.

        [1.] The truth contained in it is extorted from the lawyer's own mouth. "Now tell me," saith Christ, "which of these three was neighbour to him that fell among thieves (Luke 10:36), the priest, the Levite, or the Samaritan? Which of these did the neighbour's part?" To this the lawyer would not answer, as he ought to have done, "Doubtless, the Samaritan was;" but, "He that showed mercy on him; doubtless, he was a good neighbour to him, and very neighbourly, and I cannot but say that it was a good work thus to save an honest Jew from perishing."

        [2.] The duty inferred from it is pressed home upon the lawyer's own conscience: Go, and do thou likewise. The duty of relations is mutual and reciprocal; the titles of friends, brethren, neighbours, are, as Grotius here speaks ton pros ti—equally binding on both sides: if one side be bound, the other cannot be loose, as is agreed in all contracts. If a Samaritan does well that helps a distressed Jew, certainly a Jew does not well if he refuses in like manner to help a distressed Samaritan. Petimusque damusque vicissim—These kind offices are to be reciprocated. "And therefore go thou and do as the Samaritan did, whenever occasion offers: show mercy to those that need thy help, and do it freely, and with concern and compassion, though they be not of thy own nation and thy own profession, or of thy own opinion and communion in religion. Let thy charity be thus extensive, before thou boastest of having conformed thyself to that great commandment of loving thy neighbour." This lawyer valued himself much upon his learning and his knowledge of the laws, and in that he thought to have puzzled Christ himself; but Christ sends him to school to a Samaritan, to learn his duty: "Go, and do like him." Note, It is the duty of every one of us, in our places, and according to our ability, to succour, help, and relieve all that are in distress and necessity, and of lawyers particularly; and herein we must study to excel many that are proud of their being priests and Levites.

I bring this up at this time to set the stage for us to be thinking about what we're going to see in David. We who are Christians, who have accepted Jesus as our Lord and Savior and have the Holy Spirit living in us, should be men and women after God's own heart. This should be apparent by our actions and not by our appearance. What I mean is this.

The priest and the Levite were both religious men. They had a religious appearance, they could talk the lingo, they could recite the laws, and they knew how to play good church. But who was the one showing God's love? The Pharisees hated the Samaritans, and for Jesus to use the Samaritan as the example of the one showing God's love was totally against the grain. They would have expected the priest or the Levite to be the hero in the story. Would we have expected the same today?

Are we so wrapped up in church service—that is, in being ushers, working in children's ministries, teaching, or anything that has to do with the church—and neglecting the other important things? Are we helping our neighbor outside the church by showing love? Things like donating a car, helping to rebuild the house that was destroyed, buying some groceries, or whatever it may be.

Sometimes I think it's easier to do the big things because we get the most personal satisfaction from doing them. What about just the simple things that occur daily? Things like holding open a door or returning a grocery cart for someone, maybe just taking a minute to say hi. All these things are done for a total stranger. Remember the Samaritan was a total stranger to the man that got attacked, and Jesus referred to him as a neighbor. Can we be seen for who we are by our heart or is it by our outward appearance?

I use to do freelance work for other representatives in my industry. The first time I worked for another representative, he gave me a call a couple days after I got back from the job. Apparently, his wife worked with a single Christian woman, and she wanted to introduce me to her. So she started the conversation by saying, "Steve, I know you are a Christian because you pray before you eat your food." Oh Lord, please help me! Don't let this be the only way people recognize me as a Christian! I want people to be able to see my heart through my actions and think there goes a man after God's own heart. So let's study David's heart.

Everyone knows the story of David and Goliath. So I'm not going to spend a whole lot of time here on the obvious points that everyone talks about. But there are a few things that you have to look at in order to continue the story. Even though David was anointed to be the next king, he was still a shepherd, but he was also the musician to help Saul get relief. For we see in 1 Samuel 16:14 (NIV), "Now the Spirit of the LORD had departed from Saul, and an evil spirit from the LORD tormented him."

Now we have no idea of how the evil spirit tormented him, and it may be pure speculation to say how it did, but from the continuation of the story, you might think that the evil spirit's tormenting had to do with Saul losing his kingship. This seems to become more obvious after the story of Goliath.

> Now the Philistines gathered their forces for war and assembled at Sokoh in Judah. They pitched camp at Ephes Dammim, between Sokoh and Azekah. Saul and the Israelites assembled and camped in the Valley of Elah and drew up their battle line to meet the Philistines. The Philistines occupied one hill and the Israelites another, with the valley between them.
>
> A champion named Goliath, who was from Gath, came out of the Philistine camp. His height was six cubits and a span. He had a bronze helmet on his head and wore a coat of scale armor of bronze weighing five thousand shekels; on his legs he wore bronze greaves, and a bronze javelin was slung on his back. His spear shaft was like a weaver's rod, and its iron point weighed six hundred shekels. His shield bearer went ahead of him.
>
> Goliath stood and shouted to the ranks of Israel, "Why do you come out and line up for battle? Am I not a Philistine, and are you not the

servants of Saul? Choose a man and have him come down to me. If he is able to fight and kill me, we will become your subjects; but if I overcome him and kill him, you will become our subjects and serve us." Then the Philistine said, "This day I defy the armies of Israel! Give me a man and let us fight each other." On hearing the Philistine's words, Saul and all the Israelites were dismayed and terrified.

Now David was the son of an Ephrathite named Jesse, who was from Bethlehem in Judah. Jesse had eight sons, and in Saul's time he was very old. Jesse's three oldest sons had followed Saul to the war: The firstborn was Eliab; the second, Abinadab; and the third, Shammah. David was the youngest. The three oldest followed Saul, but David went back and forth from Saul to tend his father's sheep at Bethlehem.

For forty days the Philistine came forward every morning and evening and took his stand.

Now Jesse said to his son David, "Take this ephah of roasted grain and these ten loaves of bread for your brothers and hurry to their camp. Take along these ten cheeses to the commander of their unit. See how your brothers are and bring back some assurance from them. They are with Saul and all the men of Israel in the Valley of Elah, fighting against the Philistines."

Early in the morning David left the flock in the care of a shepherd, loaded up and set out, as Jesse had directed. He reached the camp as the army was going out to its battle positions, shouting the war cry. Israel and the Philistines were drawing up their lines facing each other. David left his things with the keeper of supplies, ran to the battle lines and asked his brothers how they were. As he was talking with them, Goliath, the Philistine champion from Gath, stepped out from his lines and shouted his usual defiance, and David heard it. Whenever the Israelites saw the man, they all fled from him in great fear.

Now the Israelites had been saying, "Do you see how this man keeps coming out? He comes out to defy Israel. The king will give great wealth to the man who kills him. He will also give him his daughter in marriage and will exempt his family from taxes in Israel."

David asked the men standing near him, "What will be done for the man who kills this Philistine and removes this disgrace from Israel? *Who is this uncircumcised Philistine that he should defy the armies of the living God?*"

They repeated to him what they had been saying and told him, "This is what will be done for the man who kills him."

When Eliab, David's oldest brother, heard him speaking with the men, he burned with anger at him and asked, "Why have you come down here? And with whom did you leave those few sheep in the wilderness? I know how conceited you are and how wicked your heart is; you came down only to watch the battle."

"Now what have I done?" said David. "Can't I even speak?" He then turned away to someone else and brought up the same matter, and the men answered him as before. What David said was overheard and reported to Saul, and Saul sent for him.

David said to Saul, "Let no one lose heart on account of this Philistine; your servant will go and fight him."

Saul replied, "You are not able to go out against this Philistine and fight him; you are only a young man, and he has been a warrior from his youth."

But David said to Saul, "Your servant has been keeping his father's sheep. When a lion or a bear came and carried off a sheep from the flock, I went after it, struck it and rescued the sheep from its mouth. When it turned on me, I seized it by its hair, struck it and killed it. Your servant has killed both the lion and the bear; this uncircumcised Philistine will be like one of them, because he has defied the armies of the living God. *The LORD who rescued me from the paw of the lion and the paw of the bear will rescue me from the hand of this Philistine.*"

Saul said to David, "Go, and the LORD be with you."

Then Saul dressed David in his own tunic. He put a coat of armor on him and a bronze helmet on his head. David fastened on his sword over the tunic and tried walking around, because he was not used to them.

"I cannot go in these," he said to Saul, "because I am not used to them." So he took them off. Then he took his staff in his hand, chose five smooth stones from the stream, put them in the pouch of his shepherd's bag and, with his sling in his hand, approached the Philistine.

Meanwhile, the Philistine, with his shield bearer in front of him, kept coming closer to David. He looked David over and saw that he was little more than a boy, glowing with health and handsome, and he despised him. He said to David, "Am I a dog, that you come at me with sticks?" And the Philistine cursed David by his gods. "Come here," he said, "and I'll give your flesh to the birds and the wild animals!"

David said to the Philistine, *"You come against me with sword and spear and javelin, but I come against you in the name of the LORD Almighty, the God of the armies of Israel, whom you have defied. This day the LORD will deliver you into my hands, and I'll strike you down and cut off your head. This very day I will give the carcasses of the Philistine army to the birds and the wild animals, and the whole world will know that there is a God in Israel. All those gathered here will know that it is not by sword or spear that the LORD saves; for the battle is the LORD's, and he will give all of you into our hands."*

As the Philistine moved closer to attack him, David ran quickly toward the battle line to meet him. Reaching into his bag and taking out a stone, he slung it and struck the Philistine on the forehead. The stone sank into his forehead, and he fell facedown on the ground.

So David triumphed over the Philistine with a sling and a stone; without a sword in his hand he struck down the Philistine and killed him.

David ran and stood over him. He took hold of the Philistine's sword and drew it from the sheath. After he killed him, he cut off his head with the sword.

When the Philistines saw that their hero was dead, they turned and ran. Then the men of Israel and Judah surged forward with a shout and pursued the Philistines to the entrance of Gath and to the gates of Ekron. Their dead were strewn along the Shaaraim road to Gath and Ekron. When the Israelites returned from chasing the Philistines, they plundered their camp.

David took the Philistine's head and brought it to Jerusalem; he put the Philistine's weapons in his own tent.

As Saul watched David going out to meet the Philistine, he said to Abner, commander of the army, "Abner, whose son is that young man?"

Abner replied, "As surely as you live, Your Majesty, I don't know."

The king said, "Find out whose son this young man is."

As soon as David returned from killing the Philistine, Abner took him and brought him before Saul, with David still holding the Philistine's head.

"Whose son are you, young man?" Saul asked him.

David said, "I am the son of your servant Jesse of Bethlehem." (1 Samuel 17:1–58) (emphasis added)

Certain things in this story leave me wondering. One was the reaction of his older brother when David was inquiring about who this *giant* was and what was going to be given to the warrior that defeated Goliath. He started to belittle him. Look at what he says in verse 28,

When Eliab, David's oldest brother, heard him speaking with the men, he burned with anger at him and asked, "Why have you come down here? And with whom did you leave those few sheep in the wilderness? I know how conceited you are and how wicked your heart is; you came down only to watch the battle."

Isn't that the way it is when someone steps out in front of the crowd. He doesn't get an "attaboy." He gets "What do you think you are going to do? You only take care of a couple sheep? You're just prideful and have a wicked heart."

Isn't this just another example of self-preservation and jealousy going on here? Looks like another "crab in the bucket" scenario. Isn't this the way it is in real life? When someone doesn't have the courage to step out in faith to do whatever needs to be done, they will use whatever means available they can to tear down the other person in order to preserve their own pride. Again we see in Eliab the same self-love we have seen in Cain of tearing down the tallest building to have the tallest building or at least to be the same-size building as all the rest.

Also watch David's language when he is talking about fighting Goliath.

He stands for God's honor. "Who is this uncircumcised Philistine that he should defy the armies of the living God?" It is unlike what is going on today where it seems like people are ashamed of God or to be associated as one of God's children. The world calls people who love Jesus "Jesus freaks" as if that were bad thing. That is understandable since they don't understand what that's all about. But what is not understandable is Christians let that bother them as if it was a bad thing; therefore, we minimize our love for Christ in order to escape the title.

> Dear friends, let us love one another, for love comes from God. Everyone who loves has been born of God and knows God. Whoever does not love does not know God, because God is love. This is how God showed his love among us: He sent his one and only Son into the world that we might live through him. This is love: not that we loved God, but that he loved us and sent his Son as an atoning sacrifice for our sins. Dear friends, since God so loved us, we also ought to love one another. No one has ever seen God; but if we love one another, God lives in us and his love is made complete in us.

This is how we know that we live in him and he in us: He has given us of his Spirit. And we have seen and testify that the Father has sent his Son to be the Savior of the world. If anyone acknowledges that Jesus is the Son of God, God lives in them and they in God. And so we know and rely on the love God has for us.

God is love. Whoever lives in love lives in God, and God in them. This is how love is made complete among us so that we will have confidence on the day of judgment: In this world we are like Jesus. *There is no fear in love. But perfect love drives out fear, because fear has to do with punishment. The one who fears is not made perfect in love.*

We love because he first loved us. Whoever claims to love God yet hates a brother or sister is a liar. For whoever does not love their brother and sister, whom they have seen, cannot love God, whom they have not seen. And he has given us this command: Anyone who loves God must also love their brother and sister. (1 John 4:7–21) (emphasis added)

Isn't this what happened on the day of Pentecost? Jesus has just been crucified, resurrected, and ascended into heaven. The apostles were basically left alone and afraid, for they did not know what the future held. Suddenly, a burst of something that seemed like wind filled the room, and they were all talking in different languages or tongues. This was the Holy Spirit.

So to listen to a lot of people or to others' teachings, you would think that the ability to speak in different languages was the power given from the Holy Spirit. I don't believe that is true. I believe that was an ability given by the Holy Spirit, but the power of the Holy Spirit was God's love or godly love which is loving others. This is why Peter was able to address the crowd publicly where before he was hiding in fear. He was given the love of God in his Spirit, the perfect love of God, and it was this love that enabled him to address a crowd in a time when he normally should have been afraid.

This same love gave Peter the ability to address the Sanhedrin in Acts 4.

> The priests and the captain of the temple guard and the Sadducees came up to Peter and John while they were speaking to the people. They were greatly disturbed because the apostles were teaching the people, proclaiming in Jesus the resurrection of the dead. They seized Peter and John and, because it was evening, they put them in jail until the next day. [4] But many who heard the message believed; so the number of men who believed grew to about five thousand.
>
> The next day the rulers, the elders and the teachers of the law met in Jerusalem. Annas the high priest was there, and so were Caiaphas, John, Alexander and others of the high priest's family. They had Peter and John brought before them and began to question them: "By what power or what name did you do this?"
>
> Then Peter, filled with the Holy Spirit, said to them: "Rulers and elders of the people! If we are being called to account today for an act of kindness shown to a man who was lame and are being asked how he was healed, then know this, you and all the people of Israel: It is by the name of Jesus Christ of Nazareth, whom you crucified but whom God raised from the dead, that this man stands before you healed. Jesus is
> "'the stone you builders rejected,
> which has become the cornerstone.'

Salvation is found in no one else, for there is no other name under heaven given to mankind by which we must be saved."

When they saw the courage of Peter and John and realized that they were unschooled, ordinary men, they were astonished and they took note that these men had been with Jesus. But since they could see the man who had been healed standing there with them, there was nothing they could say. So they ordered them to withdraw from the Sanhedrin and then conferred together. "What are we going to do with these men?" they asked. "Everyone living in Jerusalem knows they have performed a notable sign, and we cannot deny it. But to stop this thing from spreading any further among the people, we must warn them to speak no longer to anyone in this name."

Then they called them in again and commanded them not to speak or teach at all in the name of Jesus. But Peter and John replied, "Which is right in God's eyes: to listen to you, or to him? You be the judges! As for us, we cannot help speaking about what we have seen and heard."

After further threats they let them go. They could not decide how to punish them, because all the people were praising God for what had happened. For the man who was miraculously healed was over forty years old. (Acts 4:1–22)

This has to be put in perspective. This is not like they went up before a senate committee in the United States where all religious views are protected. They were in front of the same people that crucified Jesus, and they are now healing and preaching salvation in Jesus's name. If the Sanhedrin would crucify Jesus, who they themselves feared, wouldn't you think they would also do it to the followers as well? So to stand in front of the executioners and declare to them allegiance to the one they executed is what would seem to be fearless. Yet I don't believe that they were not afraid, but that they had such a fierce love for the Lord; what fear was there was overshadowed or, in John's words, "driven out" by God's love, regardless of what may happen to their personal safety.

The power of the Spirit gives us the love of God to focus on others or doing for others, and the more we focus on others, the less concern we have for ourselves. Isn't this what happens when we are sharing the gospel with nonbelievers? There is a fear of rejection, ridicule, scorn, or embarrassment from others, which in turn could be used against us.

Well, can't we do that without the Holy Spirit? There are people who are not Christians and they don't have the Holy Spirit, yet they are focused on helping others. How do you explain that? The question I raise is, are they doing it selflessly or are they doing it because of the fact that there is self-satisfaction involved?

There is no question that doing for others will make us feel better about ourselves, since it takes the focus off our problems. *Twelve-step programs* have been using that approach for years to help people overcome all types of addictions, from alcohol, drug, overeating, etc. But would they do it for no personal gain other than the love of the Father? Their motto is "Help someone else to help yourself." I am not saying this is wrong. But take a look at the people of faith.

> Some faced jeers and flogging, and even chains and imprisonment. They were put to death by stoning; they were sawed in two; they were killed by the sword. They went about in sheepskins and goatskins, destitute, persecuted and mistreated—the world was not worthy of them. They wandered in deserts and mountains, living in caves and in holes in the ground. These were all commended for their faith, yet none of them received what had been promised, since

God had planned something better for us so that
only together with us would they be made perfect. (Hebrews 11:36–40)

This may not seem relevant, yet there are martyrs all around the
world who are still persecuted for their faith today. I am sure they had
personal satisfaction that they suffered for Christ, but being sawed in
two meant that it was short-lived in this world.

I believe you can see this in Stephen in Acts 7, when he addressed
the Sanhedrin, which he was stoned to death for. Or in Paul and the
rest of the apostles, who were stoned, imprisoned, and even killed for
not relinquishing the gospel of Christ. I believe this is also what is
true with David. The other Israelites also loved God, but David loved
God and trusted God so fiercely that it overshadowed his fear, and
therefore, he faced Goliath without concern for his personal safety.

Another thing that I find amazing is the reaction from Saul.
He's asking David, "Who are you?" Saul didn't even know who David
was, even though he was the one who gave him relief from the evil
spirits. Wouldn't you think that if David's music was the one giving
him relief, he would know him very well?

Think about it, I realize that my vocabulary is not very strong,
but when I get sick, I go to the pharmacy with my prescription, and I
get the medicine that the doctor prescribes. When I first get it, rarely
can I even pronounce the name of the medicine that I need. But it
is amazing that once I get the relief from this medicine, I now know
the name of it and rarely do I forget its name and what it is used for.
Why? It was the source of my relief.

But here, Saul is getting his relief from the tempting spirits from
David, and he doesn't even know who he is. He was told earlier who
he was and where he came from, but he still doesn't know him. This
is only an indication of how much Saul is wrapped up in himself.

After Saul sent David out on military commissions and he saw
not only David's success but that the people loved David's success, he
figured that the only thing left for David to do was to take his kingdom. Get it, "*his* kingdom." God was the one who has been leading
the Israelites since the beginning of time, and Saul was appointed as

the first king, and now it is *his* kingdom, as if he had something to do with the building of it. Yes, he did unite the people and defend their country from the Philistines and he did destroy the Amalekites, even though he didn't do it the way he was supposed to. But he was appointed to do these things in the power of the Lord and not given the country as his own. First Samuel 15:1 said, "Samuel said to Saul, 'I am the one the LORD sent to anoint you king over his people Israel.'" Saul was given the position of king but not the possession of the kingdom.

This is not just an issue that Saul dealt with many years ago. This is a situation that can be seen today in the leadership of the church. I see it over and over again; the leaders of a church or a ministry tend to take over as if it is now theirs. They are put into that position to shepherd the flock, but they tend to take over as if it has now become theirs. I believe that this comes from the fact that today we have become such a success-oriented society that we are all measuring our self-worth out of our self-accomplishment. So the bigger the church or ministry, the more self-worth the leaders have of themselves.

So when your self-worth comes from your accomplishments, then it is only human nature to want to hold on to whatever it is giving you that self-worth. This creates positions of tyrants, hierarchy, and politics within the church, which in turn creates division in the house, and as Jesus said, "A house divided against itself will fall" (Luke 11:17). This is not only in a church, but in the body of Christ also.

I have a friend who told me the story of how many years ago he was trying to get a concert put together in a small community for Christian believers and anyone who wanted to attend, in hopes that the Christian believer would be able to bring a nonbelieving friend along. His plan was to get local area bands the chance to play for their exposure and for the enjoyment of the community and give the local churches the venue to present their church. He was looking for the local churches to help support this effort. They all seemed interested in helping, but there was one recurring problem that was stopping them. They wanted to know who was going to get the recognition for putting it together. Why would they care as long as they are all working together for the same effort?

My experience has been similar. I was working on a ministry where people in the same geographical area, who shared the same ideas, could find each other in order to benefit the community. The idea was rather simple. Let's say a person had an idea to renovate a house, and after it was finished, it would be given to a less fortunate family. But what if that person had a way in which he could find other Christians who were carpenters, plumbers, electricians, and people who just want to invest in a project like this, from all over the city and metropolitan area. Then they pool their resources together. How much more could they accomplish together? Instead of just doing one house, they could have done multiple houses. The pooling together of their resources would have been exponential.

But the problem I ran into was similar to my friend's. I had one pastor tell me that he could not work or allow his members to work with other Christians who did not believe the same as he did. After the shock wore off, I inquired where that came from. He responded that they were not to work with others that were not equally yoked. I thought being a Christian, we were all of the same family? But it wasn't just him.

I was also working in another city about five hours away trying to start the same thing. And I ran into the exact same problem, but in a different way. There was a group of pastors that would get together once a month to share their ideas on how to build a church. I was attending these meeting in order to develop contacts and to find support to help create a network in their city. Again I got that the pat on the back with "Good luck" and "Let me pray for you," and they sent me on my way.

While attending these meetings, it was humorous in a way to listen to them constantly pat themselves on the back because all these pastors from other denominations were able to come together in the same room. It was if they accomplish some great feat by doing this. Jesus told us that in the Sermon on the Mount in Matthew 5:43–48.

You have heard that it was said, "Love your neighbor and hate your enemy." But I tell you, love your enemies and pray for those who persecute you, that you may be children of your Father in heaven. He causes his sun to rise on the evil and the good, and sends rain on the righteous and the unrighteous. If you love those who love you, what reward will you get? Are not even the tax collectors doing that? And if you greet only your own people, what are you doing more than others? Do not even pagans do that? Be perfect, therefore, as your heavenly Father is perfect.

These pastors are supposed to be brothers in Christ, and you would have thought that they just created world peace because they could all come together without a major fight breaking out. Yet the fact of the matter is, they hadn't accomplished anything more in that area than if the Mafia families had called a truce in order to come together to deal with something that affected them all as a whole. I'm not sure I was seeing the Christian love in that.

What's more is, when they talked about building their church, their focus was not about how God was building the church; they talked about appearances, how full the church should be before you start an additional service, the parking lots, and advertisement, etc. If I didn't know any better, I would have thought I was at a business meeting with a bunch of business executives who are trying to increase the size of their business.

Now there were many good things that came out of it, like success they were having in their youth groups and teaching programs. But the thing that kept shouting out at me when I was listening to them speak is when they would say, "Here is how to grow your church" or "Here is how I built my church." It was if they owned it.

Another thing I found difficult to understand was this. Even though they would have parachurch organizations come in to explain their organizations so these churches could support their efforts, not once in the year and a half to two years that I attended these meetings did I ever hear anyone say, "Hey, let's pool our resources and accomplish something for the community." No, not once!

After listening and talking to these pastors, I believe that I figured out why it was so hard to get any cooperation outside of a pat on the back, a prayer, and a "Go get them, tiger." The fact still remains that they are human, and they too get their self-worth based on their success or level of accomplishment. So if they encouraged the members of their church to go out and seek other members of other churches to work together with, then there was a possibility that their members could start going to the other churches. This in turn would lower the appearance of the success of their church.

Then we also have to address the issue of all these building programs. I have heard in the past more nonbiblical justifications for why they have to build a new building than I even thought was possible. I can tell you story after story of how buildings that were built, which are now barely used and were built for the reason that this building was going to bring more people to the body of Christ. And nothing has been further from the truth.

I created friends in a church that was involved in the group of pastors that I was telling you about. The pastor of this church had started building a new sanctuary, even though the people I knew couldn't figure out why. He started the project and later found himself underfunded. So he started to sell parking spaces and seat spaces in order to create the revenue needed to finish the project. The same pastor during one of his presentations had exclaimed that the reason he had built the auditorium which we were in was not only for his church but for all churches to use that needed it. After hearing this, I asked him to use the auditorium to hold a concert for the community and for the purpose of letting the community know about the purpose of our ministry. He responded that there was no way he could let us use it, because if he did, he would have every church, parachurch, and ministry wanting to use it for the same reasons. What happened to his justification for building his auditorium?

It's not just him. I have seen the Bible being misrepresented, guilt, and almost any other tactic in order to justify the building of a new building. One pastor of a church I attended justified the building of a new gymnasium that the children of his church would bring their unsaved friends to play in the gym, and then the unsaved friends would bring their parents to the church, and they would find Christ in the church. He pulled together the wealthiest people in this church to commit to funding a certain portion of the project based on Ezra in the Old Testament. Then he brought that to the congregation for support and got funding for the rest.

I can remember thinking, I wonder if he would have taken the money he had collected, used it to benefit the community, like helping those who were out of work, or something similar, if he would have attracted more adults and the adults would have brought their children to church and more souls would have been won to the Lord that way, than the other way around. The problem is that he wouldn't have had the huge building as a sign of his success.

Also, pastors want to use the term "the house of God" as the justification for anything they want to do. I've seen pastors spend money on the finest of everything, justifying the cost because "this is the house of God." One church I visited had a private dining room for when his important guests came. In it they had the finest China, crystal, and silverware for the same reasoning. The thing that confuses me most is on the day that Jesus died on the cross, the curtain in the temple was torn, and now God dwells in us through this spirit, making us the house or temple of God.

Now I'm not saying that the church should look like a shack and that it should not be nicely decorated. I think that would be taking it to the other extreme. But I do believe that some of the money that we spent on the extravagant could be better spent on getting the gospel out to those who have not heard it yet. I think that would be more in line with what Jesus commanded us in Matthew 28:19, "Therefore go and make disciples of all nations, baptizing them in the name of the Father and of the Son and of the Holy Spirit."

God gave Saul the kingdom, but now Saul starts to read his own press clippings. At first, he makes a sacrifice that only the priest should have made due to the pressure that he was feeling from the unrest of the people. Then he tells Samuel that he kept the spoils of the Amalekites to sacrifice to the Lord. Basically, Saul was trying to do what God told him to, but the way that Saul wanted to do it made him look good in the process. So, was all of this done out of his love of God or his love of himself? I believe we can ask the same questions for the pastors that are doing the same thing.

When Samuel addressed Saul, look again at his answer in Samuel 15:13–23:

> When Samuel reached him, Saul said, "The LORD bless you! I have carried out the LORD's instructions."
>
> But Samuel said, "What then is this bleating of sheep in my ears? What is this lowing of cattle that I hear?"
>
> Saul answered, "The soldiers brought them from the Amalekites; they spared the best of the sheep and cattle to sacrifice to the LORD your God, but we totally destroyed the rest."
>
> "Enough!" Samuel said to Saul. "Let me tell you what the LORD said to me last night."
>
> "Tell me," Saul replied.
>
> Samuel said, "Although you were once small in your own eyes, did you not become the head of the tribes of Israel? The LORD anointed you king over Israel. And he sent you on a mission, saying, 'Go and completely destroy those wicked people, the Amalekites; wage war against them until you have wiped them out.' Why did you not obey the LORD? Why did you pounce on the plunder and do evil in the eyes of the LORD?"
>
> "But I did obey the LORD," Saul said. "I went on the mission the LORD assigned me. I completely destroyed the Amalekites and brought back Agag their king. The soldiers took sheep and cattle from the plunder, the best of what was devoted to God, in order to sacrifice them to the LORD your God at Gilgal."

But Samuel replied:

"Does the LORD delight in burnt offerings
and sacrifices as much as in obeying the LORD?
To obey is better than sacrifice, and to heed is
better than the fat of rams. For rebellion is like
the sin of divination, and arrogance like the evil
of idolatry. Because you have rejected the word of
the LORD, he has rejected you as king."

I believe that if you were to address pastors with the question of, "Are you doing what the Lord has told you to do?" they would adamantly claim that they were doing God's will. And just like Saul, they would believe that they are. And just like Saul, if you were to point out the fact that they were not being obedient or that they were doing it for their own appearances, they would become just as defensive as Saul did. I have seen people leave churches for this very reason.

But look at David. After he becomes king, he wants to build a temple for the Lord, and God basically says, "No, but I will let your son do it." It says in 2 Samuel 7:5–7,

"Go and tell my servant David, 'This is what
the LORD says: "Are you the one to build me a
house to dwell in? I have not dwelt in a house
from the day I brought the Israelites up out of
Egypt to this day. I have been moving from place
to place with a tent as my dwelling. Wherever
I have moved with all the Israelites, did I ever
say to any of their rulers whom I commanded to
shepherd my people Israel, 'Why have you not
built me a house of cedar?'"'"

If God was so worried about having a house that was made by man, then why didn't he ask the question "Why haven't you already done so?" Why did he wait 'til after the reign of David to allow it to happen? Why didn't he have them do it before if it was so important? Yes, God wanted the people to focus on his house as much as they were focusing on their houses in the first chapter of the book of Haggai, but I believe that he was more concerned with the direction of their heart and not the building. Building the temple would turn the people's focus back toward God himself in the process.

Now I am not saying that the temple wasn't important; it was very important, but only up until the time of Christ's death and resurrection. I believe that the temple that he lives in today is the temple that he is extremely concerned with, and that is because we ourselves are that temple.

It seems that if Saul had kept in perspective his position over the kingdom and not try to possess the kingdom, he would not have lived in the torment that he did during his reign. Maybe some of the worry and stress would be relieved in pastors if they would understand the same thing.

Let's not forget the heart of Jonathan either. Sometimes I don't think he gets enough publicity or credit for his godly nature and character of the person that he was. He was extremely courageous as we see in 1 Samuel 14:6–14:

> Jonathan said to his young armor-bearer, "Come, let's go over to the outpost of those uncircumcised men. Perhaps the LORD will act in our behalf. Nothing can hinder the LORD from saving, whether by many or by few."
>
> "Do all that you have in mind," his armor-bearer said. "Go ahead; I am with you heart and soul."
>
> Jonathan said, "Come on, then; we will cross over toward them and let them see us. If they say to us, 'Wait there until we come to you,' we will stay where we are and not go up to them. But if they say, 'Come up to us,' we will climb up, because that will be our sign that the LORD has given them into our hands."
>
> So both of them showed themselves to the Philistine outpost. "Look!" said the Philistines.

"The Hebrews are crawling out of the holes they were hiding in." The men of the outpost shouted to Jonathan and his armor-bearer, "Come up to us and we'll teach you a lesson."

So Jonathan said to his armor-bearer, "Climb up after me; the LORD has given them into the hand of Israel."

Jonathan climbed up, using his hands and feet, with his armor-bearer right behind him. The Philistines fell before Jonathan, and his armor-bearer followed and killed behind him. In that first attack Jonathan and his armor-bearer killed some twenty men in an area of about half an acre.

I don't even think that I could have been as brave as the armor-bearer. "Perhaps the Lord will?" I am sorry, Jonathan, but I need a little more reassurance than "perhaps."

When David killed Goliath, Jonathan could have been jealous just as David's brother Eliab was. But look at what happened instead. First Samuel 18:1–4 says,

After David had finished talking with Saul, Jonathan became one in spirit with David, and he loved him as himself. From that day Saul kept David with him and did not let him return home to his family. And Jonathan made a covenant with David because he loved him as himself. Jonathan took off the robe he was wearing and gave it to David, along with his tunic, and even his sword, his bow and his belt. This is no little thing. He took off his royal family robe, and gave him his personal sword.

But I believe the thing that reveals Jonathan's heart the most is the fact that it says he loved him as himself. This is the same thing that Jesus told us to do, which is "Love your neighbor as yourself."

This had to be harder for Jonathan than we could understand it today. He was next in line to be the king of Israel, as tradition would have it. But when Saul was tormented by the evil spirit and wanted to take David's life, Jonathan was the one who stood up for David. Even after Saul was trying to take David's life and David has to run to save it, Jonathan made a covenant with him and later on even encouraged him by telling him this in 1 Samuel 23:15–18,

> While David was at Horesh in the Desert of Ziph, he learned that Saul had come out to take his life. And Saul's son Jonathan went to David at Horesh and helped him find strength in God. "Don't be afraid," he said. "My father Saul will not lay a hand on you. You will be king over Israel, and I will be second to you. Even my father Saul knows this." The two of them made a covenant before the LORD. Then Jonathan went home, but David remained at Horesh.

Jonathan didn't have a problem with giving up his position of being king to David and being under his authority since he knew that God was with him just as God was with his father Saul. He was willing to follow the one God had anointed.

Isn't this the total opposite of what we generally see today? Many people who are leaders in the church are thinking about their position like people in the business world think about theirs. Leaders in the church are continuously jockeying themselves around in order to be in the position to move up the ladder of success.

I have a friend who is an associate pastor of the church he belongs to. There is another church that he is familiar with, whose senior pastor is well up in the years. Since he occasionally has went there to preach, they asked him if he would like to be the associate pastor of their church. He came to me saying he didn't see the point of going from one church to the other as an associate pastor. The only thing that made sense to him would be if he was to become a senior pastor; otherwise, why would he move? He asked me what I thought, and I told them that it sounded like he was making a career move rather than making a decision based on whether God wanted him to or not. Because his heart really is in the right place, he understood where I was coming from and reevaluated the decision under this light. How many would have really done that?

David took waiting on God to a whole new level. Samuel had already anointed David as king. Yet David was running from Saul to save his life. On two different instances, it appeared that God had delivered Saul into David's hand. First in 1 Samuel 24 and then again in 1 Samuel 26. All David had to do was to kill Saul, and he would become the king. He was anointed by Samuel to be the king, and Jonathan had a covenant with him to serve him. David's own men was urging David to take Saul's life because God had delivered Saul into his hand.

Yet David would not touch one of God's anointed ones, even though it was apparent that God's anointing had left Saul. This even affected Saul to the point that he claimed that David was more righteous than him and exclaimed that David would be the king. Even after Saul's death, David didn't rush to be king; he simply refused to take what seemed to already be his and waited for God to give it to him.

We see this happen over and over again within the church. I have made the same mistakes myself. It seemed as if God had told me to do something, and I ran with it rather than wait for God to move. Unfortunately and always there are consequences to pay for moving on our own timing instead of waiting on God's timing, even though it was what we were supposed to be doing in the long run.

In my short time, I've seen many associate pastors or youth pastors or just leaders in the church who didn't agree with the senior pastor split a church because they felt their calling was to lead a church and the senior pastor was not leading it correctly. So they convince a certain portion of the church to go with them and start a new church. Many times these new churches don't last very long, and the members are forced to go back to the old church or look for a new one. I heard one pastor call it the Absalom spirit. It seems to me this is the identical story of Satan wanting to have his own kingdom in heaven and convincing a third of the angels to go with him.

I bring all of this to our attention so we ask the question "Are we more like Saul today or are we more like David?" Are we wrapped up in ourselves, our ministries, our accomplishments, and our possessions just like Saul, or are we more like David who had his focus on God? I believe this is what Paul was talking about in Philippians 2:3 when he said, "Do nothing out of selfish ambition or vain conceit. Rather, in humility value others above yourselves." This could mean value others above your ambitions and success since they are all about you.

If sin is loving of ourselves rather than loving of God, then when the focus is on the success of whatever it is that we are doing and it is accomplished for the glory of ourselves rather than for the glory of God, we are actually living in sin. But since we see sin as being disobedient and not as the nature of loving ourselves, we justify are actions so then we are no longer guilty.

You say everything you do is for the glory of God? Well, would you still do it or, better yet, would you be excited if it was a huge success and someone else got the recognition? What if you started something and someone else finished it and they get the recognition, do you still get just excited?

Think about what Jesus teaches in Matthew 6:1–18:

> *Be careful not to practice your righteousness in front of others to be seen by them. If you do, you will have no reward from your Father in heaven.*
>
> So when you give to the needy, do not announce it with trumpets, as the hypocrites do in the synagogues and on the streets, to be honored by others. *Truly I tell you, they have received their reward in full.* But when you give to the needy, do not let your left hand know what your right hand is doing, ⁴ so that your giving may be in secret. *Then your Father, who sees what is done in secret, will reward you.* And when you pray, do not be like the hypocrites, for they love to pray standing in the synagogues and on the street corners to be

seen by others. Truly I tell you, they have received their reward in full. [6] But when you pray, go into your room, close the door and pray to your Father, who is unseen. *Then your Father, who sees what is done in secret, will reward you.* And when you pray, do not keep on babbling like pagans, for they think they will be heard because of their many words. Do not be like them, for your Father knows what you need before you ask him.

"This, then, is how you should pray:

"'Our Father in heaven,
hallowed be your name,
your kingdom come,
your will be done,
on earth as it is in heaven.
Give us today our daily bread.
And forgive us our debts,
as we also have forgiven our debtors.
And lead us not into temptation,
but deliver us from the evil one.'

For if you forgive other people when they sin against you, your heavenly Father will also forgive you. But if you do not forgive others their sins, your Father will not forgive your sins. When you fast, do not look somber as the hypocrites do, for they disfigure their faces to show others they are fasting. Truly I tell you, *they have received their reward in full.* But when you fast, put oil on your head and wash your face, so that it will not be obvious to others that you are fasting, but only to your Father, who is unseen; and your Father, who sees what is done in secret, will reward you.

So if Jesus was talking about being obedient, then wouldn't the act of giving, praying, and fasting been good enough? What is the point of saying you have to do them in secret? Can't we use our obedience to glorify ourselves? If sin is loving ourselves, then we are living in sin, which leads us right back to the woes of the Pharisees in Matthew 23. We always think of living in sin as the act of doing something wrong continuously, but Jesus seems always to point to the condition of our hearts.

It is easier to think that I am not living in sin because I am not committing adultery, fornicating, stealing, or whatever it may be. But what if we have twisted the meaning of what sin is?

Think of it this way. I see something that I want, and so I start the process of why I should have it and why it is not wrong for me to get it. I begin to think about how I could obtain it, and then after I justify myself in the process, I devise a plan to get it, and then I execute my plan.

Now you would naturally think that the act of stealing was the sin. But I say this is not so. The point of loving yourself so much that you would be willing to do whatever it took to satisfy yourself, regardless the harm or the neglect of the other person and God, was the sin. The act of stealing is a trespass and the harm done to the other person is the iniquity, and I will call the combination of the two the transgression.

Wouldn't this also apply if we are not talking about stealing but about buying things that we cannot afford on credit or with money that was supposed to be used for something like paying bills, food, etc.

Now someone actually taking something would obviously be stealing, but what if it isn't that obvious? Could we be stealing when we receive the glory for what we are doing, which actually robs God of his glory he deserves, since he does it all through us? Wouldn't we still be living in sin since we are doing it for the love of ourselves?

Paul writes to the Philippians about letting go of himself and his position which he could boast about, but instead, he is fighting for the goal that we all should all be striving to attain.

If someone else thinks they have reasons to put confidence in the flesh, I have more: circumcised on the eighth day, of the people of Israel, of the tribe of Benjamin, a Hebrew of Hebrews; in regard to the law, a Pharisee; as for zeal, persecuting the church; as for righteousness based on the law, faultless.

But whatever were gains to me I now consider loss for the sake of Christ. What is more, I consider everything a loss because of the surpassing worth of knowing Christ Jesus my Lord, for whose sake I have lost all things. I consider them garbage, that I may gain Christ and be found in him, not having a righteousness of my own that comes from the law, but that which is through faith in Christ—the righteousness that comes from God on the basis of faith. I want to know Christ— yes, to know the power of his resurrection and participation in his sufferings, becoming like him in his death, and so, somehow, attaining to the resurrection from the dead.

Not that I have already obtained all this, or have already arrived at my goal, but I press on to take hold of that for which Christ Jesus took hold of me. Brothers and sisters, I do not consider myself yet to have taken hold of it. But one thing I do: Forgetting what is behind and straining toward what is ahead, I press on toward the goal to win the prize for which God has called me heavenward in Christ Jesus.

All of us, then, who are mature should take such a view of things. And if on some point you think differently, that too God will make clear to you. Only let us live up to what we have already attained.

Join together in following my example, brothers and sisters, and just as you have us as a model, keep your eyes on those who live as we do.

> For, as I have often told you before and now tell you again even with tears, many live as enemies of the cross of Christ. Their destiny is destruction, their god is their stomach, and their glory is in their shame. Their mind is set on earthly things. But our citizenship is in heaven. And we eagerly await a Savior from there, the Lord Jesus Christ, who, by the power that enables him to bring everything under his control, will transform our lowly bodies so that they will be like his glorious body. (Philippians 3:4–21) (emphasis added)

That being said, even Paul seemed to have struggled with this. Think about it, when he and Barnabas in Acts 15 had a dispute, wasn't this about Paul's flesh?

> Sometime later Paul said to Barnabas, "Let us go back and visit the believers in all the towns where we preached the word of the Lord and see how they are doing." Barnabas wanted to take John, also called Mark, with them, but Paul did not think it wise to take him, because he had deserted them in Pamphylia and had not continued with them in the work. They had such a sharp disagreement that they parted company. Barnabas took Mark and sailed for Cyprus, but Paul chose Silas and left, commended by the believers to the grace of the Lord. He went through Syria and Cilicia, strengthening the churches. (Acts 15:36–41)

What if Jesus had acted the same way toward Peter, would Peter have developed into the great apostle he turned out to be? Was Paul giving John Mark the opportunity to grow up and become a stronger Christian that could evangelize those he came in contact with?

It seems that Paul could have been concerned with the success of his ministry and since John Mark had deserted them, he was afraid that John Mark would hinder the ministry's growth. Is it possible that Paul lost sight for a moment on who was building the church or that God was building it through him? This seems to be a problem in some of the churches today. It seems that pastors or church leaders lose focus on who is actually building the church. As they are getting caught up in the day-to-day activities, it starts to appear to them that they are the ones building the church, forgetting that it is Christ who said, "I will build my church" in Matthew 16:18. Yes, we are the body of Christ, the hands and the feet who do the actual work. But let's not forget that it is the Spirit that changes and convicts hearts, then adds to the church, and not by our efforts alone.

Take a look at what Paul writes in 2 Corinthians 11 and 12:

> I hope you will put up with me in a little foolishness. Yes, please put up with me! I am jealous for you with a godly jealousy. I promised you to one husband, to Christ, so that I might present you as a pure virgin to him. But I am afraid that just as Eve was deceived by the serpent's cunning, your minds may somehow be led astray from your sincere and pure devotion to Christ. For if someone comes to you and preaches a Jesus other than the Jesus we preached, or if you receive a different spirit from the Spirit you received, or a different gospel from the one you accepted, you put up with it easily enough.
>
> I do not think I am in the least inferior to those "super-apostles." I may indeed be untrained as a speaker, but I do have knowledge. We have made this perfectly clear to you in every way. Was it a sin for me to lower myself in order to elevate you by preaching the gospel of God to you free of charge? I robbed other churches by receiving support from them so as to serve you. And when

I was with you and needed something, I was not a burden to anyone, for the brothers who came from Macedonia supplied what I needed. I have kept myself from being a burden to you in any way, and will continue to do so. As surely as the truth of Christ is in me, nobody in the regions of Achaia will stop this boasting of mine. [11] Why? Because I do not love you? God knows I do!

And I will keep on doing what I am doing in order to cut the ground from under those who want an opportunity to be considered equal with us in the things they boast about. For such people are false apostles, deceitful workers, masquerading as apostles of Christ. And no wonder, for Satan himself masquerades as an angel of light. It is not surprising, then, if his servants also masquerade as servants of righteousness. Their end will be what their actions deserve.

I repeat: Let no one take me for a fool. But if you do, then tolerate me just as you would a fool, so that I may do a little boasting. In this self-confident boasting I am not talking as the Lord would, but as a fool. Since many are boasting in the way the world does, I too will boast. You gladly put up with fools since you are so wise! In fact, you even put up with anyone who enslaves you or exploits you or takes advantage of you or puts on airs or slaps you in the face. To my shame I admit that we were too weak for that!

Whatever anyone else dares to boast about—I am speaking as a fool—I also dare to boast about. Are they Hebrews? So am I. Are they Israelites? So am I. Are they Abraham's descendants? So am I. Are they servants of Christ? (I am out of my mind to talk like this.) I am more. I have worked much harder, been in prison more frequently, been flogged more severely, and been exposed to death again and again. Five times I received from the Jews the forty lashes minus one. Three times I was beaten with rods, once I was pelted with stones, three times I was shipwrecked, I spent a night and a day in the open sea, I have been constantly on the move. I have been in danger from rivers, in danger from bandits, in danger from my fellow Jews, in danger from Gentiles; in danger in the city, in danger in the country, in danger at sea; and in danger from false believers. I have labored and toiled and have often gone without sleep; I have known hunger and thirst and have often gone without food; I have been cold and naked. Besides everything else, I face daily the pressure of my concern for all the churches. Who is weak, and I do not feel weak? Who is led into sin, and I do not inwardly burn?

If I must boast, I will boast of the things that show my weakness. The God and Father of the Lord Jesus, who is to be praised forever, knows that I am not lying. In Damascus the governor under King Aretas had the city of the Damascenes guarded in order to arrest me. But I was lowered in a basket from a window in the wall and slipped through his hands. (2 Corinthians 11:1–33)

I must go on boasting. Although there is nothing to be gained, I will go on to visions and revelations from the Lord. I know a man in Christ who fourteen years ago was caught up to the third heaven. Whether it was in the body or out of the body I do not know—God knows. And I know that this man—whether in the body or apart from the body I do not know, but God knows—was caught up to paradise and heard inexpressible things, things that no one is permitted to tell. I will boast about a man like that, but I will not boast about myself, except about my weaknesses. Even if I should choose to boast, I would not be a fool, because I would be speaking the truth. But I refrain, so no one will think more of me than is warranted by what I do or say, or because of these surpassingly great revelations. Therefore, in order to keep me from becoming conceited, I was given a thorn in my flesh, a messenger of Satan, to torment me. Three times I pleaded with the Lord to take it away from me. But he said to me, "My grace is sufficient for you, for my power is made perfect in weakness." Therefore I will boast all the more gladly about my weaknesses, so that Christ's power may rest on me. That is why, for Christ's sake, I delight in weaknesses, in insults, in hardships, in persecutions, in difficulties. For when I am weak, then I am strong.

I have made a fool of myself, but you drove me to it. I ought to have been commended by you, for I am not in the least inferior to the "super-apostles," even though I am nothing. I persevered in demonstrating among you the marks of a true apostle, including signs, wonders and miracles. How were you inferior to the other churches, except that I was never a burden to you? Forgive me this wrong! (2 Corinthians 12:1–13)

Now by what I am going to say, I am not in any way diminishing what Paul has done or his humility or what he endured for the sake of Christ. Paul is my favorite biblical hero. Think about it, how many people would be stoned and left dead and then would go back to the same city to preach? I would be crying to God, "I thought you told me to go in there, look I got a hang nail. Why would you let a teacher of your Word endure such punishment?" I'm sure you think that I am utilizing hyperbole here, but I am afraid that it is really closer to the truth than I want to admit.

I also realize he was defending himself to others who were claiming to be the true Christian and trying to discredit him. But it could seem that Paul goes into a very long explanation and resorted to sarcasm to explain himself to the Corinthians. The truth is, no one drove Paul to make a fool of himself. Besides, he states in his first letter to the Corinthians that if he only preaches the Gospel, then he has no reason to boast. This could give us insight to what the thorn in the flesh actually was. I realize this has been a topic that has numerous different explanations, so please allow me to explain mine.

He said he was given a thorn in the flesh, a messenger from Satan. I believe that the first thing to consider is that the messenger himself was the actual thorn. In the Old Testament passages of Numbers 33:55 and Judges 2:3, the people "of the land" or "of the nations" are spoken of as being "thorns in your sides." In Joshua 23:13, the people are referred to as "thorns in your eyes." People today refer to others as a thorn in the side when they are dealing with difficult people. So it wouldn't be abnormal for Paul to refer to the messenger as a thorn in his flesh.

Then next thing is, what does a messenger do? They relay a message. This message was to torment Paul. So it had to do with something in his mind, even though he refers to it as the flesh. Paul uses the term *flesh* when he differentiated the difference of the things of the Spirit and the things of the mind in his letter to the Romans. So then "the thorn in the flesh" would refer to the tormenting message of the mind.

So what was the message he received? The same message that Eve, you and me, and every other human gets from Satan. He wants us to focus on our wants or look at ourselves and our accomplishments with pride or feel sorry for ourselves because of the trials and hardships that we have endured. He basically wants us to love ourselves. He wants us to be singing "I did it my way!" This is what I have been referring to as the "nature of man," "sin," or referred to as "the sin of the world."

Paul knew what was right, and since he was still human, he had to fight sin, just like the rest of us. If you look for it, you can see his fight in his ministry and in his letters.

I believe that the point could be argued that Paul did seek some justification for not using the rights of an apostle. Read the first letter that he sent to the Corinthians.

> Am I not an apostle [a special messenger]? Am I not free [unrestrained and exempt from any obligation]? Have I not seen Jesus our Lord? Are you [yourselves] not [the product and proof of] my workmanship in the Lord?
>
> Even if I am not considered an apostle [a special messenger] by others, at least I am one to you; for you are the seal [the certificate, the living evidence] of my apostleship in the Lord [confirming and authenticating it].
>
> This is my [real ground of] defense [my vindication of myself] to those who would put me on trial and cross-examine me.
>
> Have we not the right to our food and drink [at the expense of the churches]?
>
> Have we not the right also to take along with us a Christian sister as wife, as do the other apostles and the Lord's brothers and Cephas [Peter]?
>
> Or is it only Barnabas and I who have no right to refrain from doing manual labor for a livelihood [in order to go about the work of the ministry]?
>
> [Consider this:] What soldier at any time serves at his own expense? Who plants a vineyard and does not eat any of the fruit of it? Who tends a flock and does not partake of the milk of the flock?

Do I say this only on human authority and as a man reasons? Does not the Law endorse the same principle?

For in the Law of Moses it is written, You shall not muzzle an ox when it is treading out the corn. Is it [only] for oxen that God cares?

Or does He speak certainly and entirely for our sakes? [Assuredly] it is written for our sakes, because the plowman ought to plow in hope, and the thresher ought to thresh in expectation of partaking of the harvest.

If we have sown [the seed of] spiritual good among you, [is it too] much if we reap from your material benefits?

If others share in this rightful claim upon you, do not we [have a still better and greater claim]? However, we have never exercised this right, but we endure everything rather than put a hindrance in the way [of the spread] of the good news (the Gospel) of Christ.

Do you not know that those men who are employed in the services of the temple get their food from the temple? And that those who tend the altar share with the altar [in the offerings brought]?

[On the same principle] the Lord directed that those who publish the good news [the Gospel] should live [get their maintenance] by the Gospel.

But I have not made use of any of these privileges, nor am I writing this [to suggest] that any such provision be made for me [now]. For it would be better for me to die than to have anyone make void and deprive me of my [ground for] glorifying [in this matter].

For if I [merely] preach the Gospel, that gives me no reason to boast, for I feel compelled of necessity to do it. Woe is me if I do not preach the glad tidings [the Gospel]!

For if I do this work of my own free will, then I have my pay [my reward]; but if it is not of my own will, but is done reluctantly and under compulsion, I am [still] entrusted with a [sacred] trusteeship and commission.

What then is the [actual] reward that I get? Just this: that in my preaching the good news [the Gospel], I may offer it [absolutely] free of expense [to anybody], not taking advantage of my rights and privileges [as a preacher] of the Gospel.

For although I am free in every way from anyone's control, I have made myself a bond servant to everyone, so that I might gain the more [for Christ].

To the Jews I became as a Jew, that I might win Jews; to men under the Law, [I became] as one under the Law, though not myself being under the Law, that I might win those under the Law.

To those without [outside] law I became as one without law, not that I am without the law of God and lawless toward Him, but that I am [especially keeping] within and committed to the law of Christ, that I might win those who are without law.

To the weak [wanting in discernment] I have become weak [wanting in discernment] that I might win the weak and overscrupulous. I have [in short] become all things to all men, that I might by all means [at all costs and in any and every way] save some [by winning them to faith in Jesus Christ].

And I do this for the sake of the good news [the Gospel], in order that I may become a participator in it and share in its [blessings along with you].

Do you not know that in a race all the runners compete, but [only] one receives the prize? So run [your race] that you may lay hold [of the prize] and make it yours.

Now every athlete who goes into training conducts himself temperately and restricts himself in all things. They do it to win a wreath that will soon wither, but we [do it to receive a crown of eternal blessedness] that cannot wither.

Therefore I do not run uncertainly [without definite aim]. I do not box like one beating the air and striking without an adversary.

But [like a boxer] *I buffet my body [handle it roughly, discipline it by hardships] and subdue it, for fear that after proclaiming to others the Gospel and things pertaining to it, I myself should become unfit [not stand the test, be unapproved and rejected as a counterfeit].* (1 Corinthians 9:1–27 AMP) (emphasis added)

He had to control the flesh just like an overeater, alcoholic, or anyone else that has a problem in a certain area of their life.

I am a recovered alcoholic and drug addict. I have experienced the physical withdrawals of alcohol and drugs. But there is more to recovery than just that. There is the retraining of the mind. You have to retrain almost every aspect of your life—how you think, what you do in social settings, who you hang around with, how you respond to tragic situations or boredom. Anything can trigger your mind to want to use alcohol or drugs, and you have to learn how to keep the flesh or the mind into submission of doing the right thing versus the thing that it wants to do or from falling back into old behavior.

Overcoming the thorn wasn't a problem for Paul alone, for Peter had the same issue. First, let's look at what happened to him when he was still with Jesus. Everyone wants to focus on the time in Matthew and Mark when Jesus first told the disciples that he was going to be crucified and Peter rebuked Jesus for it. Jesus tells him in Matthew 16:23, "Jesus turned and said to Peter, 'Get behind me, Satan! You are a stumbling block to me; you do not have in mind the concerns of God, but merely human concerns.'" This is the same thing that I believe a lot of Christians, especially leaders in the church, would hear today if they were really listening to what the Spirit was telling them.

But to me, that is not the biggest zinger that Peter got. In the last chapter of John, Peter decides to do what he knows how to and goes fishing, and the other disciples go with him. Jesus appears on the bank with cooked fish for breakfast, and they all ate what may have been the breakfast for champions of that day. I guess it was because they wanted the benefits of omega-3 the fish have.

After they were done eating, the story continues as follows.

> When they had finished eating, Jesus said to Simon Peter, "Simon son of John, do you love me more than these?"
>
> "Yes, Lord," he said, "you know that I love you."
>
> Jesus said, "Feed my lambs."
>
> Again Jesus said, "Simon son of John, do you love me?"
>
> He answered, "Yes, Lord, you know that I love you."
>
> Jesus said, "Take care of my sheep."
>
> The third time he said to him, "Simon son of John, do you love me?"
>
> Peter was hurt because Jesus asked him the third time, "Do you love me?" He said, "Lord, you know all things; you know that I love you."
>
> Jesus said, "Feed my sheep. Very truly I tell you, when you were younger you dressed yourself

and went where you wanted; but when you are old you will stretch out your hands, and someone else will dress you and lead you where you do not want to go." Jesus said this to indicate the kind of death by which Peter would glorify God. Then he said to him, "Follow me!"

Peter turned and saw that the disciple whom Jesus loved was following them. [This was the one who had leaned back against Jesus at the supper and had said, "Lord, who is going to betray you?"] When Peter saw him, he asked, "Lord, what about him?"

Jesus answered, "If I want him to remain alive until I return, what is that to you? You must follow me." Because of this, the rumor spread among the believers that this disciple would not die. But Jesus did not say that he would not die; he only said, "If I want him to remain alive until I return, what is that to you?" (John 21:15–23)

Oh, that had to hurt. It hurts me to read it. Peter had to think, *Why did I ask?* Oh, to get an answer from the Lord. "What is that to you?" This is such a powerful statement because it addresses sin in its very core. What we are supposed to be doing is following the path that God has for us, not concerning ourselves with the path that he has chosen for everyone else.

I think this is so powerful to me because I hear it so much. I have to buffet my body or rather beat it into my head that it doesn't make one iota of a minuscule difference what God has others doing; it only matters that I am following him. That is the hardest part, when you have to put it into action because as James tells us in James 2:14–26:

What good is it, my brothers and sisters, if someone claims to have faith but has no deeds? Can such faith save them? Suppose a brother or a

REDISCOVERING GOD'S LOVE

sister is without clothes and daily food. If one of you says to them, "Go in peace; keep warm and well fed," but does nothing about their physical needs, what good is it? In the same way, faith by itself, if it is not accompanied by action, is dead.

But someone will say, "You have faith; I have deeds."

Show me your faith without deeds, and I will show you my faith by my deeds. You believe that there is one God. Good! Even the demons believe that—and shudder.

You foolish person, do you want evidence that faith without deeds is useless? Was not our father Abraham considered righteous for what he did when he offered his son Isaac on the altar? You see that his faith and his actions were working together, and his faith was made complete by what he did. And the scripture was fulfilled that says, "Abraham believed God, and it was credited to him as righteousness," and he was called God's friend. You see that a person is considered righteous by what they do and not by faith alone.

In the same way, was not even Rahab the prostitute considered righteous for what she did when she gave lodging to the spies and sent them off in a different direction? As the body without the spirit is dead, so faith without deeds is dead.

So how can you be following God if you are not acting on it?

Now Peter should be given some consideration since he didn't have the Holy Spirit living in him at the time that the two previous situations happened. Yet look at what happened after the day of Pentecost and after he was well into his ministry.

When Cephas came to Antioch, I opposed him to his face, because he stood condemned.

For before certain men came from James, he used to eat with the Gentiles. But when they arrived, he began to draw back and separate himself from the Gentiles because he was afraid of those who belonged to the circumcision group. The other Jews joined him in his hypocrisy, so that by their hypocrisy even Barnabas was led astray.

When I saw that they were not acting in line with the truth of the gospel, I said to Cephas in front of them all, "You are a Jew, yet you live like a Gentile and not like a Jew. How is it, then, that you force Gentiles to follow Jewish customs?

"We who are Jews by birth and not sinful Gentiles know that a person is not justified by the works of the law, but by faith in Jesus Christ. So we, too, have put our faith in Christ Jesus that we may be justified by faith in Christ and not by the works of the law, because by the works of the law no one will be justified.

"But if, in seeking to be justified in Christ, we Jews find ourselves also among the sinners, doesn't that mean that Christ promotes sin? Absolutely not! If I rebuild what I destroyed, then I really would be a lawbreaker.

"For through the law I died to the law so that I might live for God. I have been crucified with Christ and I no longer live, but Christ lives in me. The life I now live in the body, I live by faith in the Son of God, who loved me and gave himself for me. I do not set aside the grace of God, for if righteousness could be gained through the law, Christ died for nothing!" (Galatians 2:11–21)

Peter's, whom Paul refers to as Cephas, hypocrisy shows he was concerned with his appearance and his acceptance of his Jewish peers rather than treating or loving everyone the same. Because of his sin, even other Christians followed his example, like Barnabas.

Here's the thing. The thorn in the flesh is that same for Paul, Peter, you, and me. It is the message of Satan that creates the desire to focus on or satisfy the love of ourselves over anything or anyone else, especially God. Wasn't this the way that Jesus was tempted in the desert?

> Then Jesus was led by the Spirit into the wilderness to be tempted by the devil. After fasting forty days and forty nights, he was hungry. The tempter came to him and said, "If you are the Son of God, tell these stones to become bread."
>
> Jesus answered, "It is written: 'Man shall not live on bread alone, but on every word that comes from the mouth of God.'"
>
> Then the devil took him to the holy city and had him stand on the highest point of the temple. "If you are the Son of God," he said, "throw yourself down. For it is written:
>
> "'He will command his angels concerning you,
>
> and they will lift you up in their hands,
>
> so that you will not strike your foot against a stone.'"
>
> Jesus answered him, "It is also written: 'Do not put the Lord your God to the test.'"
>
> Again, the devil took him to a very high mountain and showed him all the kingdoms of the world and their splendor. "All this I will give you," he said, "if you will bow down and worship me."
>
> Jesus said to him, "Away from me, Satan! For it is written: 'Worship the Lord your God, and serve him only.'"
>
> Then the devil left him, and angels came and attended him. (Matthew 4:1–11)

Jesus was tempted the same way that we are. The devil was trying to get him to focus on himself. What else does the devil have to tempt us with? If the love of self is sin and all transgressions are the result of sin, then the only thing that the devil has to tempt you with is the love of yourself.

You're hungry? Use your power to get something to eat. When we are going through trials and hardships, we wonder if God is there with us to protect us. The devil said, "Hey, test God. He said he would command his angels to protect you." Jesus had a mission to accomplish. It was to take back the world the devil stole. The devil offered it to him if Jesus would only bow down and worship him. If Jesus would have done any of these things he would have sinned, for he would have focused on the satisfaction of himself rather than the will of the Father.

It is in the middle of the fight to do what is right that we see the need for something greater than ourselves to help us overcome whatever it is that we are fighting. Humility comes in when we realize that it is by the power of God given to us through the Holy Spirit that helps us to accomplish what it is that we are fighting against and not by our power to do so. It doesn't matter if it is God directly affecting us and doing it all or just some of it or if it is by another Christian helping us, we can overcome the thorn in the flesh when we rely on the power of the Spirit.

That's why Paul writes this to the Romans in Romans 8.

> Therefore, there is now no condemnation for those who are in Christ Jesus, because through Christ Jesus the law of the Spirit who gives life has set you free from the law of sin and death. For what the law was powerless to do because it was weakened by the flesh, God did by sending his own Son in the likeness of sinful flesh to be a sin offering. And so he condemned sin in the flesh, in order that the righteous requirement of the law might be fully met in us, who do not live according to the flesh but according to the Spirit.

Those who live according to the flesh have their minds set on what the flesh desires; but those who live in accordance with the Spirit have their minds set on what the Spirit desires. The mind governed by the flesh is death, but the mind governed by the Spirit is life and peace. The mind governed by the flesh is hostile to God; it does not submit to God's law, nor can it do so. Those who are in the realm of the flesh cannot please God.

You, however, are not in the realm of the flesh but are in the realm of the Spirit, if indeed the Spirit of God lives in you. And if anyone does not have the Spirit of Christ, they do not belong to Christ. But if Christ is in you, then even though your body is subject to death because of sin, the Spirit gives life because of righteousness. And if the Spirit of him who raised Jesus from the dead is living in you, he who raised Christ from the dead will also give life to your mortal bodies because of his Spirit who lives in you.

Therefore, brothers and sisters, we have an obligation—but it is not to the flesh, to live according to it. For if you live according to the flesh, you will die; but if by the Spirit you put to death the misdeeds of the body, you will live.

For those who are led by the Spirit of God are the children of God. The Spirit you received does not make you slaves, so that you live in fear again; rather, the Spirit you received brought about your adoption to sonship. And by him we cry, "Abba, Father." The Spirit himself testifies with our spirit that we are God's children. Now if we are children, then we are heirs—heirs of God and co-heirs with Christ, if indeed we share in his sufferings in order that we may also

share in his glory. I consider that our present sufferings are not worth comparing with the glory
that will be revealed in us. For the creation waits
in eager expectation for the children of God to be
revealed. For the creation was subjected to frus-
tration, not by its own choice, but by the will of
the one who subjected it, in hope that the creation itself will be liberated from its bondage to
decay and brought into the freedom and glory of
the children of God.

We know that the whole creation has been
groaning as in the pains of childbirth right up
to the present time. Not only so, but we ourselves, who have the firstfruits of the Spirit, groan
inwardly as we wait eagerly for our adoption to
sonship, the redemption of our bodies. For in
this hope we were saved. But hope that is seen is
no hope at all. Who hopes for what they already
have? But if we hope for what we do not yet have,
we wait for it patiently.

In the same way, the Spirit helps us in our
weakness. We do not know what we ought to
pray for, but the Spirit himself intercedes for us
through wordless groans. And he who searches
our hearts knows the mind of the Spirit, because
the Spirit intercedes for God's people in accordance with the will of God.

And we know that in all things God works
for the good of those who love him, who have
been called according to his purpose. For those
God foreknew he also predestined to be con-
formed to the image of his Son, that he might be
the firstborn among many brothers and sisters.
And those he predestined, he also called; those he
called, he also justified; those he justified, he also
glorified. (Romans 8:1–30)

So since we have the Spirit living in us, then we no longer have to live according to the flesh. If we are no longer living according to the flesh, then the thorn no longer has any power over us. That doesn't mean that the thorn will not be there; we just won't pay it any attention since our focus is on the mind of the Spirit and not on the mind of the flesh.

This is a very simple illustration of how I first learned this in my own life. I felt the need to quit, or should I say God was prompting me to quit smoking. I decided that I didn't want to quit on the weekend, because that was the largest chance that I would have to be around other smokers, and I didn't want the temptation of this, especially on the first day or so of me quitting. So I wanted to start in the middle of the week. Problem was that on the day I decided to quit, I still had a pack of cigarettes left, and there was something wrong with the idea of just throwing them away. Since I couldn't quit midday, and since I smoked a pack in half a day, I bought enough cigarettes to finish my last pack at the end of a day. This day would be Thursday, and that meant that I was going to quit on Friday, the day that I especially didn't want to quit on.

I didn't change plans. I woke up Friday morning, and on my knees, I said to the Father, "I know I need to quit, and you know I need to quit, so I will do everything that I can to do so, but then I need you to do whatever it is that you need to do." Then I started my day. That evening, I was in a smoky environment, and I thought to myself, *Hey, you did good today. You haven't had any cigarettes, so you can have one this evening and start the process over tomorrow.* Then I heard a voice in my inner being that was as loud as if I heard it with my ears. "Steve, people that don't smoke don't have a cigarette at the end of the day." That was God doing the part that I wasn't able to do. He gave me a voice of reason.

I had a decision to make right then. Do I listen to his voice of reason, or do I do it my way? Thankfully, I did listen, and though there were times that were tough, I haven't had a cigarette since. Does the thorn ever come back to try and tempt me? Not anymore, for I have set my mind on the fact that I don't smoke, I don't want to smoke, and there is no reason for me to ever pick up a cigarette ever again. James 4:7 tells us to "Submit yourselves, then, to God. Resist the devil, and he will flee from you." So after a time, the thorn left me with this temptation.

You may think that is too simple, but think about the amount of people who still smoke and are on oxygen so they can breathe. What about the alcoholic who still drinks even though it has cost him everything? Or the workaholic that loses his family because of his love of his career. Or let's not forget the person that ruins his family for the lust of someone other than his spouse. You may think that I am talking about those who are of the world, but these are examples of people that are supposed to be living by the Spirit and not according to the flesh. Yet every one of these are yielding to the thorn in the flesh rather than being focused on the strength of the Spirit.

This leads us back to David. It is evident that he had the heart of God. Look at how he took the kingdom and how he handled his men.

> David and his men reached Ziklag on the third day. Now the Amalekites had raided the Negev and Ziklag. They had attacked Ziklag and burned it, and had taken captive the women and everyone else in it, both young and old. They killed none of them, but carried them off as they went on their way.
>
> When David and his men reached Ziklag, they found it destroyed by fire and their wives and sons and daughters taken captive. So David and his men wept aloud until they had no strength left to weep. David's two wives had been captured—Ahinoam of Jezreel and Abigail, the widow of Nabal of Carmel. David was greatly distressed because the men were talking of stoning him; each one was bitter in spirit because of his sons and daughters. But David found strength in the LORD his God.
>
> Then David said to Abiathar the priest, the son of Ahimelek, "Bring me the ephod." Abiathar

brought it to him, and David inquired of the LORD, "Shall I pursue this raiding party? Will I overtake them?"

"Pursue them," he answered. "You will certainly overtake them and succeed in the rescue."

David and the six hundred men with him came to the Besor Valley, where some stayed behind. Two hundred of them were too exhausted to cross the valley, but David and the other four hundred continued the pursuit.

They found an Egyptian in a field and brought him to David. They gave him water to drink and food to eat—part of a cake of pressed figs and two cakes of raisins. He ate and was revived, for he had not eaten any food or drunk any water for three days and three nights.

David asked him, "Who do you belong to? Where do you come from?"

He said, "I am an Egyptian, the slave of an Amalekite. My master abandoned me when I became ill three days ago. We raided the Negev of the Kerethites, some territory belonging to Judah and the Negev of Caleb. And we burned Ziklag."

David asked him, "Can you lead me down to this raiding party?"

He answered, "Swear to me before God that you will not kill me or hand me over to my master, and I will take you down to them."

He led David down, and there they were, scattered over the countryside, eating, drinking and reveling because of the great amount of plunder they had taken from the land of the Philistines and from Judah. David fought them from dusk until the evening of the next day, and none of them got away, except four hundred young men who rode off on camels and fled. David recovered everything the Amalekites had taken, including his two wives. Nothing was missing: young or old, boy or girl, plunder or anything else they had taken. David brought everything back. He took all the flocks and herds, and his men drove them ahead of the other livestock, saying, "This is David's plunder."

Then David came to the two hundred men who had been too exhausted to follow him and who were left behind at the Besor Valley. They came out to meet David and the men with him. As David and his men approached, he asked them how they were. But all the evil men and trouble-makers among David's followers said, "Because they did not go out with us, we will not share with them the plunder we recovered. However, each man may take his wife and children and go."

David replied, "No, my brothers, you must not do that with what the LORD has given us. He has protected us and delivered into our hands the raiding party that came against us. Who will listen to what you say? The share of the man who stayed with the supplies is to be the same as that of him who went down to the battle. All will share alike." David made this a statute and ordinance for Israel from that day to this.

When David reached Ziklag, he sent some of the plunder to the elders of Judah, who were his friends, saying, "Here is a gift for you from the plunder of the LORD's enemies." (1 Samuel 30:1–26)

David made sure that even the ones that were tired got a fair share of the plunder, and then he sent some to friends. Even when he hears of Saul's death, he wept for him. I would like to think I was as good as that, but I seriously doubt that I would weep for a man that put me on the run for my life, when I was trying to do nothing but good for him. Then he made good on the vow with Jonathan with the receiving into the kingdom of Mephibosheth, after Jonathan was dead. So it is apparent that David didn't have his focus on himself, rather he had the heart of God. But look at what happens when he turns his heart from God and focuses it on himself.

First off, let's look at the real root of the problem before we go into the actual scene. In 2 Samuel 8:4, it says, "David captured a thousand of his chariots, seven thousand charioteers and twenty thousand foot soldiers. He hamstrung all but a hundred of the chariot horses." We see that David was following the law God set down in Deuteronomy 17:16, "The king, moreover, must not acquire great numbers of horses for himself or make the people return to Egypt to get more of them, for the LORD has told you, 'You are not to go back that way again.'" So he hamstrung all the horses except for one hundred in keeping in line with that law. Yet it also says in Deuteronomy 17:17, "He must not take many wives, or his heart will be led astray. He must not accumulate large amounts of silver and gold." So what happened with this one? Did horses not have as much value as the wives and wealth? Let's face it, David had at least eight wives and ten concubines, and probably more. I guess there was a loophole of how many is "not many?" But he knew that God did establish one man and one woman back in Genesis. Also, how much is large amount of gold and silver? Though David wasn't as bad as his son Solomon, I think David's love or lust for women and bling helped shaped Solomon into what he eventually became. The nut doesn't fall far from the tree, as they say.

So here is how the account goes in 2 Samuel 11:

> In the spring, at the time when kings go off to war, David sent Joab out with the king's men and the whole Israelite army. They destroyed the Ammonites and besieged Rabbah. But David remained in Jerusalem.
>
> One evening David got up from his bed and walked around on the roof of the palace. From the

roof he saw a woman bathing. The woman was very beautiful, and David sent someone to find out about her. The man said, "She is Bathsheba, the daughter of Eliam and the wife of Uriah the Hittite." Then David sent messengers to get her. She came to him, and he slept with her. (Now she was purifying herself from her monthly unclean-ness.) Then she went back home. The woman conceived and sent word to David, saying, "I am pregnant."

So David sent this word to Joab: "Send me Uriah the Hittite." And Joab sent him to David. When Uriah came to him, David asked him how Joab was, how the soldiers were and how the war was going. Then David said to Uriah, "Go down to your house and wash your feet." So Uriah left the palace, and a gift from the king was sent after him. But Uriah slept at the entrance to the palace with all his master's servants and did not go down to his house.

David was told, "Uriah did not go home." So he asked Uriah, "Haven't you just come from a military campaign? Why didn't you go home?"

Uriah said to David, "The ark and Israel and Judah are staying in tents, and my commander Joab and my lord's men are camped in the open country. How could I go to my house to eat and drink and make love to my wife? As surely as you live, I will not do such a thing!"

Then David said to him, "Stay here one more day, and tomorrow I will send you back." So Uriah remained in Jerusalem that day and the next. At David's invitation, he ate and drank with him, and David made him drunk. But in the eve-ning Uriah went out to sleep on his mat among his master's servants; he did not go home.

In the morning David wrote a letter to Joab and sent it with Uriah. In it he wrote, "Put Uriah out in front where the fighting is fiercest. Then withdraw from him so he will be struck down and die."

So while Joab had the city under siege, he put Uriah at a place where he knew the strongest defenders were. When the men of the city came out and fought against Joab, some of the men in David's army fell; moreover, Uriah the Hittite died.

Joab sent David a full account of the battle. He instructed the messenger: "When you have finished giving the king this account of the battle, the king's anger may flare up, and he may ask you, 'Why did you get so close to the city to fight? Didn't you know they would shoot arrows from the wall? Who killed Abimelek son of Jerub-Besheth? Didn't a woman drop an upper millstone on him from the wall, so that he died in Thebez? Why did you get so close to the wall?' If he asks you this, then say to him, 'Moreover, your servant Uriah the Hittite is dead.'"

The messenger set out, and when he arrived he told David everything Joab had sent him to say. The messenger said to David, "The men overpowered us and came out against us in the open, but we drove them back to the entrance of the city gate. Then the archers shot arrows at your servants from the wall, and some of the king's men died. Moreover, your servant Uriah the Hittite is dead."

David told the messenger, "Say this to Joab: 'Don't let this upset you; the sword devours one as well as another. Press the attack against the city and destroy it.' Say this to encourage Joab."

When Uriah's wife heard that her husband
was dead, she mourned for him. After the time
of mourning was over, David had her brought to
his house, and she became his wife and bore him
a son. But the thing David had done displeased
the LORD. (1 Samuel 11:1–27)

So every time I hear this story or the explanation of David, I
hear them talk about the sin of adultery or the sin murder, but as
I have been saying, I believe he sinned when he was so focused on
getting what he wanted that he didn't consider the hurting of others
in the process. When he asked who this woman was, he was told that
it was Uriah the Hittite's wife. That should have been the end right
there. David knew better than to take another man's wife; he had
Michal taken from him. Besides that, if this would have made it better, which it didn't, this wasn't just somebody he really didn't know;
Uriah had been with him a long time.

So when David sent for her, he didn't do it to make her his wife.
He wanted to satisfy his lust, and it didn't matter what the cost was
to anyone else. He wanted what he wanted, and he wanted it now.
Sounds like the culture we live in today.

Yet he doesn't stop there. It wasn't bad enough that he took
Uriah's wife, but when she conceived, instead of admitting his fault,
he tried to cover his tracks. Mark 4:22 tells us, "For whatever is hidden is meant to be disclosed, and whatever is concealed is meant to
be brought out into the open." I believe that if we are looking, we
can see the hand of God showing up to use this to point out David's
sin. God never stopped calling David a man after his own heart, even
though David's heart wasn't totally on him. What God did was allow
David enough rope to hang himself so that when the time was right,
he would reveal the sin in him.

This leaves the question of how can God be considered loving
if he would allow Uriah to die in order to reveal sin in David's life.
There are two points that I would like to make to this question.

Before I get started, let's take a look at 2 Samuel 12:1–12:

> The LORD sent Nathan to David. When he came to him, he said, "There were two men in a certain town, one rich and the other poor. The rich man had a very large number of sheep and cattle, but the poor man had nothing except one little ewe lamb he had bought. He raised it, and it grew up with him and his children. It shared his food, drank from his cup and even slept in his arms. It was like a daughter to him.
>
> "Now a traveler came to the rich man, but the rich man refrained from taking one of his own sheep or cattle to prepare a meal for the traveler who had come to him. Instead, he took the ewe lamb that belonged to the poor man and prepared it for the one who had come to him."
>
> David burned with anger against the man and said to Nathan, "As surely as the LORD lives, the man who did this must die! He must pay for that lamb four times over, because he did such a thing and had no pity."
>
> Then Nathan said to David, "You are the man! This is what the LORD, the God of Israel, says: 'I anointed you king over Israel, and I delivered you from the hand of Saul. I gave your master's house to you, and your master's wives into your arms. I gave you all Israel and Judah. And if all this had been too little, I would have given you even more.'"

Look at what God had told David concerning all that he had. If I had been David, what I would have expected to hear from God would have been something like this: "Look at all I gave you, wasn't that enough? What more did you want, you selfish inconsiderate?"

But he didn't. He said, "Hey, look at all I gave you, and if you wanted more, you could have had it too." What an offer.

> Why did you despise the word of the LORD by doing what is evil in his eyes? You struck down Uriah the Hittite with the sword and took his wife to be your own. You killed him with the sword of the Ammonites. Now, therefore, the sword will never depart from your house, because you despised me and took the wife of Uriah the Hittite to be your own.'
>
> "This is what the LORD says: 'Out of your own household I am going to bring calamity on you. Before your very eyes I will take your wives and give them to one who is close to you, and he will sleep with your wives in broad daylight. You did it in secret, but I will do this thing in broad daylight before all Israel.'"
>
> Then David said to Nathan, "I have sinned against the LORD." Nathan replied, "The LORD has taken away your sin. You are not going to die. But because by doing this you have shown utter contempt for the LORD, the son born to you will die." (2 Samuel 12:9–14)

So David had to pay a consequence for his transgression. God didn't just let him off the hook. Yet at the same time, God was merciful in the process, for God could have taken David's life, worse yet God could have not pardoned his sin, and David could have been separated for eternity from God. I think that this is where we miss the point so many times also. When our sin results in a transgression, there are consequences that we too have to deal with. Yes, our sin is forgiven, thanks to Christ, but that doesn't mean that there are no consequences for the action taken. The degree of the consequence is left up to the Father to decide, which sometimes the consequences can be our own death. Yet God is merciful that he will look at the death of his son as the atonement for our sin, and he allows us to live in eternity with him, regardless of our sin.

But now, not only did Uriah die, but an innocent baby died too. How can we see a just or a merciful God when he let two people—and if you continue to read, there will be more—die because of David, when he let David live? Where is the justice in that?

David understood it. Continue to read 2 Samuel 12:15–23:

> After Nathan had gone home, the LORD struck the child that Uriah's wife had borne to David, and he became ill. David pleaded with God for the child. He fasted and spent the nights lying in sackcloth on the ground. The elders of his household stood beside him to get him up from the ground, but he refused, and he would not eat any food with them.
>
> On the seventh day the child died. David's attendants were afraid to tell him that the child was dead, for they thought, "While the child was still living, he wouldn't listen to us when we spoke to him. How can we now tell him the child is dead? He may do something desperate."
>
> David noticed that his attendants were whispering among themselves, and he realized the child was dead. "Is the child dead?" he asked.
>
> "Yes," they replied, "he is dead."
>
> Then David got up from the ground. After he had washed, put on lotions and changed his clothes, he went into the house of the LORD and worshiped. Then he went to his own house, and at his request they served him food, and he ate.
>
> His attendants asked him, "Why are you acting this way? While the child was alive, you fasted and wept, but now that the child is dead, you get up and eat!"

He answered, "While the child was still alive, I fasted and wept. I thought, 'Who knows? The LORD may be gracious to me and let the child live.' But now that he is dead, why should I go on fasting? Can I bring him back again? I will go to him, but he will not return to me."

David knew that he had to deal with the loss of his son. Wouldn't that have been more painful than if he would have died himself? If he would have died and got to be with God whom he loved, wouldn't that have been better than having to deal with the pain for losing his son and later on his sons? David knew that his son was with God the Father and that someday he would be with him. He didn't want to deal with the pain, but when God wouldn't allow him to keep his son, then he knew where he would be.

The same goes for Uriah. God knew that Uriah would be with him. What we Christian seem to forget is that the end result is supposed to be spending eternity with him. I heard it said that "we all want to go to heaven, but no one wants to die to get there."

In this area, I feel kind of like Paul, who said in Philippians 1:21–26,

For to me, to live is Christ and to die is gain. If I am to go on living in the body, this will mean fruitful labor for me. Yet what shall I choose? I do not know! I am torn between the two: I desire to depart and be with Christ, which is better by far; [24] but it is more necessary for you that I remain in the body. Convinced of this, I know that I will remain, and I will continue with all of you for your progress and joy in the faith, so that through my being with you again your boasting in Christ Jesus will abound on account of me.

I realize that the best thing that can happen to me is that I die and get to be with Jesus in eternity. Even though I'm not ready to die just yet, because the way that I figure it is that when I leave this *rock*, I have all eternity to be with him, so I want to accomplish as much as I can for him while I am still here, and I would like to stick around as long as possible to do so.

Yet I know Christians who have lost loved ones and they are bitter against God for it. Their focus is on God taking their loved one away from them rather than the fact that their loved one is with him. So instead of just grieving the loss of them, they also turn bitter toward God.

Though I admit that I have never lost anyone as close as a spouse, child, parent, or sibling, I have had some painful losses in my life. So I don't address this topic at all flippantly. I just think that the way that we are viewing the issue of death is a worldly view and not one of a Christian perspective. Our goal is not that we live a dream life here on earth. Rather, that we get to spend a dream eternity in heaven, with the one that loves us more than we can ever possibly love him. So when God takes our loved ones home to be with him, shouldn't it be more of a mixed feeling of sorrow of saying good-bye for now and joy of their returning home?

If we don't take this view of death, how do we stay true to our faith in the purpose of Christ's death and the promise of eternal life? This is why Christ came, isn't it? So when he gives the promise to our loved ones and we get bitter at him for doing so, aren't we only thinking of ourselves? We could say that their life got cut short, but if God calls you to be with him, isn't that the amount of life that you are supposed to have? Doesn't that also mean that they don't have to experience any more of the sorrows that this life brings? They received the promise, not a death sentence. It's like they won a one-way trip to paradise, yet we get mad at the one who offered it and that they took it. Shouldn't we consider the joy of paradise?

Let's not forget, as David didn't, that we too will be with them in paradise; they just got there first. We should have a great expectation of joining them there, and it will happen—I am finding out—sooner than we think. I found this out as I get older, time keeps getting faster, or as it says in Psalm 89:47, "Remember how fleeting is my life. For what futility you have created all humanity!" Or in Job

14:1–2, "Mortals, born of woman, are of few days and full of trouble. They spring up like flowers and wither away; like fleeting shadows, they do not endure."

What we should be doing is what David did, and that was to keep going on in life. Second Samuel 12:24–25 says,

> Then David comforted his wife Bathsheba, and he went to her and made love to her. She gave birth to a son, and they named him Solomon. The LORD loved him; and because the LORD loved him, he sent word through Nathan the prophet to name him Jedidiah.

The other thing that we should take note of is that the consequences of David's actions because of sin were also caused by David's sin, again considering sin as the love of ourselves. Here's what I mean. God told David through Nathan in 2 Samuel 12:10–12,

> Now, therefore, the sword will never depart from your house, because you despised me and took the wife of Uriah the Hittite to be your own. This is what the LORD says: "Out of your own household I am going to bring calamity on you. Before your very eyes I will take your wives and give them to one who is close to you, and he will sleep with your wives in broad daylight. You did it in secret, but I will do this thing in broad daylight before all Israel."

Now there are different ways to view this. God could have caused this to happen or God could have not prevented it from happening. Remember David had the ear of God. Had he not stolen Uriah's wife, God may have prevented this from happening, but what did transpire was another result of David's sin.

David's son Amnon, the son of Ahinoam of Jezreel, fell in love, or so he claimed, with David's daughter Tamar, the sister of Absalom, who is the son of Maakah, daughter of Talmai king of Geshur. This is all taking into the account of David's many wives. Before I go any further and discuss David's part, I want to focus on the details of this story, because there is a very interesting point that I think should be noted.

The story starts in 2 Samuel 13:1:20 as follows:

> In the course of time, Amnon son of David fell in love with Tamar, the beautiful sister of Absalom son of David.
>
> Amnon became so obsessed with his sister Tamar that he made himself ill. She was a virgin, and it seemed impossible for him to do anything to her.
>
> Now Amnon had an adviser named Jonadab son of Shimeah, David's brother. Jonadab was a very shrewd man. He asked Amnon, "Why do you, the king's son, look so haggard morning after morning? Won't you tell me?"
>
> Amnon said to him, "I'm in love with Tamar, my brother Absalom's sister."
>
> "Go to bed and pretend to be ill," Jonadab said. "When your father comes to see you, say to him, 'I would like my sister Tamar to come and give me something to eat. Let her prepare the food in my sight so I may watch her and then eat it from her hand.'"
>
> So Amnon lay down and pretended to be ill. When the king came to see him, Amnon said to him, "I would like my sister Tamar to come and make some special bread in my sight, so I may eat from her hand."
>
> David sent word to Tamar at the palace: "Go to the house of your brother Amnon and prepare some food for him." So Tamar went to the house of her brother Amnon, who was lying

down. She took some dough, kneaded it, made the bread in his sight and baked it. Then she took the pan and served him the bread, but he refused to eat.

"Send everyone out of here," Amnon said. So everyone left him. Then Amnon said to Tamar, "Bring the food here into my bedroom so I may eat from your hand." And Tamar took the bread she had prepared and brought it to her brother Amnon in his bedroom. But when she took it to him to eat, he grabbed her and said, "Come to bed with me, my sister."

"No, my brother!" she said to him. "Don't force me! Such a thing should not be done in Israel! Don't do this wicked thing. What about me? Where could I get rid of my disgrace? And what about you? You would be like one of the wicked fools in Israel. Please speak to the king; he will not keep me from being married to you." But he refused to listen to her, and since he was stronger than she, he raped her.

Then Amnon hated her with intense hatred. In fact, he hated her more than he had loved her. Amnon said to her, "Get up and get out!"

"No!" she said to him. "Sending me away would be a greater wrong than what you have already done to me."

But he refused to listen to her. He called his personal servant and said, "Get this woman out of my sight and bolt the door after her." So his servant put her out and bolted the door after her. She was wearing an ornate robe, for this was the kind of garment the virgin daughters of the king wore. Tamar put ashes on her head and tore the ornate robe she was wearing. She put her hands on her head and went away, weeping aloud as she went. Her brother Absalom said to her, "Has that Amnon, your brother, been with you? Be quiet for now, my sister; he is your brother. Don't take this thing to heart." And Tamar lived in her brother Absalom's house, a desolate woman.

Isn't it amazing that he hated her even more than how much he thought that he loved her, after he satisfied his own lust. She even offered herself to him to be his wife, but that was not the way he wanted her, indicating that he was only concerned with pleasing himself and not taking account of her well-being at all. This should be a wake-up call to all of those who are in a relationship and are being pressured to do things that they know they shouldn't or don't want to do. Any time someone is forcing you to or trying to manipulate you to do something, then they are concerned with their needs, and they do not have any respect for yours, regardless of how they make it seem. Eventually this can and often does lead to a total disrespect for you altogether.

Rape in those days wasn't like today in this country, where there are women who have been raped and still go on to live a relatively normal life. Not so back then. The woman's chances of an honorable wedding end. According to the customs and laws of that time, when a woman's virginity was taken by rape, then the rapist was required to take her as his wife, which was her right, unless the father objected (Exodus 22:16–17). If the woman was not married, then she basically lived the life of a single widow for the rest of her life.

So after Amnon raped her, the reason she was begging him to have her as his wife was because she knew that she would spend the rest of her life single and in disgrace. Here is the thing, so did Amnon, the one that supposedly loved her so much, yet he didn't care. If he was concerned about her to any degree, he wouldn't have left her in this situation.

That is why it doesn't make any sense to me when I find Christians who are living together without the commitment of a lifelong marriage, especially when they do so for many years. The fact that they do not respect you enough to give you a commitment is the evidence that they are concerned with themselves and not you. Or as the saying goes, "Why buy the cow, when the milk is free?" They may say that they care and they may even act as if they do, but do they really or are they giving you enough of themselves to keep you from going anywhere?

This leads me to the question of why anyone would want to be in a relationship with a person that is more focused on their own wants and needs than you and your needs. Based on what Paul taught us in Ephesians 5 on how men and women should treat each other as a married couple, how can a man love a woman like Christ loved the church when he won't give her a commitment in the first place? Better yet, why does a Christian woman settle for a man that will not love her like Christ loved the church? This works vice versa for a man as well.

I was talking to one person, and she told me that she knew that she was being used but that she was using him as well. "So then, the two wrongs make it right?" I asked. Show me where that logic has been proven to be rational.

So when Tamar tells Absalom about this incident, he has even more reason to want revenge than say a brother would today. "And Absalom never said a word to Amnon, either good or bad; he hated Amnon because he had disgraced his sister Tamar" (2 Samuel 13:22).

What adds injury to insult is the fact that when David was told, we see that he gets angry. "When King David heard all this, he was furious" (2 Samuel 13:21). So you would think that a certain head would roll, wouldn't you? But nowhere can we see that David did anything about it.

Actually if you were to go back and study the ancient Greek translation called the Septuagint, you would see a sentence that states, "But he would not hurt Amnon because he was his eldest son and he loved him."

Back in Genesis 37, in the story of Joseph and his brothers, Jacob loved Joseph more than the other brothers, and what was worse is that he showed it for all to see. This caused animosity between Joseph and his brothers, to the point of his brothers, first, trying to kill him but instead selling him into slavery. Who was the real person to blame for this animosity? I think it was Jacob.

Well, that being the case, when David did nothing to rectify the situation between Tamar and Amnon, then wasn't it like he was playing favorites with Amnon and disregarding his other child? This would put David into the category of a great king, but an irresponsible father.

Go back to 1 Samuel 30, and remember how he fairly treated his men when they got tired and couldn't finish the pursuit. They still received their share of the plunder. Yet when dealing with his own family, he can't seem to fairly treat his own children. Isn't there something wrong when you can deal with those outside your family better than you deal with our own?

I talked about this earlier, but I believe that it could be expounded on here again. Who was David really loving when he didn't take the appropriate actions regarding his family? The Septuagint stated that it was because he was the eldest and that he loved him is why he did nothing. So there was the risk that he could have lost the love of his son if he would have dealt with him in the proper manner. This of course would have been painful for David to bear. Rather than dealing with his children the way that he ought to have, he ignored the problem hoping it would go away. But by doing nothing, David ended up losing both Amnon and then later Absalom in the process, along with all the other problems that were created.

There is always the risk that in the process of disciplining, the child will rebel against the parent. So the parent can refuse to discipline the child, because of the fear of losing the love of the child. But who is the parent really loving, themselves or the child? Proverbs 22:6 tells us to "Start children off on the way they should go, and even when they are old they will not turn from it." So the discipline is a vital part of loving the child, even though the child may not understand it at the time.

Yet we all know situations where there are children that go astray even though they were brought up in a Christian home. How could this be when the Bible clearly states that he will not turn from it? Well, I believe that it has to do with the child's ability to make their own choices. I know; I was such a child.

Here is the difference though. Since I had the Christian background, I knew where to turn when the bottom of my life fell out, just like the story of the prodigal son when he came to his senses and realized where he came from. So when you give your children the correct upbringing and they rebel against you for doing so, then they have a starting point to refer back to when the timing is right.

Today, however, we are allowing the children to bring up the parents, and we have a society of narcissistic and hedonistic people, because their whole upbringing has been based on them getting what they want, not what they need. Therefore, they do not have a true reference of what life is all about.

So am I saying that they are the victims of their upbringings? Yes and no. Yes, if you were not trained the correct way, then your early years would reflect that. But a huge *no* because as the saying goes, "Shame on my parents for who I was, and shame on me for who I am." For anyone to stay in that childlike state of mind is guilty of their own lack of growth. Especially when there is enough evidence to prove that this is not the way to live and that we have in us a moral compass that points to another direction. Yet there still are many people that actually live that way.

Think about it, the minute Adam and Eve ate the apple, they knew something was wrong. No one was there pointing a finger at them to make them feel guilty. They went into hiding because they knew that there was something wrong in themselves. It was internal, not external from someone else. Not only was there no one to point the finger at them, but no one was there who taught them how to start blaming someone else for their actions. Something they had, which was love, was twisted and used in a manner that it was not intended to be used. This left them feeling ashamed, and they felt the need to hide from it.

Amazingly there are many people that live in their own head and go through life thinking that they are the only one that matters or they are the center of their universe. They live their lives as if their pleasure, satisfaction, and self-preservation is what life is all about.

Yet deep down, they know there is something wrong in themselves, just like Adam and Eve felt.

How can they possibly continue to live their whole life like this and never find the truth? The answer to this question is, they make money, careers, or other things their idol or god. Paul tells us through his letter in 1 Timothy 6:10 (AMP), "For the love of money is a root of all evils; it is through this craving that some have been led astray and have wandered from the faith and pierced themselves through with many acute [mental] pangs." I believe that this could be stated another way: "Money is what we use to try and fulfill the love of ourselves and, through this craving, have wandered from the truth and are left with our own mental anguish."

Let's think of it this way, what the apple was going to do for Eve, money, careers, relationships are supposed to do for us. And Satan to this very day uses this apple to tempt us to continue our love relationship with ourselves. There are countless things in this world to try and use to satisfy our love relationship with ourselves—homes, cars, trips, gadgets, and the list continues to grow. But then, when you get a house, garage, and a storage unit of things collected, we can start to work on our looks. We can add on things, cut things off, tuck things in, and stretch them tight again, all so that we feel better about ourselves or, should I say, that we can love ourselves again. Now I believe in working out and looking the best that I can for health reasons, but that too can become just as much a love addiction as using surgery.

The more we continue this relationship, the more the need grows. What helps fuel this need? Other people's need for money and things. Society invents more ways and things to offer to make more money so they too can get their apple and have their own love relationship with themselves, and the process continues on indefinitely. Here is the sad thing. Eventually there are those who acquire great wealth and many things only to find out that the hole they were trying to fill is larger than any man can fill. They are left empty and desperate, and many end their life with their own hands, thinking there is no way that they can fix their hopeless situation.

And in a sense, they are right, not in that ending their life is the right thing to do, but there is no way that they or any other man can fix it. This finely is the first time that they come to the absolute truth. No amount of money, things, or relationships will ever fix this situation, no matter how hard you try. Only God can, and I believe that God allows us to go through all of this to get us to the point of finally realizing what this truth really is.

But there are people who are no longer trying to attempt this impossible feat because they have learned the truth. They are the true followers of Christ. They know the way out of this thought process, even if they haven't been raised with parents that were truly acting as a parent should. I use the word *true* here on purpose, for as you will see as I get deeper into this, there are those who claim to be followers and yet have not learned what the truth actually means.

My point here is the fact that David was a man after God's own heart, and he dealt with his own men and people with this heart. But he didn't use the same heart to deal with his own children. If David would have been a father the way God created us to parent, then his children would have had a better chance of making better decisions. Also, if David would have focused on giving his love to his children rather than being concerned whether they loved him or not, he may not have lost them in the process.

Yet today we are making the same mistakes that David made. Today, people are focused more on their career than they are on their families and losing both in the process. They are so concerned with their dealing in the business market or within their sphere of influence, yet they don't have the same interest or fair dealings within their own families. Eventually they start to lose the members of their own family, and they wonder what happened. They lose wives, children, even parents and siblings all in the name of personal success, and this is usually in the form of their career or business. But when they retire, their success amounts to a trophy on the shelf of accomplishments, to find out later that they have no one or very few to share it with. The old phrase says that "On their death bed they never say I wish would have I spent more time at the office. But they always say that I wish I would have spent more time with the ones they love." What they failed to realize is that, yes, we can make huge differences in the world through our occupation or vocation, but the lasting and longer-reaching impact can come through our families.

Think about it this way. There is a desire in most people to leave an impression on this earth when they leave it. This impression can be good or bad, and it is intended to affect the largest group of people possible. I refer to bad also because why else would people who are despondent walk into a store or restaurant and start shooting everybody they can and then turn the gun on themselves? They knew they were going to die, because they leave suicide notes beforehand. If they weren't trying to make an impression, why didn't they just kill themselves and leave everyone else alone? It usually boils down to they want their life or better yet their death to have a purpose or make a statement, and the more people that are influenced, or in this case negatively affected, the more impact the statement has.

This can be said for the positive aspect too. The more good or positive things we do for others, the more the desire to affect as many people as possible. Unfortunately, anything can be taken to extremes to the point of what once was a good thing has now been turned into a negative, for the fact that it was expanded beyond its intended purpose. Their intentions were in the right place; they just wanted to have a positive effect on as many people as possible. This can be similarly seen in economics, known as the law of diminishing return.

So the question I have is, do you affect more people by your vocation or by your family? There is a study that was done by A. E. Winship, Jukes-Edwards, "A Study in Education and Heredity" (Harrisburg, Pa., 1900), who used the study of Richard L. Dugdale in 1871 and 1874. The basis of this study was to study the descendants of two families, one being the descendants of Jonathan Edwards compared to the descendants of a Max Jukes. Max is not the name of a real person but the name given a certain man whose descendants were studied.

According to Dugdale's description of Max, he was a man who grew up hating school, hating work, and only wanting to hunt and fish which being a good shot helped. He was vulgar, yet he was very jolly and love to tell stories, and he was anything but religious.

A. E. Winship, on the other hand, studied a man named Jonathan Edwards. Edwards was hardworking, God-fearing, and Bible-believing. He inspired "The Great Awakening" through his sermons and is given credited for "erecting the standard of Orthodoxy for enlightened Protestant Europe." He served briefly as president of Princeton University where he believed in leading by example and taught people to be responsible for their daily actions.

Naturally, like all fathers do, Juke and Edwards had an impact on their immediate families, but what about the generations to follow? Here is the outcome of these two studies.

Dugdale estimated that of the approximately 1,200 descendants of Max Juke, 300 were convicts, 27 were murderers, 190 were prostitutes, and 509 were either alcoholics or drug addicts. He estimated that the Jukes had cost the State of New York almost 1.3 million dollars to house, institutionalize, and treat the family of deviants.

Compare this to A. E. Winship estimation that of the 1,400 descendants of Jonathan Edwards included 13 college presidents, 86 college professors, 430 ministers, 314 war veterans, 75 authors, 100 lawyers, 30 judges, 66 physicians, and 80 holders of public office, including three US senators, seven congressman, mayors of three large cities, governors of three states, a vice president of the United States, and a controller of the United States treasury.

Now as always, there are those who debate the accuracy of the numbers concerning the results of the studies of both men. What I think is not debatable is that each man had an impact on his descendants. Each man's traits were passed down through several generations, so we can adapt our father's or forefather's traits.

I have seen this played out in my own life, but the difference is that I was trying to not let it happen. Here is what I mean. When I was in my teenage years, I basically hated my dad. He wasn't an evil man; he was a product of his upbringing just like everyone else is. He did have a problem with alcohol, but he quit drinking after he became ill with a sickness where alcohol actually complicated the problem. After he got better, he decided not to return to the drink. This is good and bad at the same time. What I mean is, even though it is not a good thing to do, people use alcohol to cope with problems or circumstances in their lives. So if you take away the alcohol, then they have to substitute something else to replace it, especially when they do not learn how to cope with their problems in a healthy manner. Unfortunately, my dad used anger as his coping method.

Now it is not all my dad's fault. He used to tell me when I was sixteen that I needed to move out on my own while I still knew everything, which is a pretty good picture of my state of mind. So naturally there was a lot of fighting going on between us. I don't need to get into this any deeper, but I want you to understand that we didn't have a warm father-son relationship at that time. Jumping ahead, both my dad and I have overcome our personal issues and grown up tremendously, so now we have created a close relationship that I treasure.

Where I am going is that through all of this, I solemnly swore on a stack of Bibles, on the temple, and even the gold in the temple that I would never be like my dad. Years later after I had been on my own for a while, imagine the horror that I was confronted with when I heard my dad's voice literally come out of my mouth. Now it may not have sounded like my dad's voice to anyone else, but to my ears, it sounded exactly like him. I couldn't believe it. Not only that, but then I realized that a lot of things that I was doing was like my dad, even after my solemn oath.

Now the good thing of all of this is my dad has more very admirable traits along with those few that were not so admirable. Thank God, some of them got passed down to me also, so I was not at a complete loss. My point is even though I didn't want to be like him, I still had many of his traits, both positive and negative in nature, that I received without me even knowing about it.

Also, it may appear from reading this condensed summary that Edwards was a man of great wealth and that his children had a better chance of being successful, but actually, the opposite is true. Edwards was actually ousted from his pulpit by the ecclesiastical council for a controversial sermon he had given to the youth regarding the use of their speech. This was the source of his income. So he eventually took a pastoral position outside of an Indian village, which by the way is where he did most of his famous writings. When he died of small pox at age fifty-six as the president of Princeton, he left his children without any fortune, and six of his children were under the age of twenty-one. So they did not have a fortune to build upon, and they all basically had to start from scratch.

What he did leave them was a desire to expand their intellectual capacity with a continuous devotion to training, a vigor for life, and a good moral character to build it all on. This not only propelled his immediate family on but those of future generations also.

I say all of this to all of those men and women who believe that they are going to make their biggest contribution to the world by their occupation or vocation, not considering the fact that yes they may have an impact on those that are around them, but is that impact going to be seen for generations to come?

David was a man after God's own heart. When he dealt with his men and even his own self, he did so with the heart of God. Unfortunately, he didn't do so when he dealt with his own children, and this in turn was seen generations afterward. Look at his son Solomon. God granted Solomon wisdom—such wisdom has never been known to man before or after himself—yet he ended up making the same mistake David had, which later ended up being his demise also. The mistake was his obsession for women. Let's face it, with seven hundred wives and three hundred concubines, he could be with a different woman every night for almost three years. Think about it, he must have had group anniversary days with his wives. But wasn't this a trait that was passed down from father to son, just not in the same proportion?

I used to work selling urethane coating to the entertainment industry. One of the products that we had was a patented rock replication process. We took a mold of a particular rock or rock cliff and then would spray a series of different urethanes into this mold to duplicate an exact replica of the rock we molded, which made it extremely light. This first mold made was considered a first-generation mold. If we took the duplicated rock and made a mold of it, this mold would then become a second generation mold. So then if we did the same thing with a rock from the second-generation mold and made yet another mold, this would then be a third-generation mold. This continues on the farther you duplicate this process.

The problem with molds is that with each new generation, there is a loss of detail from the original. So the rock created out of a second-generation mold has less detail in it than a rock created out of the first-generation mold. If you continue to pull a mold off the previous generational mold, somewhere down the line, you lose so much detail that you only have a small resemblance of the original rock.

Don't we see the same thing when we are viewing the picture of mankind? The farther a generation goes without some type of growing process or a positive change that keeps this process from happening, the worst future generation continue to deteriorate. Every time one generation lacks discipline in an area, future generations tend to lack even more. I believe that you can see this in the way that men respond to women today in this country. Years ago, men were way more chivalrous than they are today. Men held open the doors, would stand and remove their hat when a woman entered the room, would pull out the chair, walk on the outside of the sidewalk, give their coat to a woman when she's cold—draping it over her shoulders—give up their seat, etc. Today, most men don't even consider any of these things. Why? Well, they haven't seen them being done by their elders, so it doesn't make sense to think that they would do them either. Or the fact that when you do these things, the reaction from women are not always positive since they have never seen it either, and they think you are being a chauvinistic person. So what was considered as an act of respect is now lost or, at the very least, well hidden.

I believe that this can be seen in the Edwards family as well. If the son of Jonathan had molded himself off his father, then he would have produced a son who had lost detail in the process. Just like if we mold ourselves after our own fathers, then we would produce sons who also lost detail. The more this was duplicated, the more loss of detail there would be, until there would only be a small resemblance of the original rock. So what Jonathan had to do was to teach his sons how to mold themselves into first-generation molds so they could teach it to their sons and be passed down to future generations

The question would then be, who could we possibly use to be the rock we are to be molded to?

JESUS

I started all of this making a claim that Jesus had to die the way that he did, because if he would have died any other way, he would have been self-serving and therefore sinned. Now that I am into it this far, I want to explore that even deeper.

When I hear the story of redemption through the blood of Christ, I always hear of how he was perfect and how he had to be perfect in order to be the sacrifice for our sin. When I hear this, it is always stated in a way that would infer the idea that he never did anything wrong and that actually his being perfect was because of his keeping perfect obedience to the law, which I still believe he did. But I also believe that if we were to study the life and teachings of Jesus, we would actually see that he was perfect, but his perfection was perfect love and that his perfect obedience was because of his love. God is perfect love, and since he is God, he is perfect love. So the actual statement that Jesus "was perfect" is not stated correctly, but that he "is perfect"—perfect love, that is. So what is perfect love?

Jesus stated to us that he came to serve and not be served in Mark 10:45, "For even the Son of Man did not come to be served, but to serve, and to give his life as a ransom for many." And that is the definition of God's perfect love. God's perfect love is to serve outward for the benefit of others, so perfect love is serving others.

So in the beginning, we are created in God's image, which is defined by a love that flows outwardly to others. Adam and Eve distorted that image by listening to the devil and misdirecting their love toward themselves. So then it would take God himself to restore that image so that we had an example we could follow. The father did that through his son Jesus.

For who else could show us God's love or the way we are to love but God himself? Who could we have used as the example to follow? Abraham, Isaac, Jacob, David, Moses, Jeremiah? I don't think so, since they also had their moments of self-love. So the only one that we have who has totally lived his life out of love for others has been Christ himself.

Look at what Paul tells us in 1 Corinthians 11:1: "Follow my example, as I follow the example of Christ." So how do we follow Paul's example? Well, Paul was saying that he was making himself to be a first-generation mold of Christ, and so then if we are to be following Paul's example, we too are supposed to be making ourselves a first-generation mold of Christ. If we were to make ourselves a mold of Paul, then we would lose detail in the process. If we make ourselves to be a mold of anyone other than Christ, we are going to lose detail in the process also. And you don't know how much detail has already been lost, so what you may become is only a small resemblance of the original rock.

Some may refer to this as modeling. The *Encarta Dictionary* definition of modeling is "The demonstration of a way of behaving to somebody, especially a child, in order for that behavior to be imitated." The reason I prefer *molded* rather than *modeling* is for the fact that we can imitate the actions of Christ, and I don't want to imitate Christ; my desire should be to be an exact duplicate of Christ.

This is the danger of only following a preacher and obeying everything that he tells you rather than studying the Word for yourself and becoming what the Bible instructs you to become. Second Timothy 2:15 (AMP) says,

> Study and be eager and do your utmost to present yourself to God approved [tested by trial], a workman who has no cause to be ashamed, correctly analyzing and accurately dividing [rightly handling and skillfully teaching] the Word of Truth.

You have to know the word for yourself, so you make sure that you are making yourself from a mold of Christ that hasn't lost any detail.

When I hear others teach about serving in the body or in the church, it is always taught in the manner of being obedient to the teaching of Christ. Yet pay attention to what Christ says in John 14:15, "If you love me, keep my commands." Notice that he didn't say, "Keep my commands, and you will love me." If he had, then he would have been saying that being obedient was the way to love him. How do we know this? I refer back to what I said earlier, does love come from obedience, or is it the other way around? Jesus then tells us in John 14:21, "Whoever has my commands and keeps them is the one who loves me." So the evidence of our love is shown from our obedience, not that our love comes from obedience. We should be focused on changing our hearts to love like God does and not merely focusing on being obedient.

The Pharisees were practicing the laws, and Jesus chastises them for not doing them in love. Weren't they being obedient to the law? Yes, and then again no. They were going through the motion without the right notion of the purpose of the law, the same as they were in the days of Malachi. Jesus tells us that the summation of all the laws and the prophets are to love God with all our heart and mind and to love our neighbor as ourselves, so how could they be obedient when they were not acting in love? If we are serving in the local churches or wherever and it is done out of the guilt trip from a pastor or anybody else for that matter and not from out of the heart of love, are we doing anything different?

Think about the area of tithing. I am going to address this in a roundabout way, so bear with me. But I think tithing is used in a nonbiblical way today in most churches since we don't live under the law of the old covenant but under the commandment or law of Christ, which again is "Love one another as I have loved you."

Jesus tells us in Matthew 5:17, "Do not think that I have come to abolish the Law or the Prophets; I have not come to abolish them but to fulfill them," which some believe that the laws are still in place. But they seem to quit reading too soon. Matthew 5:18 says, "For truly I tell you, until heaven and earth disappear, not the smallest letter, not the least stroke of a pen, will by any means disappear from

the Law until everything is accomplished." Didn't that happen after
Christ's death and resurrection? All was fulfilled.

Listen to the writer of Hebrews in chapter 8 verses 7 to 13.

> For if there had been nothing wrong with
> that first covenant, no place would have been
> sought for another. But God found fault with the
> people and said:
> "The days are coming, declares the Lord,
> when I will make a new covenant
> with the people of Israel
> and with the people of Judah.
> It will not be like the covenant
> I made with their ancestors
> when I took them by the hand
> to lead them out of Egypt,
> because they did not remain faithful to my
> covenant,
> and I turned away from them,
> declares the Lord.
> This is the covenant I will establish with the
> people of Israel
> after that time, declares the Lord.
> I will put my laws in their minds
> and write them on their hearts.
> I will be their God,
> and they will be my people.
> No longer will they teach their neighbor,
> or say to one another, 'Know the Lord,'
> because they will all know me,
> from the least of them to the greatest.
> For I will forgive their wickedness
> and will remember their sins no more."
> By calling this covenant "new," *he has made*
> *the first one obsolete*; and what is obsolete and

outdated will soon disappear. (Hebrews 8:7–13) (emphasis added)

Even Paul confirms this writing to the Ephesians in chapter 2 verses 11 to 18.

> Therefore, remember that formerly you who are Gentiles by birth and called "uncircumcised" by those who call themselves "the circumcision" [that done in the body by the hands of men]— remember that at that time you were separate from Christ, excluded from citizenship in Israel and foreigners to the covenants of the promise, without hope and without God in the world. But now in Christ Jesus you who once were far away have been brought near through the blood of Christ.
>
> For he himself is our peace, who has made the two one and has destroyed the barrier, the dividing wall of hostility, *by abolishing in his flesh the law with its commandments and regulations.* His purpose was to create in himself one new man out of the two, thus making peace, and in this one body to reconcile both of them to God through the cross, by which he put to death their hostility. He came and preached peace to you who were far away and peace to those who were near. For through him we both have access to the Father by one Spirit. (Ephesians 2:11–18) (emphasis added)

In order for him to create the two men into one, he abolished the law in his flesh. So then we no longer have a law to live by. Well, if that is the case, then we should be able to read about this in other parts of the Bible also.

Look at how Peter found out about this in his account with God in Acts 10.

At Caesarea there was a man named Cornelius, a centurion in what was known as the Italian Regiment. He and all his family were devout and God-fearing; he gave generously to those in need and prayed to God regularly. One day at about three in the afternoon he had a vision. He distinctly saw an angel of God, who came to him and said, "Cornelius!"

Cornelius stared at him in fear. "What is it, Lord?" he asked.

The angel answered, "Your prayers and gifts to the poor have come up as a memorial offering before God. Now send men to Joppa to bring back a man named Simon who is called Peter. He is staying with Simon the tanner, whose house is by the sea."

When the angel who spoke to him had gone, Cornelius called two of his servants and a devout soldier who was one of his attendants. He told them everything that had happened and sent them to Joppa.

About noon the following day as they were on their journey and approaching the city, Peter went up on the roof to pray. He became hungry and wanted something to eat, and while the meal was being prepared, he fell into a trance. He saw heaven opened and something like a large sheet being let down to earth by its four corners. It contained all kinds of four-footed animals, as well as reptiles and birds. Then a voice told him, "Get up, Peter. Kill and eat."

"Surely not, Lord!" Peter replied. "I have never eaten anything impure or unclean."

The voice spoke to him a second time, "Do not call anything impure that God has made clean."

This happened three times, and immediately the sheet was taken back to heaven.

While Peter was wondering about the meaning of the vision, the men sent by Cornelius found out where Simon's house was and stopped at the gate. They called out, asking if Simon who was known as Peter was staying there.

While Peter was still thinking about the vision, the Spirit said to him, "Simon, three men are looking for you. So get up and go downstairs. Do not hesitate to go with them, for I have sent them."

Peter went down and said to the men, "I'm the one you're looking for. Why have you come?"

The men replied, "We have come from Cornelius the centurion. He is a righteous and God-fearing man, who is respected by all the Jewish people. A holy angel told him to ask you to come to his house so that he could hear what you have to say." Then Peter invited the men into the house to be his guests.

The next day Peter started out with them, and some of the believers from Joppa went along. The following day he arrived in Caesarea. Cornelius was expecting them and had called together his relatives and close friends. As Peter entered the house, Cornelius met him and fell at his feet in reverence. But Peter made him get up. "Stand up," he said, "I am only a man myself."

While talking with him, Peter went inside and found a large gathering of people. He said to them: "You are well aware that it is against our law for a Jew to associate with or visit a Gentile. But God has shown me that I should not call anyone impure or unclean. So when I was sent for, I came without raising any objection. May I ask why you sent for me?"

Cornelius answered: "Three days ago I was in my house praying at this hour, at three in the afternoon. Suddenly a man in shining clothes stood before me and said, 'Cornelius, God has heard your prayer and remembered your gifts to the poor. Send to Joppa for Simon who is called Peter. He is a guest in the home of Simon the tanner, who lives by the sea.' So I sent for you immediately, and it was good of you to come. Now we are all here in the presence of God to listen to everything the Lord has commanded you to tell us."

Then Peter began to speak: "I now realize how true it is that God does not show favoritism but accepts from every nation the one who fears him and does what is right. You know the message God sent to the people of Israel, announcing the good news of peace through Jesus Christ, who is Lord of all. You know what has happened throughout the province of Judea, beginning in Galilee after the baptism that John preached— how God anointed Jesus of Nazareth with the Holy Spirit and power, and how he went around doing good and healing all who were under the power of the devil, because God was with him.

"We are witnesses of everything he did in the country of the Jews and in Jerusalem. They killed him by hanging him on a cross, but God raised him from the dead on the third day and caused him to be seen. He was not seen by all the people, but by witnesses whom God had already chosen—by us who ate and drank with him after he rose from the dead. He commanded us to preach to the people and to testify that he is the one whom God appointed as judge of the living and the dead. All the prophets testify about him that everyone who believes in him receives forgiveness of sins through his name."

While Peter was still speaking these words, the Holy Spirit came on all who heard the message. The circumcised believers who had come with Peter were astonished that the gift of the Holy Spirit had been poured out even on Gentiles. For they heard them speaking in tongues and praising God.

Then Peter said, "Surely no one can stand in the way of their being baptized with water. They have received the Holy Spirit just as we have." So he ordered that they be baptized in the name of Jesus Christ. Then they asked Peter to stay with them for a few days. (Acts 10:1–48)

This whole story needs to be picked apart. First off, God tells Peter to eat food that is forbidden to be eaten by the law. If the law was still in place, then God would be commanding Peter to break the law. James tells us in James 1:13–15,

When tempted, no one should say, "God is tempting me." For God cannot be tempted by evil, nor does he tempt anyone; but each person is tempted when they are dragged away by their own evil desire and enticed. Then, after desire has conceived, it gives birth to sin; and sin, when it is full-grown, gives birth to death.

So if God doesn't tempt anyone to do evil, then he is not going to command anyone to do evil either, and anyone that breaks the law is considered evil. That means that either the vision Peter had was out of his own evil desires, like he was craving a reptile for desert but knew he shouldn't have one, or God was telling him that he no longer was bound by the law. I believe that the rest of the story would prove that the latter of the two was true.

Think about it, Peter then invited Gentiles to come and eat with him, and then he went to a Gentile's home. Both of these were against the law also. And then we read what Peter says in Acts 10:34–35, "Then Peter began to speak: 'I now realize how true it is that God does not show favoritism but accepts from every nation the one who fears him and does what is right.'"

The laws were written to God's chosen people, the Jews, not the Gentiles, so they never did live under the law, even though they did live under a law which we see Paul writes about in Romans 2:14–15,

> Indeed, when Gentiles, who do not have the law, do by nature things required by the law, they are a law for themselves, even though they do not have the law. They show that the requirements of the law are written on their hearts, their consciences also bearing witness, and their thoughts sometimes accusing them and at other times even defending them.

It was the law written on their heart, which was "Love one another as I have loved you."

Again, the nature of God is love, and since man was created in the image of God, the nature of man is love. God's love is a love of going outward or giving to another. But man's love got distorted when Adam and Eve sinned and turned their love on themselves. Yet that isn't the way that it was intended; the way that it was intended has never changed. Then God created a set of laws for a chosen nation that was to be a guide to live by and help change their heart to live in love. The people of other nations didn't have the laws to help them to live in this manner, but they still had the law of love written in their heart. The problem is that even when they did the right things (even defending them), they still had sin on them for what man can do anything totally for another without doing something also for himself. Only one man can claim this, and his name is Jesus.

So since God commanded Peter to do what was considered breaking the law and God wouldn't tempt or command us to do anything evil, then it is obvious that the law no longer existed. That is because we no longer live by the law; we now live by grace.

Again I use the story of Paul rebuking Peter for living a double standard. One minute he is living by grace, and when his Jew buddies show up, he starts following the law.

> When I saw that they were not acting in line with the truth of the gospel, I said to Cephas in front of them all, "You are a Jew, yet you live like a Gentile and not like a Jew. How is it, then, that you force Gentiles to follow Jewish customs?
>
> "We who are Jews by birth and not sinful Gentiles know that a person is not justified by the works of the law, but by faith in Jesus Christ. So we, too, have put our faith in Christ Jesus that we may be justified by faith in Christ and not by the works of the law, because by the works of the law no one will be justified.
>
> "But if, in seeking to be justified in Christ, we Jews find ourselves also among the sinners, doesn't that mean that Christ promotes sin? Absolutely not! If I rebuild what I destroyed, then I really would be a lawbreaker.
>
> "For through the law I died to the law so that I might live for God. I have been crucified with Christ and I no longer live, but Christ lives in me. The life I now live in the body, I live by faith in the Son of God, who loved me and gave himself for me. I do not set aside the grace of God, for if righteousness could be gained through the law, Christ died for nothing!" (Galatians 2:14–21)

Paul doesn't stop there either. He goes on in Galatians 3.

You foolish Galatians! Who has bewitched you? Before your very eyes Jesus Christ was clearly portrayed as crucified. I would like to learn just one thing from you: Did you receive the Spirit by the works of the law, or by believing what you heard? Are you so foolish? After beginning by means of the Spirit, are you now trying to finish by means of the flesh? Have you experienced so much in vain—if it really was in vain? So again I ask, does God give you his Spirit and work miracles among you by the works of the law, or by your believing what you heard? So also Abraham "believed God, and it was credited to him as righteousness."

Understand, then, that those who have faith are children of Abraham. Scripture foresaw that God would justify the Gentiles by faith, and announced the gospel in advance to Abraham: "All nations will be blessed through you." So those who rely on faith are blessed along with Abraham, the man of faith.

For all who rely on the works of the law are under a curse, as it is written: "Cursed is everyone who does not continue to do everything written in the Book of the Law." Clearly no one who relies on the law is justified before God, because "the righteous will live by faith." The law is not based on faith; on the contrary, it says, "The person who does these things will live by them." Christ redeemed us from the curse of the law by becoming a curse for us, for it is written: "Cursed is everyone who is hung on a pole." He redeemed us in order that the blessing given to Abraham might come to the Gentiles through Christ Jesus, so that by faith we might receive the promise of the Spirit. (Galatians 3:1–14)

Then he continues in Galatians 5.

> It is for freedom that Christ has set us free. Stand firm, then, and do not let yourselves be burdened again by a yoke of slavery.
>
> Mark my words! I, Paul, tell you that if you let yourselves be circumcised, Christ will be of no value to you at all. Again I declare to every man who lets himself be circumcised that he is obligated to obey the whole law. You who are trying to be justified by the law have been alienated from Christ; you have fallen away from grace. For through the Spirit we eagerly await by faith the righteousness for which we hope. For in Christ Jesus neither circumcision nor uncircumcision has any value. The only thing that counts is faith expressing itself through love. (Galatians 5:1–6)

Now you may be thinking that that only applies to circumcision, but how can that be? If you are following the law, any part of it, you are living under the bondage of the law and not by the freedom given through Christ called grace.

Look at what Paul tells us concerning our giving in 2 Corinthians 9:7 (AMP),

> Let each one [give] as he has made up his own mind and purposed in his heart, not reluctantly or sorrowfully or under compulsion, for God loves [he takes pleasure in, prizes above other things, and is unwilling to abandon or to do without] a cheerful [joyous, "prompt to do it"] giver [whose heart is in his giving].

If you are giving according to a law, how are you making up your mind to what to give? Isn't the law telling you what you must give? Oh, yeah, I remember 10 percent is the minimum to give, and you make up your mind on how much more. No, you decide in your heart without compulsion or reluctance on how much to give, not based on a law, since we do not live by the law anymore but by grace.

Well, is it okay to use 10 percent as a gauge? If that is what you feel in your heart to give. But you are not under a law to do so.

I can remember when I was going through an extremely rough time in my life and I didn't have barely enough to make ends meet. I was on my way to church, which taught tithing. I was like, "God, what do I do? I don't have enough to make ends meet and tithe this week?" I was asking how much I should give when I got this thought that I should only give one dollar. I immediately shut that down as the flesh or the devil or whatever, but it couldn't have been from God. So I kept asking. Then I saw a semi going down the road with a big number 1 on it; then, I saw a sign with the number 1 on it, and then another sign. It was like everywhere I looked, the number 1 kept appearing to the point I finally said, "Okay, I am only going to give one dollar." When it was time to put it into the offering plate, I had the toughest time putting in only one dollar. The guilt of not putting in more was powerful. Why? Because I was trying to keep a law that no longer exist.

Now there are other times that I didn't have it and gave it anyways, and God has seen to it that I had what I needed, but I had what I needed both times. I think that the way that we view giving is not even close to the way that the early church viewed it. Here are two stories why.

First is the story of the widow's mite. Both Luke and Mark tell the story, but I am going to use Luke this time. Luke 21:1–4,

> And He looked up and saw the rich putting their gifts into the treasury, and He saw also a certain poor widow putting in two mites. So He said, "Truly I say to you that this poor widow has put in more than all; 4 for all these out of their abundance have put in offerings for God, but she out of her poverty put in all the livelihood that she had."

They gave their offerings, and she gave it all. Now you may be thinking, "Well yeah, but that was a certain circumstance. I mean if all you have is a couple of pennies or whatever, then when you are giving it all, you are still not giving a lot." Well, according to Jesus, she gave more than all of the others because she did give all she had.

Jesus was trying to point out the condition of the widow's heart—she was living as she was created to be. She was loving God, not herself, with everything she had, and so was the early church. I believe that if you were to study the New Testament under this light, you would see that this is part of the gospel that they shared. Read what Paul says the other apostles told him to do. Galatians 2:8–10 says,

> For God, who was at work in Peter as an apostle to the circumcised, was also at work in me as an apostle to the Gentiles. James, Cephas and John, those esteemed as pillars, gave me and Barnabas the right hand of fellowship when they recognized the grace given to me. They agreed that we should go to the Gentiles, and they to the circumcised. All they asked was that we should *continue to remember the poor*, the very thing I had been eager to do all along.

Let's look at this story in Acts 4:32–35,

> All the believers were one in heart and mind. No one claimed that any of their possessions was their own, but they shared everything they had. With great power the apostles continued to testify to the resurrection of the Lord Jesus. And God's grace was so powerfully at work in them all that there were no needy persons among them. For from time to time those who owned land or houses sold them, brought the money from the

sales and put it at the apostles' feet, and it was distributed to anyone who had need.

The first thing that I want to point out is when you are reading Acts, it is a detailed story of how the early church got its start. Therefore, when you read about the events like Jesus's ascension to heaven, the picking of Matthias, the day of Pentecost, or Peter and John speaking to the Sanhedrin, Luke gives you a detailed account of what occurred. Yet here, he barely mentions it but for the reason of setting up for the story of Ananias and Sapphira.

This may be because he mentioned it before in Acts 2:42–47 (emphasis added):

> They devoted themselves to the apostles' teaching and to fellowship, to the breaking of bread and to prayer. Everyone was filled with awe at the many wonders and signs performed by the apostles. All the believers were together and had everything in common. *They sold property and possessions to give to anyone who had need.* 46 Every day they continued to meet together in the temple courts. They broke bread in their homes and ate together with glad and sincere hearts, praising God and enjoying the favor of all the people. And the Lord added to their number daily those who were being saved.

Yet even here it barely gets honorable mention. He barely talks about the breaking of the bread. Why? Could it be because that is naturally what they did?

Since I have been chasing rabbit holes throughout this whole thing, then I might as well chase this one. Why is it that we only partake of the Lord's supper in the church house on Sunday and not when we come together in our homes? They met in the temple courts, but they broke bread together in their homes when they came together to eat. Yet today, when we eat together, we call that breaking of bread. If you study verse 42 and verse 46, you will see that there is a difference between the two. I have never been in another Christian's home where we broke bread and remember the Lord's death before we ate. Why not? How did this become a ceremony and for some churches only on the second or third or whatever Sunday of the month?

Going back to where I was, it seems that when you are reading about the early church selling of property and not considering anything as (exclusively) being their own, he was stating the fact as if it was common knowledge, so then there was no need to get into detail since they all were doing that anyway.

Consider the rest of the story in Acts 5:1–11. First, they give an example of Barnabas selling his field and giving it to the apostles. Then Luke tells the story of a couple that it appears they did the same thing.

> Now a man named Ananias, together with his wife Sapphira, also sold a piece of property. With his wife's full knowledge he kept back part of the money for himself, but brought the rest and put it at the apostles' feet.
>
> Then Peter said, "Ananias, how is it that Satan has so filled your heart that you have lied to the Holy Spirit and have kept for yourself some of the money you received for the land? Didn't it belong to you before it was sold? And after it was sold, wasn't the money at your disposal? What made you think of doing such a thing? You have not lied just to human beings but to God."
>
> When Ananias heard this, he fell down and died. And great fear seized all who heard what had happened. Then some young men came forward, wrapped up his body, and carried him out and buried him.
>
> About three hours later his wife came in, not knowing what had happened. Peter asked

her, "Tell me, is this the price you and Ananias got for the land?"

"Yes," she said, "that is the price."

Peter said to her, "How could you conspire to test the Spirit of the Lord? Listen! The feet of the men who buried your husband are at the door, and they will carry you out also."

At that moment she fell down at his feet and died. Then the young men came in and, finding her dead, carried her out and buried her beside her husband. Great fear seized the whole church and all who heard about these events. (Acts 5:1–11)

Okay, so what just happened here? Well, think about it. Luke gave us an idea of how the church was viewing themselves and then gave us an actual story to get the idea of how it was done. The Christians of that time understood that they were to deny the love relationship that they had with themselves including their belongings and to now live as Christ, their Lord, commanded them to, which was to live their lives for the good of others. There was no fanfare; they were doing this straight from the heart.

But there is a difference in the story of Ananias and Sapphira. They gave it, but they gave it for the glory of themselves to satisfy the love of themselves and not from the heart. Why else would they have given a portion of it and then tell Peter it was all? As Peter told them, it was theirs to do with as they wished. It would have been different if Ananias had come with the money and said, "Here, Peter, I sold my field, but the house needs a new roof [or whatever], and I kept enough to take care of that, but here is the rest."

The issue was not the amount that they gave; it was the condition of heart that they gave it with. Can you imagine if nothing would have happened after everyone knew they had lied? Instead, there was great fear among them. Can you imagine what would happen today if the same thing happened to people that are doing things for the glory of themselves? We would see whole nations drop dead in an instant.

So the thing that I want to know is, why is it that today we preach tithing and back then they gave what was needed? But they didn't give to one local church; they gave it to the people of the body of Christ that were in need in whatever the location. But this isn't even the whole truth, because in Acts 4:32, it states, "No one claimed that any of their possessions where their own." You can't give something away that wasn't yours to give. Since they didn't claim ownership of any possessions, they merely redistributed it.

So am I saying that we should all sell what we have and give it all away? No, the Amplified Bible uses the word *exclusively* when it describes ownership. It says in Acts 4:32 (AMP), "Now the company of believers was of one heart and soul, and not one of them claimed that anything which he possessed was [exclusively] his own, but everything they had was in common and for the use of all." I believe that this is a good way of looking at it, either because it makes sense or because I don't really want to sell the things that I own. Oh, wretched man that I am.

I believe that when the heart is right, then we can use everything that the Lord gives us with great joy, but we can have the same joy of giving it away if the Lord asks us to. If God gives me a brand-new full-dressed Harley, I can assure you that I would ride it not only with a smile on my face but laughing with great joy. If I wasn't the wretched man that I am, then I would give it away with the same joy and laughter that I accepted it with, because someone else will get to experience the same joy that I did. I wouldn't be looking at it as if God took it away from me. I look forward to the day that I can grow that far.

Yes, I realize that even Job was in great distress when everything he had was taken from him. But what it also showed us is his acknowledgment of God. Yet he didn't have the Holy Spirit living in him to help him; we do. So we should even have a better spirit about it than Job did (more on the Holy Spirit later). Isn't that how Paul came to the realization in Philippians 4:10–13,

> I rejoiced greatly in the Lord that at last you renewed your concern for me. Indeed, you were concerned, but you had no opportunity to show it. I am not saying this because I am in need,

for I have learned to be content whatever the circumstances. I know what it is to be in need, and
I know what it is to have plenty. I have learned
the secret of being content in any and every situation, whether well fed or hungry, whether living
in plenty or in want. I can do all this through
him who gives me strength.

What about the blessings that come from my giving? Okay, let's
discuss this deeper. Everyone who wants to use this argument does so
based on "The seed planted is the harvest that is returned." Galatians
6:7 says, "Do not be deceived: God cannot be mocked. A man reaps
what he sows." See it says it right there. Well, let's look at the rest of it.

Brothers and sisters, if someone is caught in
a sin [I believe this should have been interpreted as
transgression], you who live by the Spirit should
restore that person gently. But watch yourselves,
or you also may be tempted. Carry each other's
burdens, and in this way you will fulfill the law of
Christ. If anyone thinks they are something when
they are not, they deceive themselves. Each one
should test their own actions. Then they can take
pride in themselves alone, without comparing
themselves to someone else, for each one should
carry their own load. Nevertheless, the one who
receives instruction in the word should share all
good things with their instructor.

Do not be deceived: God cannot be mocked.
A man reaps what he sows. *Whoever sows to please
their flesh, from the flesh will reap destruction;
whoever sows to please the Spirit, from the Spirit
will reap eternal life.* Let us not become weary in
doing good, for at the proper time we will reap
a harvest if we do not give up. Therefore, as we
have opportunity, let us do good to all people,

especially to those who belong to the family of
believers. (Galatians 6:1–10) (emphasis added)

He was talking about the consequences of sin, which is what we
have seen in the life of David.

Again, we can look at Luke 6:38, where it says, "Give, and it
will be given to you. A good measure, pressed down, shaken together
and running over, will be poured into your lap. For with the measure
you use, it will be measured to you." Okay, but back up one sentence.
As I said before, read it in the context that it was written. He was
talking about judging others. Luke 6:37–38 says,

> Do not judge, and you will not be judged.
> Do not condemn, and you will not be con-
> demned. Forgive, and you will be forgiven. Give,
> and it will be given to you. A good measure,
> pressed down, shaken together and running over,
> will be poured into your lap. For with the mea-
> sure you use, it will be measured to you.

There are other similar passages that are being used to make this
point. But let's go back to the teachings of Jesus in Matthew 6:19–34:

> Do not store up for yourselves treasures
> on earth, where moths and vermin destroy, and
> where thieves break in and steal. But store up for
> yourselves treasures in heaven, where moths and
> vermin do not destroy, and where thieves do not
> break in and steal. For where your treasure is,
> there your heart will be also.
>
> The eye is the lamp of the body. If your eyes
> are healthy, your whole body will be full of light.
> But if your eyes are unhealthy, your whole body
> will be full of darkness. If then the light within
> you is darkness, how great is that darkness!

No one can serve two masters. Either you will hate the one and love the other, or you will be devoted to the one and despise the other. You cannot serve both God and money.

Therefore I tell you, do not worry about your life, what you will eat or drink; or about your body, what you will wear. Is not life more than food, and the body more than clothes? Look at the birds of the air; they do not sow or reap or store away in barns, and yet your heavenly Father feeds them. Are you not much more valuable than they? Can any one of you by worrying add a single hour to your life?

And why do you worry about clothes? See how the flowers of the field grow. They do not labor or spin. Yet I tell you that not even Solomon in all his splendor was dressed like one of these. If that is how God clothes the grass of the field, which is here today and tomorrow is thrown into the fire, will he not much more clothe you—you of little faith? So do not worry, saying, "What shall we eat?" or "What shall we drink?" or "What shall we wear?" For the pagans run after all these things, and your heavenly Father knows that you need them. But seek first his kingdom and his righteousness, and all these things will be given to you as well. Therefore do not worry about tomorrow, for tomorrow will worry about itself. Each day has enough trouble of its own.

Here is Luke's version of what Jesus says in Luke 12:15, "Then he said to them, 'Watch out! Be on your guard against all kinds of greed; life does not consist in an abundance of possessions.'" He also adds this to the end of his version in Luke 12:32–34,

Do not be afraid, little flock, for your Father has been pleased to give you the kingdom. *Sell your possessions and give to the poor. Provide purses for yourselves that will not wear out, a treasure in heaven that will never fail, where no thief comes near and no moth destroys.* For where your treasure is, there your heart will be also.

So the early church was just doing what the Lord commanded them to.

Did you notice that it didn't say, "So do not worry about what you will eat or drink or even wear [or in this day, car to drive, house you will live in, etc.], for your heavenly Father knows that you tithe or give or both, and so he will take care of you in accordance to your giving." No, what he did say was quit focusing on those things and focus on being righteous.

Now righteousness is being in right standing with God. The question is then, how are we in right standing with God? Through justification by accepting Jesus Christ as our Savior.

But now apart from the law the righteousness of God has been made known, to which the Law and the Prophets testify. This righteousness is given through faith in Jesus Christ to all who believe. There is no difference between Jew and Gentile, for all have sinned and fall short of the glory of God, and all are justified freely by his grace through the redemption that came by Christ Jesus. God presented Christ as a sacrifice of atonement, through the shedding of his blood—to be received by faith. He did this to demonstrate his righteousness, because in his forbearance he had left the sins committed beforehand unpunished—he did it to demonstrate his righteousness at the present time, so as to be just and the one who justifies those who have faith in Jesus. (Romans 3:21–26)

But what does this really mean?

Romans 6:23 tells us, "For the wages of sin is death, but the gift of God is eternal life in Christ Jesus our Lord." Or the way that I am explaining it is that the wages of your love relationship with yourself is death, both physically and spiritually. Spiritual death is the separation of ourselves from God. Isaiah 59:1–2 says, "Surely the arm of the LORD is not too short to save, nor his ear too dull to hear. But your iniquities have separated you from your God; your sins have hidden his face from you, so that he will not hear." Jesus's death then became a ransom for us all.

It has always been taught that he did this by his death on the cross, which is true. His death was the atonement for our sin. But I believe that there is more to it than that. He also lived a sacrificed life for us while he was on this earth. Think about it, could you or do you know of any other man whose total existence was for the benefit of mankind? Especially since everything on this earth is his and he didn't take advantage of it. So his life and his death was a sacrifice on our behalf. Matthew 20:28 says, "Just as the Son of Man did not come to be served, but to serve, and to give his life as a ransom for many." We always think of his sacrificial death, yet his whole life was given to us.

John writes in his letter of 1 John 5:1–5:

> Everyone who believes that Jesus is the Christ is born of God, and everyone who loves the father loves his child as well. This is how we know that we love the children of God: by loving God and carrying out his commands. In fact, this is love for God: to keep his commands. And his commands are not burdensome, for everyone born of God overcomes the world. This is the victory that has overcome the world, even our faith. Who is it that overcomes the world? Only the one who believes that Jesus is the Son of God.

Paul tells us in Romans 10:5–13:

> Moses writes this about the righteousness that
> is by the law: "The person who does these things
> will live by them." But the righteousness that is by
> faith says: "Do not say in your heart, 'Who will
> ascend into heaven?' [that is, to bring Christ down]
> or 'Who will descend into the deep?'" [that is, to
> bring Christ up from the dead]. But what does it
> say? "The word is near you; it is in your mouth
> and in your heart," that is, the message concerning
> faith that we proclaim: If you declare with your
> mouth, "Jesus is Lord," and believe in your heart
> that God raised him from the dead, you will be
> saved. For it is with your heart that you believe
> and are justified, and it is with your mouth that
> you profess your faith and are saved. As Scripture
> says, "Anyone who believes in him will never be
> put to shame." For there is no difference between
> Jew and Gentile—the same Lord is Lord of all and
> richly blesses all who call on him, for, "Everyone
> who calls on the name of the Lord will be saved."

So those who believe that Jesus is the Son of God and believes
that God raised him from the dead to be the atonement of our sin,
they will be saved. But what about the part where we are to be calling
Jesus "our Lord"? What does it mean to call Jesus *Lord*?

Here is the definition that I got from the Strong's Greek dictionary:

> G2962
> κύριος
> kurios
> koo'-ree-os
> From κῦρος kuros (supremacy); supreme in
> authority, that is, (as noun) controller; by implica-

tion Mr. (as a respectful title):—God, Lord, master, Sir.

So one could use the term *lord* out of respect as you would use the word *gentleman*, but that is not the case here, evidently. Paul was referring to the word *lord* in the sense of saying that I am turning my freedom of will or my life over to the control of the Son of God, who is Jesus Christ. So when you trust Jesus for the atonement of your sin, you are in right standing with God the Father, and you no longer are guilty of your sin. What's better yet is you live under the protection of God's grace, no longer being condemned under the burden of the law. Then we give up our life to follow Jesus as our Lord and his example of living, which is the same as his command to love one another as he loved us.

Paul tells us in Romans 5:

> Therefore, since we have been justified through faith, we have peace with God through our Lord Jesus Christ, through whom we have gained access by faith into this grace in which we now stand. And we boast in the hope of the glory of God. Not only so, but we also glory in our sufferings, because we know that suffering produces perseverance; perseverance, character; and character, hope. And hope does not put us to shame, because God's love has been poured out into our hearts through the Holy Spirit, who has been given to us.
>
> You see, at just the right time, when we were still powerless, Christ died for the ungodly. Very rarely will anyone die for a righteous person, though for a good person someone might possibly dare to die. But God demonstrates his own love for us in this: While we were still sinners, Christ died for us.

Since we have now been justified by his blood, how much more shall we be saved from God's wrath through him! For if, while we were God's enemies, we were reconciled to him through the death of his Son, how much more, having been reconciled, shall we be saved through his life! Not only is this so, but we also boast in God through our Lord Jesus Christ, through whom we have now received reconciliation.

Therefore, just as sin entered the world through one man, and death through sin, and in this way death came to all people, because all sinned—

To be sure, sin was in the world before the law was given, but sin is not charged against anyone's account where there is no law. Nevertheless, death reigned from the time of Adam to the time of Moses, even over those who did not sin by breaking a command, as did Adam, who is a pattern of the one to come.

But the gift is not like the trespass. For if the many died by the trespass of the one man, how much more did God's grace and the gift that came by the grace of the one man, Jesus Christ, overflow to the many! Nor can the gift of God be compared with the result of one man's sin: The judgment followed one sin and brought condemnation, but the gift followed many trespasses and brought justification. For if, by the trespass of the one man, death reigned through that one man, how much more will those who receive God's abundant provision of grace and of the gift of righteousness reign in life through the one man, Jesus Christ!

Consequently, just as one trespass resulted in condemnation for all people, so also one righteous act resulted in justification and life for all people. For just as through the disobedience of the one man the many were made sinners, so also through the obedience of the one man the many will be made righteous.

The law was brought in so that the trespass might increase. But where sin increased, grace increased all the more, so that, just as sin reigned in death, so also grace might reign through righteousness to bring eternal life through Jesus Christ our Lord. (Romans 5:1–21)

So if we no longer live under a law but by grace, are we free to murder, steal, covet our neighbor's wife or goods, etc.? I'll let Paul answer that first.

What shall we say, then? Shall we go on sinning so that grace may increase? By no means! We are those who have died to sin; how can we live in it any longer? Or don't you know that all of us who were baptized into Christ Jesus were baptized into his death? We were therefore buried with him through baptism into death in order that, just as Christ was raised from the dead through the glory of the Father, we too may live a new life.

For if we have been united with him in a death like his, we will certainly also be united with him in a resurrection like his. For we know that our old self was crucified with him so that the body ruled by sin might be done away with, that we should no longer be slaves to sin—because anyone who has died has been set free from sin.

Now if we died with Christ, we believe that we will also live with him. For we know that since Christ was raised from the dead, he cannot die again; death no longer has mastery over him. The death he died, he died to sin once for all; but the life he lives, he lives to God.

In the same way, count yourselves dead to sin but alive to God in Christ Jesus. Therefore do not let sin reign in your mortal body so that you obey its evil desires. Do not offer any part of yourself to sin as an instrument of wickedness, but rather offer yourselves to God as those who have been brought from death to life; and offer every part of yourself to him as an instrument of righteousness. For sin shall no longer be your master, because you are not under the law, but under grace. (Romans 6:1–14)

Okay, so here is my answer. Sin is the loving of self. Sin separated us eternally from God. Being a slave to sin was a hard life to live. By God's mercy and grace, he sends his son to be the redemption for us. Galatians 4:4–5 says, "But when the set time had fully come, God sent his Son, born of a woman, born under the law, to redeem those under the law, that we might receive adoption to sonship." Now we are back in righteousness with the Father. That being the case, now we want to go back to the state that we were in before of loving ourselves or living in sin? Okay, is that crazy or what?

I'll let Paul continue in Romans 6:15–23:

What then? Shall we sin because we are not under the law but under grace? By no means! Don't you know that when you offer yourselves to someone as obedient slaves, you are slaves of the one you obey—whether you are slaves to sin, which leads to death, or to obedience, which leads to righteousness? But thanks be to God that, though you used to be slaves to sin, you have come to obey from your heart the pattern of teaching that has now claimed your allegiance.

You have been set free from sin and have become slaves to righteousness.

I am using an example from everyday life because of your human limitations. Just as you used to offer yourselves as slaves to impurity and to ever-increasing wickedness, so now offer yourselves as slaves to righteousness leading to holiness. When you were slaves to sin, you were free from the control of righteousness. What benefit did you reap at that time from the things you are now ashamed of? Those things result in death! But now that you have been set free from sin and have become slaves of God, the benefit you reap leads to holiness, and the result is eternal life. For the wages of sin is death, but the gift of God is eternal life in Christ Jesus our Lord.

The *Matthew Henry's Concise Commentary* says it this way:

The apostle having at large asserted, opened, and proved, the great doctrine of justification by faith, for fear lest any should suck poison out of that sweet flower, and turn that grace of God into wantonness and licentiousness, he, with a like zeal, copiousness of expression, and cogency of argument, presses the absolute necessity of sanctification and a holy life, as the inseparable fruit and companion of justification; for, wherever Jesus Christ is made of God unto any soul righteousness, he is made of God unto that soul sanctification, 1 Cor. 1:30. The water and the blood came streaming together out of the pierced side of the dying Jesus. And what God hath thus joined together let not us dare to put asunder.

Sometimes it seems hard to live free from sin, or should I say loving ourselves, but then are we forgetting how hard it was to live for ourselves? Jesus tells us in Matthew 11:28–29,

> Come to me, all you who are weary and burdened, and I will give you rest. Take my yoke upon you and learn from me, for I am gentle and humble in heart, and you will find rest for your souls. For my yoke is easy and my burden is light.

If you would actually analyze the facts, it is easier to live for Christ than it is to live for ourselves.

Knowing this, how could you be continuing to live in sin if you are claiming that Jesus is your Lord? For if he is your Lord, then you would be doing what he has commanded you to do. For Jesus said in John 14:15, "If you love me, keep my commands." This was his command in John 13:34, "A new command I give you: Love one another. As I have loved you, so you must love one another." This is the opposite of sin.

Yet as we will see, today in the church, the children of God continue to live in sin anyway. They are living lives that are focused on themselves. The focus is on how God will take care of their needs rather than on how they can be of service to God. *I'm just as guilty as the rest!*

The first question that should be raised is, how did Jesus love us? He did it selflessly, for others, without concern for himself. So if we do not love one another like Jesus did, then we are still living in sin and have not repented. Paul tells us in 1 Corinthians 6:19–20, "Do you not know that your bodies are temples of the Holy Spirit, who is in you, whom you have received from God? You are not your own; you were bought at a price. Therefore honor God with your bodies." But how can we stop sinning?

Well, one way that people think they can do this is to avoid all situations that would cause them to sin, considering that sin is their actions of disobedience. If we view sin in this manner, then the way we could avoid sinning is to avoid the situation in which we keep ourselves from committing the action. But if sin is not the action, the action is the trespass, which causes the inequity, and sin is the condition of the heart, better known as the love of self or what could be referred to as being hard-hearted, then avoidance of the situation doesn't keep us from sinning, rather it keeps us from committing the transgression. So we can avoid all circumstances and live in a box and still be living in sin. The action of living in the box could be a proof of that sin. How? Let's look at some different stories of Jesus.

> Later on there was a Jewish festival [feast] for which Jesus went up to Jerusalem.
>
> Now there is in Jerusalem a pool near the Sheep Gate. This pool in the Hebrew is called Bethesda, having five porches (alcoves, colonnades, doorways).
>
> In these lay a great number of sick folk—some blind, some crippled, and some paralyzed [shriveled up]—waiting for the bubbling up of the water.
>
> For an angel of the Lord went down at appointed seasons into the pool and moved and stirred up the water; whoever then first, after the stirring up of the water, stepped in was cured of whatever disease with which he was afflicted.
>
> There was a certain man there who had suffered with a deep-seated and lingering disorder for thirty-eight years.
>
> When Jesus noticed him lying there [helpless], knowing that he had already been a long time in that condition, He said to him, "Do you want to become well?" [Are you really in earnest about getting well?]
>
> The invalid answered, "Sir, I have nobody when the water is moving to put me into the pool; but while I am trying to come [into it] myself, somebody else steps down ahead of me."

Jesus said to him, "Get up! Pick up your bed [sleeping pad] and walk!"

Instantly the man became well and recovered his strength and picked up his bed and walked. But that happened on the Sabbath.

So the Jews kept saying to the man who had been healed, It is the Sabbath, and you have no right to pick up your bed [it is not lawful].

He answered them, "The Man Who healed me and gave me back my strength, He Himself said to me, 'Pick up your bed and walk!'"

They asked him, "Who is the Man Who told you, 'Pick up your bed and walk?'"

Now the invalid who had been healed did not know who it was, for Jesus had quietly gone away [had passed on unnoticed], since there was a crowd in the place.

Afterward, when Jesus found him in the temple, He said to him, "See, you are well! Stop sinning or something worse may happen to you."

The man went away and told the Jews that it was Jesus Who had made him well. (John 5:1–15 AMP)

Put this into the proper prospective. Let's say you are in the hospital with a terminal form of cancer. Somebody walks up to you, and you know that they have the power to heal you. The first thing that comes out of their mouth is, "Do you want to become well?" Wouldn't you want to kind of come out of your skin saying, "Of course I want to be well" or at least be a bit sarcastic and go, "No, I'm enjoying myself. I just want to lay here and endure this pain. I heard it builds character, even though I won't have it for long."

But that is not the way the old man was. Every time I read the passage, I can almost literally hear the whine in his voice. Yet after he was healed, Jesus told him to go and stop sinning. What is the guy doing? Having wild pool parties? He has been like this for thirty-eight years, what could he have possibly done? How about feeling sorry for himself? Isn't that a form of loving one's self?

Truthfully though, wouldn't that seem like a heartless thing to ask? Doesn't everyone want to be healed or have the challenge in their life removed?

Well, imagine how shocked I was the first time that I found out that this is not true. I was talking to a friend of mine who was bound to a wheelchair. Once during a conversation about his situation, we came across the issue of healing. I asked him if he believed in healing and what he would do if he was healed, and he shocked me with his response.

He told me he didn't want to be healed even if he could. He explained that there was a certain level of comfort in his condition. What did come with his condition was additional help, attention, and care that he wouldn't have if he could move normally again. He was familiar with how to live life in his situation, so he was afraid that if he had to live a normal life, he wouldn't be able to manage as well as he could the way that he is now.

I am finding out that he is not alone. There are many people that are living in situations that are less than desirable and are always complaining about them, yet they do nothing whatsoever to get themselves out of it. This is because either they don't know how or that they really don't want to because they have found a certain level of comfort in their current situation. So for Jesus to ask this seemingly insensitive question, what he was really doing was addressing his sin. His sin was the same as all of us, the sin of loving ourselves, and it revealed itself through self-pity.

Then there is the story in Luke 5:17–26:

> One day Jesus was teaching, and Pharisees and teachers of the law were sitting there. They had come from every village of Galilee and from Judea and Jerusalem. And the power of the Lord was with Jesus to heal the sick. Some men came carrying a paralyzed man on a mat and tried to take him into the house to lay him before Jesus.

When they could not find a way to do this because of the crowd, they went up on the roof and lowered him on his mat through the tiles into the middle of the crowd, right in front of Jesus.

When Jesus saw their faith, he said, "Friend, your sins are forgiven."

The Pharisees and the teachers of the law began thinking to themselves, "Who is this fellow who speaks blasphemy? Who can forgive sins but God alone?"

Jesus knew what they were thinking and asked, "Why are you thinking these things in your hearts? Which is easier: to say, 'Your sins are forgiven,' or to say, 'Get up and walk'? But I want you to know that the Son of Man has authority on earth to forgive sins." So he said to the paralyzed man, "I tell you, get up, take your mat and go home." Immediately he stood up in front of them, took what he had been lying on and went home praising God. Everyone was amazed and gave praise to God. They were filled with awe and said, "We have seen remarkable things today."

The guy was paralyzed. What could he have possibly been doing wrong, where he committed a sin in the traditional thinking of sin? But again, if sin is the loving of self, then he easily could have been guilty of self-pity also.

Then there are situations where someone is guilty of sin not because they did something, but because they didn't do something.

Now on his way to Jerusalem, Jesus traveled along the border between Samaria and Galilee. As he was going into a village, ten men who had leprosy met him. They stood at a distance and called out in a loud voice, "Jesus, Master, have pity on us!" When he saw them, he said, "Go, show yourselves to the priests." And as they went, they were cleansed. One of them, when he saw he was healed, came back, praising God in a loud voice. He threw himself at Jesus' feet and thanked him—and he was a Samaritan. Jesus asked, "Were not all ten cleansed? Where are the other nine? Has no one returned to give praise to God except this foreigner?" Then he said to him, "Rise and go; your faith has made you well." (Luke 17:11–19)

Isn't it funny also how Luke points out the fact that he was a Samaritan, so I can only presume the others were Jews? Here is the thing, nine out of ten didn't even consider coming back to thank Jesus for this miracle that completely changed their plot in life; they got what they wanted and went about their way. So the failure to give thanks to God for the blessings that he bestows on our life would be a transgression against him and the evidence that we still are living in sin.

It would seem that if sin is the action of disobedience, then as long as you go about your business and you are not doing harm to anyone else, you are not sinning. But if sin is not the action of being disobedient, rather the loving of self, then you going about your business could be the trespass you are committing.

I hear of so many different crimes these days that are being committed out in the open, and no one does anything to stop them for fear of getting involved. Some of this is due to a society that has created a victim mentality and has punished people that were trying to help out. When I was a kid and I did something wrong, I first got in trouble with the person who saw me, but then I got in trouble with my parents. Today if you correct a child who is not your own for doing something wrong, you will hear about it from the kid's parent.

I once saw the neighbor's kids pointing a BB gun at another neighbor's garage. Before they were able to get a shot off, I quickly asked, "Hey, what are you guys doing? Don't you know that will put a hole in the siding?" Next thing I know I saw their dad come over to tell me that the BBs were plastic and that he didn't appreciate me yelling at his kids. Well, first off, the truth is I wasn't yelling. Second, there was no way of knowing that they were plastic since the gun looked like a regular BB gun. Third, I'm sure the other neighbor doesn't want his siding used for target practice. And last but not least, if the gun would have made holes, then I was actually saving the kids from making a big mistake and my neighbor from having to fix his siding. But the only thing that the kid's dad could see was the fact that I was trying to correct his kids. Even though, I would rather take the chance of getting my head bitten off while protecting everyone in the process instead of not having done anything, which would have saved my head, and seeing the damage done instead, but it does tend to make you not want to do anything.

Now we can go through life minding our own business, only focused on ourselves, or we can stand up for what is right, in a correct manner, helping to protect those who need the help. This doesn't matter if it is feeding the poor, taking care of the sick, or protecting a group of people who are in harm's way and can't protect themselves.

What about the people who just need to see that there is another way to live outside of the way they are living? This can be from a simple life adjustment to a total life overhaul. At one time, I was in need of a life overhaul. If I hadn't had a group of people, and particularly a certain few persons who would take the time out of their life to invest it into mine, there is no question that I would not be here today, because I was plotting my suicide when they intervened. What if they would have went about their business and paid no attention to me? I would have been a short article on the daily newspaper at most, and that would have been it. Another life totally wasted because no one took their time to care.

I like the way that *The Message* translates Paul's letter to the Philippians in 2:1–11:

> If you've gotten anything at all out of fol-
> lowing Christ, if his love has made any difference
> in your life, if being in a community of the Spirit
> means anything to you, if you have a heart, if you

care—then do me a favor: Agree with each other, love each other, be deep-spirited friends. Don't push your way to the front; don't sweet-talk your way to the top. Put yourself aside, and help others get ahead. Don't be obsessed with getting your own advantage. Forget yourselves long enough to lend a helping hand.

Think of yourselves the way Christ Jesus thought of himself. He had equal status with God but didn't think so much of himself that he had to cling to the advantages of that status no matter what. Not at all. When the time came, he set aside the privileges of deity and took on the status of a slave, became human! Having become human, he stayed human. It was an incredibly humbling process. He didn't claim special privileges. Instead, he lived a selfless, obedient life and then died a selfless, obedient death—and the worst kind of death at that—a crucifixion.

Because of that obedience, God lifted him high and honored him far beyond anyone or anything, ever, so that all created beings in heaven and on earth—even those long ago dead and buried—will bow in worship before this Jesus Christ, and call out in praise that he is the Master of all, to the glorious honor of God the Father. (Philippians 2:1–11)

This is how we know what love is: Jesus Christ laid down his life for us. And we ought to lay down our lives for our brothers and sisters. If anyone has material possessions and sees a brother or sister in need but has no pity on them, how can the love of God be in that person? Dear children, let us not love with words or speech but with actions and in truth. (1 John 3:16–18)

What good is it, my brothers and sisters, if someone claims to have faith but has no deeds? Can such faith save them? 15 Suppose a brother or a sister is without clothes and daily food. If one of you says to them, "Go in peace; keep warm and well fed," but does nothing about their physical needs, what good is it? In the same way, faith by itself, if it is not accompanied by action, is dead.

But someone will say, "You have faith; I have deeds. Show me your faith without deeds, and I will show you my faith by my deeds." (James 3:14–18)

So the failure to act can be living in sin if the definition of sin is the loving of oneself to the point that our focus is only on the meeting of our needs and disregarding the needs of others around us who need our help.

PROBLEMS IN THE CHURCH

In today's society though, this can be tough to discern. It seems that panhandling has become a profession in itself. I have had many instances where I gave to someone, only to find out that this was the way that they were making a living, not that they were in a situation that called for special assistance. I know someone that stopped to help a guy who was on the side of the road with a sign that said, "Will work for food." He was a small contractor and told the guy to get in and he would pay him a day's wages to help him do something like pull wire or such. The guy said, "No way, I'm not going to work that hard." What's sad is that it wasn't that hard of work.

Today we live in an entitlement society that believes the world owes them something just for showing up or being born. But the Apostle Paul tells us in 2 Thessalonians 3:6–15:

> In the name of the Lord Jesus Christ, we command you, brothers and sisters, to keep away from every believer who is idle and disruptive and does not live according to the teaching you received from us. For you yourselves know how you ought to follow our example. We were not idle when we were with you, nor did we eat anyone's food without paying for it. On the contrary, we worked night and day, laboring and toiling so that we would not be a burden to any of you. We did this, not because we do not have the right to such help, but in order to offer ourselves as a model for you to imitate. For even when we were

with you, we gave you this rule: *"The one who is unwilling to work shall not eat."*

We hear that some among you are idle and disruptive. They are not busy; they are busybodies. Such people we command and urge in the Lord Jesus Christ to settle down and earn the food they eat. And as for you, brothers and sisters, never tire of doing what is good.

Take special note of anyone who does not obey our instruction in this letter. Do not associate with them, in order that they may feel ashamed. Yet do not regard them as an enemy, but warn them as you would a fellow believer.

I believe that these are words that we should not only live by but give by.

As the Bible says in Deuteronomy 15:11, "There will always be poor people in the land. Therefore I command you to be open-handed toward your brothers and toward the poor and needy in your land." Also, it is written in Proverbs 14:31, "He who oppresses the poor shows contempt for their Maker, but whoever is kind to the needy honors God."

Actually that was what the church did before the 1900s. The church was where the poor looked to for their needs. I believe this is the way that it should be. First Corinthians 8:6 (AMP) (emphasis added) says, "Yet for us there is [only] one God, the Father, *Who is the Source of all things* and for Whom we [have life], and one Lord, Jesus Christ, through and by Whom are all things and through and by Whom we [ourselves exist]." God is the source, and he used the church to administer to the needs of the poor.

Before the 1930s, there were poorhouses and such, but the condition of the poorhouses were kept less-than-desirable to discourage people from staying poor. Then in the 1930s came the Great Depression. People were starving, had no money, and nowhere to go. The government stepped in to help by supplying bread and soup lines. They created unemployment benefits. They did what they thought was best to help the Americans get back on their feet. There is a debate going on even to this day whether or not this was a good thing. I am not going to even touch that issue, for this is not the platform to be doing so, remembering this is a synopsis of a complicated subject. But even if it was a good thing, like any good thing, there comes other challenges that are not so good. Here's what I mean.

Every good program has a purpose for its existence. There is a need, and the program is supposed to supply a solution to that need. When that need has been satisfied, the program has no purpose or life left to it. The program that the government started was to help citizens to get through a tough time 'til they could get back on their feet again. It was not intended to be a continuous welfare system. It was designed to get the country back on a growth cycle.

In order to have a program to supply the needs that the program is supposed to supply, it takes people. So the government had to hire people to administer the program. Well, if the program has lived out its purpose, then there is no need for the program and likewise no need for the people to administer the program. So the only natural thing for the people who administer the program to do is to look for other areas to use the program. Well, as the Bible says, there will always be poor people among us, so it was not hard to figure out how to keep the program going.

This in turn created different types of problems. First off, the poor started looking at the government as the source of their provision. It was not God who was feeding them; it was the government that was feeding them. This created dependency on the government to take care of their needs. Not only that, they now didn't use the gifts that God gave them to create their own ability to provide for themselves. Remember, necessity is the mother of invention. So if the government is providing all necessities, then you have no reason to go out and look elsewhere to provide need. A case in point is that I am not getting better at spelling when I have spellchecker to do it for me. If I had to look up every word the old way, it would stick in my mind better. But because I am human and I still like the easier, softer way, I use it, but I am not getting much better at spelling either.

Now I am not trying to be an economics expert, nor am I saying that everyone that is in the situation of receiving aid is in that position because they want to, so please put down the rocks and listen. You can't deny that there are a lot of people that are, and have been for generations, living off the system because it is easier than fighting to improve their situation out in the world.

But they are not the only people that are dependent on the system. So are the people that administrate the system. If there are no poor people, then there is no reason for their existence. So they want to keep the people who depend on them dependent on them, so they have a purpose for their job's existence.

The politician who tells you he is for the poor people is lying. If he really was for the poor people, he would be focused more on the training and creating more opportunities for the poor than just throwing more of the taxpayers' money at them. The saying goes, "Feed a man a fish, and he eats for a day," then he will have to come back every day and get another and another, and you will be able to control him with the supply of the fish. "Teach a man to fish, and he can feed himself for a lifetime." But then, he doesn't need you, so you lost that control. Makes sense that if I want to keep control and be reelected every term, then I have to keep feeding them fish, not teach them how to fish so that I am always needed. Who do you think the politician is loving?

Another problem is that for several generations, the church has not been the main source of help to the poor, and so the poor don't associate God as the source of all their needs. Now you have lost an important part of ministering to the poor, not in just their material needs but their spiritual needs as well. The government can't satisfy their spiritual needs, and so they are not only in *financial bondage*, but they are spiritually and emotionally deprived as well.

Again, I stress the point that I am not an expert of economics, and I don't have all the answers or know all the history to the situation that I am about to describe. I am talking in general while trying to set the stage for another point.

The same problem with the elderly has happened. The government installed a program in the late 1700s and more so in the mid-

1800s to supply the needs of injured war veterans and the widows of deceased war veterans. Then came the 1930s, and there was no way to take care of all of the elderly citizens. The formation of the social security was created to support those who were too old to work.

But rather than set up a program to help the people get a secure investment or savings program going for future generations, they used the idea of taxation of the worker and giving to the elderly based on past payments to the program. It makes sense, except for the fact of the baby boomer that came after World War II. This is the largest generation there has ever been, so there will be more baby boomers in retirement than workers to support them. Let's not forget to mention the robbing and misuse of Social Security funds. Now there is a good possibility that there will not be Social Security around for today's children when they are the elderly.

Now since the government is having problems taking care of all the poor and the elderly, they are cutting back on the amount of payments and the number of recipients who receive these payments.

So where do all these other people go to look for help? Well, the church of course. I have had conversations with several pastors who tell me that the church is being sought out more and more to help with the poor and the elderly. They are not sure what they are going to do. My response to them is "That's great." Of course, they look at me like I am stupid, but then I explain why.

You have to be living under a rock if you cannot tell that Satan and his cronies have been working overtime to attack the body of Christ. You see it over and over again in many different arenas.

Well, an easy way that Satan can come after us is though politics or economics. So if the people depend on the government to take care of their needs and he can control the government, then he has control of a certain group of people in the country.

But if the people are coming to the church for their support, then the church can direct them to God who is the source. Now that God is the source and not the government, you strip the power from the government because of their dependency of that support. In turn, you also strip Satan of his power to work through the government, which also strips him of his power of those people in the country.

Now I can hear the Christians saying, "How are we going to be able to pay for all of this?" My answer is this: "Are we going to live according to God's Word or not?" I think this a fair question.

God's word tells us in 2 Corinthians 9:8–15:

> And God is able to bless you abundantly, so that in all things at all times, having all that you need, you will abound in every good work. As it is written:
>
> "They have freely scattered their gifts to the poor; their righteousness endures forever."
>
> Now he who supplies seed to the sower and bread for food will also supply and increase your store of seed and will enlarge the harvest of your righteousness. You will be enriched in every way so that you can be generous on every occasion, and through us your generosity will result in thanksgiving to God.
>
> This service that you perform is not only supplying the needs of the Lord's people but is also overflowing in many expressions of thanks to God. Because of the service by which you have proved yourselves, others will praise God for the obedience that accompanies your confession of the gospel of Christ, and for your generosity in sharing with them and with everyone else. And in their prayers for you their hearts will go out to you, because of the surpassing grace God has given you. Thanks be to God for his indescribable gift!

So by that bit of information, I would have to say that God will be the one who will give us the availability to meet the needs of those we serve. How? you ask.

By getting the money into the hands of the Christians with the right hearts, who are not living in sin or should I say loving self, so they will be able to administer to the poor and elderly. Now that we have people who are in need looking to God, they will be giving thanksgiving and honor to the one who truly deserves it, which is God and not the government.

Jesus taught us what to do in Matthew 10:39, "Whoever finds his life will lose it, and whoever loses his life for my sake will find it."

Isn't that the message that he was trying to explain to the rich young ruler in Mark 10:17–22?

> As Jesus started on his way, a man ran up to him and fell on his knees before him. "Good teacher," he asked, "what must I do to inherit eternal life?"
>
> "Why do you call me good?" Jesus answered. "No one is good—except God alone. You know the commandments: 'You shall not murder, you shall not commit adultery, you shall not steal, you shall not give false testimony, you shall not defraud, honor your father and mother.'"
>
> "Teacher," he declared, "all these I have kept since I was a boy."
>
> Jesus looked at him and loved him. "One thing you lack," he said. "Go, sell everything you have and give to the poor, and you will have treasure in heaven. Then come, follow me."
>
> At this the man's face fell. He went away sad, because he had great wealth.
>
> Jesus looked around and said to his disciples, "How hard it is for the rich to enter the kingdom of God!" (Mark 10:17–22)

He just told him to do the same thing that God told Abraham to do in Genesis. Jesus told him that he must be willing to lay it all down for him.

There are those who want to take the concept of being prosperous in the body and make it a sin. Yet John tells us in 3 John 1:2

(AMP), "Beloved, I pray that you may prosper in every way and [that your body] may keep well, even as [I know] your soul keeps well and prospers." Well, that would make sense, since how else do you think that the poor will be fed or the people will get Bibles or the children educated? Do you think that it is all done from trading goats and chickens? No, it takes money. So you would think that you would want true Christians to have the money to share in this manner.

Now here is where the problem comes in. People use the verse of 3 John 1:2 out of context. They take the prosperity they are given and use or abuse it for themselves to satisfy the love of themselves. They go out and buy cars and houses and get into debt over their heads and then act as if they are putting on a good display on how good God is and how he is working in their lives. Then they give a small portion away to the kingdom of God.

This is the opposite of what John wrote to his friend Gaius in 3 John 1.

> The elder,
>
> To my dear friend Gaius, whom I love in the truth.
>
> Dear friend, I pray that you may enjoy good health and that all may go well with you, even as your soul is getting along well. It gave me great joy when some believers came and testified about your faithfulness to the truth, telling how you continue to walk in it. I have no greater joy than to hear that my children are walking in the truth.
>
> Dear friend, you are faithful in what you are doing for the brothers and sisters, even though they are strangers to you. They have told the church about your love. Please send them on their way in a manner that honors God. It was for the sake of the Name that they went out, receiving no help from the pagans. We ought therefore to show hospitality to such people so that we may work together for the truth.

I wrote to the church, but Diotrephes, who loves to be first, will not welcome us. So when I come, I will call attention to what he is doing, spreading malicious nonsense about us. Not satisfied with that, he even refuses to welcome other believers. He also stops those who want to do so and puts them out of the church.

Dear friend, do not imitate what is evil but what is good. Anyone who does what is good is from God. Anyone who does what is evil has not seen God. Demetrius is well spoken of by everyone—and even by the truth itself. We also speak well of him, and you know that our testimony is true.

I have much to write you, but I do not want to do so with pen and ink. I hope to see you soon, and we will talk face to face.

Peace to you. The friends here send their greetings. Greet the friends there by name. (3 John 1:1–14)

Did you ever wonder what "walking in the truth" was? He couldn't have been talking about the death and resurrection of Christ, because he states that "he has no greater joy than his children are walking in the truth," so Gaius was one of his children or one of John's disciples in the church. Once you accept Christ, you have already committed to follow him as your Lord.

John's letter was to thank Gaius for his support to the other brothers and sisters in the church. Also, John is warning Gaius about Diotrephes's love of himself, which is what sin is. So with all things considered, then wouldn't it make sense that walking in the truth was what Jesus told us to do in Matthew, Mark, and Luke? Luke 9:23 says, "Then he said to them all: 'Whoever wants to be my disciple must deny themselves and take up their cross daily and follow me.'" Or the same thing that I have been saying all along, that we must stop the love relationship with ourselves and to direct that love to God through others.

> Jesus looked around and said to his disciples, "How hard it is for the rich to enter the kingdom of God!"
> The disciples were amazed at his words. But Jesus said again, "Children, how hard it is to enter the kingdom of God! It is easier for a camel to go through the eye of a needle than for someone who is rich to enter the kingdom of God."
> The disciples were even more amazed, and said to each other, "Who then can be saved?"
> Jesus looked at them and said, "With man this is impossible, but not with God; all things are possible with God." (Mark 10:23–27)

Maybe the reason that it is so hard getting through the narrow gate is because we try to hang on to all the stuff that God has given us or in some cases just went out and got on our own. The point I am trying to show here is that Jesus told us to lay down our life and follow him. He used the rich young ruler, or as God showed us through Abraham, that we have to be willing to let go of the possession that we have and trust God to take care of us or whatever the case may be. God may give you a nice Mercedes, but he may give it to you so that you can bless someone else with it. The point is that you don't get so attached to it that if God wants to use it for something or someone other than you, you will let go of it.

Then you always have the people who want to guilt-trip you if you don't give everything away, because you are not acting in the manner of a Christian. Well, did you notice that God was very specific in what it was that Abraham was supposed to give up? Abraham was a very wealthy man. God made it very specific what and how he was supposed to give it up. You could be doing things that are not in the will of God by going on a rampage and just giving everything that you own away. Don't let other people tell you what to do; wait for God to give you the command of what to do. But if he tells you to give up everything, then we also need to be willing to do so.

Now look at what Jesus says will happen as we continue on in Mark 10:28–31:

> Then Peter spoke up, "We have left every-
> thing to follow you!"
> "Truly I tell you," Jesus replied, "no one who
> has left home or brothers or sisters or mother or
> father or children or fields for me and the gospel
> will fail to receive a hundred times as much in
> this present age: homes, brothers, sisters, moth-
> ers, children and fields—along with persecu-
> tions—and in the age to come eternal life. But
> many who are first will be last, and the last first."

Here is where the rich young ruler missed the ship. Jesus says that you will receive in return a hundred times the amount that you gave up for him. And he says, "Now in this time" and when you get to heaven. But I believe again that it is important that we are giving up in our lives what it is that God wants us to give up, not the things that we want to give up or are told by someone else to give up.

Isn't this called worship? Aren't you sacrificing something that means a lot to you because of your love of God? The laying down your life or a part of your life to follow God is a type of worship. You hold him in the highest regard, high enough that you are willing to give him your all. I believe that this is the highest form of worship there is.

This brings to mind another issue that shows that the body of Christ is living in sin that I would like to mention. It involves the judgmental attitudes that people have toward those who have a lot of money or a wealthier lifestyle than themselves.

There are those people in the body who are always pointing a finger at the wealthy people and judging them on the way they live their lives or the things that they have. What I wonder about is, "Where do these judgmental people get the right?" I hear them say things like "They have an enormous house. I think it is a bit too much. They could get by with half as much as they have. If they had half as much, it would be okay, but what they have now is over the limit."

Now I need to know something. Where is the limit? What book of the Bible is it in? Is it possibly in the book of "Jealousy"? I have never found the limit. Are you suggesting that God put limits on how much his people can have? Okay, the Joneses are a B category family. Here is their limit. First off, doesn't it say in Proverbs 13:22, "A good man leaves an inheritance to his children's children, But the wealth of the sinner is stored up for the righteous"? So then good men are to leave an inheritance not only for our children but for our grandchildren as well. Doesn't it take wealth to do this?

Who are we to judge another man's wealth? How do we know the circumstances of his situation? Isn't that totally against what Jesus told us to do? Besides, let's think of this.

Let's say that there's a man that has a $20 million income. He has good write-offs and his tax bill is let's say $6 million. (You can tell already that this isn't my income today. I have no idea what it would be. Besides, I think the government wants $19.5 million of it.) Let's say that he goes out and buys a $2 million estate and also spends $1 million on cars and vacations and living expenses.

Right now most people would be warming up the pointing finger and getting ready to yell, "That's over the limit!" But hold on a minute.

Let's say he banks $3 million in his savings and he gives the rest of his income to the church that year, which is $8 million. Now here is what most people would say, "Well, if he would have gotten a house that costs half as much and spent only half as much on his enjoyment, then he could have given $1.5 million dollars more to charity."

Okay, but let's look at the next year. Let's say his income didn't increase. So $6 million comes right off the top. Then let's say he uses $1 million this year to live and that's all he needs. Why? Because the house and all the cars, toys, and memberships are paid off. He banks

$3 million in the savings and gives the $10 million away. Okay, now let's look at most people's situation.

Let's say you have a $100,000 income, even though most people don't. Let's say you too have tax advantages that you can get your tax bill to say $30,000. Let's also make sure you give to your church, $12,000 (I am sure that most people don't). You save $10,000 (again most don't). Most people with that kind of income live in a $250,000 to $300,000 house with a fifteen- to thirty-year mortgage. They would have a minimum of two cars, not to mention a toy or two to play with. That leaves you a $55,000 to make the mortgage, car and toy payments, along with the monthly bills and memberships, and take vacations.

The next year, you do it again the same as last year, and it continues basically the same every year after that, except for yearly raises and such. So you give up basically 12 percent of your income to the church, and the rest goes to maintaining your lifestyle.

The first guy, he spends an enormous amount of money, especially the first year, yet he gave away roughly 40 percent of his income to the church. But this is the important point. Then next year, he spent an enormous amount, yet he still gave away 50 percent of his income to the church. Why, because he was still living below his means.

Now if he would have bought so many houses that he would be making payments on all of them and not been able to give more that 10 to 20 percent, then he would be doing the same thing as most people. But people can't see how much was given away; they can only see the material things that he has, so they judge him on what they see, not on what he does.

Besides, couldn't you have stayed in a $150,000 or an $80,000 house?

"Well, that is ridiculous. There is nothing wrong with having a nice home for my family."

You're right, he probably feels the same, and you would too if you were in his income bracket. Besides, he is living under a biblical truth, which is "Keep out of debt and *owe no man* anything, except to love one another; for he who loves his neighbor [who practices loving others] has fulfilled the Law [relating to one's fellowmen, meeting all its requirements]" (Romans 13:8 AMP) (emphasis added). Can you say the same thing?

Now the coin flips the other way also. If you are the one who has the money and you are not generous with it, beware. What God has given to you to use, he can take away in an instant. If you're not being a good steward with what God has given you, he can give it to someone who is. Or you could find yourself with a hard heart and be left with a pile of money and miserable in the process. I am not saying that you have to give all your money away to be happy. But I am saying that people who are always focused on loving themselves can be the most miserable people there are. A poor person who is always doing something for someone else, or in other words loving others, can be the happiest people around. This is the most gratifying feeling that there is because it is the way that God created us to be. That is what God did for us—he loved us so much that he gave. He gave his only Son.

Think about this. If God wants to take away a rich man's wealth, he can do it in a blink of an eye. He did it to King Nebuchadnezzar.

Nebuchadnezzar got the big head, and God put him out to pasture to eat grass with the cattle and wild animals until he got his act together; then, God put him back in the throne (see Daniel 4:28–37). Think about how powerful that is. He drove him out of the kingdom to live with the cattle and wild animals, eating grass. There is going to have to be something extremely powerful to make me want to eat grass. But then, he restores him back in the kingdom after he comes to his senses. You don't think that God could do the same thing today?

Folks, it's not the money! It's the heart. At the same time, if God told the wealthy man to give up that house or that income, and he did, isn't his heart right? Question for you is, would you give up yours? I believe that is also why we don't have more money in the body of Christ. Jesus says in Matthew 6:21 (KJV), "For where your treasure is, there will your heart be also." So if your money is being spent on all the toys that you can make payments on, it says that is where your heart will be. If your treasure is going to take care of others, to help spread the Word, or to strengthen the body, then your heart will be in that. More people today are trying to keep up with the unsaved Joneses. So it is natural that if the Joneses' hearts are in their material possessions and you are doing the same thing as the Joneses, then you are following them down the path of the world. This is the opposite that we are told to be as Christians. Even though we live in this world, we are not to conform to the world's ways (see Titus 2:12).

So it is important that the body of Christ does prosper so we can do the work that we are supposed to be doing.

WHERE IS UNITY IN THE BIBLE?

As I explained earlier, I was working on an idea for the body of Christ to put down doctrinal differences and come together to change the moral, economical, and social conditions in this country. During this time, I had the opportunity to talk to others in the body of Christ, and I am amazed at the different types of responses that I received.

When I talk to pastors and church leaders, their first response usually was "You have no idea how big a project this is that you are taking on." Then the next response is "What makes you different than the last person that tried this?" But when the conversation comes to an end, it had been a positive experience that they all would like to see happen and a "go get 'em, tiger," and we will see how it turns out.

When I talked to lay people, they usually were excited and explain how tired they were of dealing with the war within the body. They were also tired of the fact that they felt like they were being forced more and more to hide their beliefs because of people of the world claiming they were being offended. They felt they had no way or no one to do anything about it, and this is just the way that it is.

It is also amazing to me the number of people that when I asked them if they were Christians, they gave me answers such as, "Well, I'm a Baptist," or Methodist or Catholic. I would ask them, "Isn't that Christian?" and they would have to think about it. They didn't identify with being a Christian as much as they did with their church affiliation.

There are questions that continues to arise. Are we supposed to be in unity? How can I be associated with a church that teaches wrong doctrine? How can I worship with people who do not believe the truth (as I understand it)? Which makes me wonder, are we teaching the wrong message? Are people relating more to being a part of their church than to being a part of the body of Christ? Have we lost focus on the importance of who we really are?

Let's address this question first: "Are we supposed to be unified?" Well, if we are or are not, then I would have to believe that the way to find out would be in the Bible and that it would give the answer either way.

Let's start in John. Unification was prophesied before the death of Jesus. If you remember, when Jesus had raised Lazarus from the dead, there was quite a stir going on, and the Jewish leaders were getting worried that the Jews were starting to put their faith in Jesus.

> So the chief priests and Pharisees called a meeting of the council [the Sanhedrin] and said, "What are we to do? For this Man performs many signs [evidences, miracles]. If we let Him alone to go on like this, everyone will believe in Him and adhere to Him, and the Romans will come and suppress and destroy and take away our [holy] place and our nation [our temple and city and our civil organization]." But one of them, Caiaphas, who was the high priest that year, declared, "You know nothing at all! Nor do you understand or reason out that it is expedient and better for your own welfare that one man should die on behalf of the people than that the whole nation should perish [be destroyed, ruined]." (John 11:47–50 AMP)

That is common knowledge. We all know this part, but what needs to be point out is this:

> Now he did not say this simply of his own accord [he was not self-moved]; but being the high priest that year, he prophesied that Jesus was to die for the nation, *And not only for the nation*

*but also for the purpose of uniting into one body the
children of God who have been scattered far and
wide.* (John 11:51–52) (emphasis added).

So what I am pointing out is that it was prophesied that he was
to die, not only for the nation of Israel but for the gathering of all of
the children together into one body. We are the children. Now some
of you may say, "Yeah, but he was talking about when we are gathered up and going on to heaven." Okay, then let's look at what Jesus
had to say about it.

Jesus himself taught us that if we are divided, we could not stand.

Then one was brought to Him who was
demon-possessed, blind and mute; and He
healed him, so that the blind and mute man
both spoke and saw. And all the multitudes
were amazed and said, "Could this be the Son
of David?" Now when the Pharisees heard it
they said, "This fellow does not cast out demons
except by Beelzebub, the ruler of the demons."
But Jesus knew their thoughts, and said to them:
"Every kingdom divided against itself is brought
to desolation, and every city or house divided
against itself will not stand. If Satan casts out
Satan, he is divided against himself. How then
will his kingdom stand? And if I cast out demons
by Beelzebub, by whom do your sons cast them
out? Therefore they shall be your judges. But if I
cast out demons by the Spirit of God, surely the
kingdom of God has come upon you. Or how
can one enter a strong man's house and plunder
his goods, unless he first binds the strong man?
And then he will plunder his house. He who
is not with Me is against Me, and he who does
not gather with Me scatters abroad. (Matthew
12:22–30 NKJV)

Notice he said every kingdom that is divided will not stand. That tells me that it doesn't matter if it is God's kingdom or if it is the world's kingdom. It will not stand. I hope this is a message that we in the United States get a grasp on soon. But here is the thing. When we are all in heaven, there is not going to be any division, so he must have been talking about here on this earth.

Another thing to notice is that the same teaching can be found in three out of the four Gospels. It is also in Mark 3:20–27 and in Luke 11:14–23. So I would get the impression that this is a teaching that God wanted us to understand.

Also if you pay attention to verse 30, you will note that it says, "He who is not with Me is against Me, and he who does not gather with Me scatters abroad." Couldn't this also mean that if we are not working toward unifying the body, we are then working against him? It is what Jesus wanted. Where do I get this?

Look at how Jesus prayed for his disciples right before he was to be arrested and put to death.

> I have revealed you to those whom you gave me out of the world. They were yours; you gave them to me and they have obeyed your word. Now they know that everything you have given me comes from you. For I gave them the words you gave me and they accepted them. They knew with certainty that I came from you, and they believed that you sent me. I pray for them. I am not praying for the world, but for those you have given me, for they are yours. All I have is yours, and all you have is mine. And glory has come to me through them. I will remain in the world no longer, but they are still in the world, and I am coming to you. Holy Father, protect them by the power of your name—the name you gave me—so that *they may be one as we are one.* (John 17:6–17 NIV) (emphasis added)

So he was praying for the disciples who were going to still be in the world that they may be as one, just as the Father and Jesus are one. But he didn't stop there.

Then immediately after praying for the disciples, he continued to pray for all of the believers as follows:

> My prayer is not for them alone. I pray also for those who will believe in me through their message, *that all of them may be one, Father, just as you are in me and I am in you.* May they also be in us so that the world may believe that you have sent me. I have given them the glory that you gave me, *that they may be one as we are one: I in them and you in me. May they be brought to complete unity to let the world know that you sent me and have loved them even as you have loved me.* Father, I want those you have given me to be with me where I am, and to see my glory, the glory you have given me because you loved me before the creation of the world. Righteous Father, though the world does not know you, I know you, and they know that you have sent me. I have made you known to them, and will continue to make you known in order that the love you have for me may be in them and that I myself may be in them. (John 17:20–26 NIV) (emphasis added)

So he was not just praying that the disciples are acting as one, but that all of the believers are acting as one. Why? Verse 23 said, "May they be brought to complete unity to let the world know that you sent me and have loved them even as you have loved me." When we act as one, then we let the world know that Jesus was sent and that the Father loves them. But there is something that I want to point out also relating to Jesus's prayer in John 17:20–26.

Let's just say that I decided that I wanted to become pregnant and have a baby as a man. I started to ask God that he help me get pregnant. Not only that, I also had other Christians praying in faith that I get pregnant and have a baby. Would I get pregnant?

Naturally the answer is no. And why is that? I am a man. God created woman to bear children, so I don't have the right plumbing; if I had the right plumbing, then I wouldn't be a man. I would be a woman. It would be like trying to have water and not have the wet. So we would be praying in vain for something that is not going to happen.

Given that this is true, would it make sense that Jesus would pray prayers that would be in vain? I would believe that there isn't or ever was a man on this earth who would know how to pray a more effectual prayer than God himself.

So when I hear people in the body say that we are not supposed to be unified or, better yet, that it is impossible that we can be unified because of all the different diversity in the church, I have a question for them: Why would Jesus pray that all the believers are one, as him and the Father are one, if there is no way that it can be accomplished? It wouldn't make sense for him to pray such a prayer. Wouldn't it make sense that it is not only possible, but that this is what God wants since the one who prayed it was God himself?

Let's continue to look at what the rest of the New Testament has to say.

It seems very interesting that when you read about the day of Pentecost, it mentions that they were all unified. In the King James Version of Acts 2:1, it states, "And when the day of Pentecost was fully come, they were all with one accord in one place." Now why would this version of the Bible say "with one accord" if it was just trying to state that they were in one place?

Here is what the *Matthew Henry's Concise Commentary* has to say:

> We cannot forget how often, while their Master was with them there were strifes among the disciples which should be the greatest; but now all these strifes were at an end. They had prayed more together of late. Would we have the Spirit poured out upon us from on high, let us

be all of one accord. And notwithstanding differences of sentiments and interests, as there were
among those disciples, let us agree to love one
another; for where brethren dwell together in
unity, there the Lord commands his blessing.

Also, you will see that Paul was telling us the same thing.
Paul tells us in 2 Corinthians 13:11 (AMP),

Finally, brethren, farewell [rejoice]! Be
strengthened [perfected, completed, made what
you ought to be]; be encouraged and consoled and
comforted; be of the same [agreeable] mind one
with another; live in peace, and [then] the God
of love [Who is the Source of affection, good-
will, love, and benevolence toward men] and the
Author and Promoter of peace will be with you.

Wait, are you seeing what I am seeing? Paul said that "when"
we are of the same and agreeable mind and that we are in peace with
each other, "then" the God of love and the author and promoter of
peace will be with you. What would stop us from being at peace with
each other? How about living in sin or the love of ourselves?

ARE WE STOPPING GOD?

This leads me to a question: Would the Holy Spirit be able to do more and operate more in the body if we were all of "one accord"? Let's think about this: Are we hindering the power of God working throughout the body because we are not of "one mind"?

Now I am not saying that God isn't moving in the world today. It can easily be seen that he is. What I am saying is, could there be more done? Are we hindering God from doing all that he wants to do because we are not living in peace with each other or in another sense living in sin?

Let's face it. It seems like every time that I get into a conversation with a fellow Christian, we are always talking about what we believe is right and not right. I have to literally work at not discussing our differences and focus on the similarities. Why is it so important that we are right? Is this stopping the Holy Spirit from operating in our lives?

I have a friend who says nothing positive about a well-known TV preacher. I don't want to mention any names. He claims that this preacher has very little to offer and that the little that the preacher does have to offer you have to pick through so many bones that it isn't worth the time it takes to get to the meat. Now at the same time, I have another friend who had a daughter in the hospital with a very serious illness. It was so serious that my friend and his wife were in a frightened state of mind. This same preacher happened to be in town and was led by the Lord to go and lay hands on their daughter, which this preacher did. My friend tells me how you could just feel the power of the Holy Spirit fill the room and not only was his daughter healed, but the patient next to her asked to have hands laid on her, and she was healed as well. Now here you have two people being healed by the power of the Holy Spirit through this preacher, not to mention the huge ministry that this preacher has or all the different missions that are running because of this preacher. Yet we have people, just like my friend, who want to badmouth this person because they don't agree with the teaching. What about the fruit?

Wouldn't it make more sense for my friend to come to a more peaceful conclusion? "Hey, I don't agree with the teaching, but the ministry is producing positive fruit, so God must be using this preacher, and I will just accept the fact that if it is okay with God, then it's okay with me." Look at what Paul says in 1 Corinthians 3:1–23.

> Brothers and sisters, I could not address you as people who live by the Spirit but as people who are still worldly—mere infants in Christ. I gave you milk, not solid food, for you were not yet ready for it. Indeed, you are still not ready. *You are still worldly. For since there is jealousy and quarreling among you, are you not worldly? Are you not acting like mere humans?* For when one says, "I follow Paul," and another, "I follow Apollos," are you not mere human beings?
>
> What, after all, is Apollos? And what is Paul? Only servants, through whom you came to believe—as the Lord has assigned to each his task. I planted the seed, Apollos watered it, but God has been making it grow. So neither the one who plants nor the one who waters is anything, but only God, who makes things grow. The one who plants and the one who waters have one purpose, and they will each be rewarded according to their own labor. For we are co-workers in God's service; you are God's field, God's building. (1 Corinthians 3:1–9) (emphasis added)

Couldn't this read, "I follow the Baptist, I follow the Methodist or Catholic or Lutherans, even nondenominational"? Again I quote from the *Matthew Henry's Concise Commentary*:

> The most simple truths of the gospel, as to man's sinfulness and God's mercy, repentance towards God, and faith in our Lord Jesus Christ, stated in the plainest language, suit the people better than deeper mysteries. Men may have much doctrinal knowledge, yet be mere beginners in the life of faith and experience. Contentions and quarrels about religion are sad evidences of carnality. True religion makes men peaceable, not contentious. But it is to be lamented, that many who should walk as Christians, live and act too much like other men. Many professors, and preachers also, show themselves to be yet carnal, by vain-glorious strife, eagerness for dispute, and readiness to despise and speak evil of others.

It sounds like he could have been writing about us today. Paul continues:

> By the grace God has given me, I laid a foundation as a wise builder, and someone else is building on it. But each one should build with care. For no one can lay any foundation other than the one already laid, which is Jesus Christ. If anyone builds on this foundation using gold, silver, costly stones, wood, hay or straw, their work will be shown for what it is, because the Day will bring it to light. It will be revealed with fire, and the fire will test the quality of each person's work. If what has been built survives, the builder will receive a reward. If it is burned up, the builder will suffer loss but yet will be saved—

even though only as one escaping through the flames. (1 Corinthians 3:10–15).

Again in this case, I can't say it better than Matthew Henry.

> The ministers about whom the Corinthians contended, were only instruments used by God. We should not put ministers into the place of God. He that planteth and he that watereth are one, employed by one Master, trusted with the same revelation, busied in one work, and engaged in one design. They have their different gifts from one and the same Spirit, for the very same purposes; and should carry on the same design heartily. Those who work hardest shall fare best. Those who are most faithful shall have the greatest reward. They work together with God, in promoting the purposes of his glory, and the salvation of precious souls; and He who knows their work, will take care they do not labour in vain. They are employed in his husbandry and building; and He will carefully look over them.

So we are employed by the same Master. We work to accomplish his purpose with the different talents and gifts that he gives us, and he makes sure that we don't labor in vain. Wow, that means that we don't have to go around and judge and condemn those for what they are doing, but that we can focus on what it is that God has planned for us to do in our own walk. That seems to take a load off my mind, so then I can walk in peace.

Wonder what else Paul says?

> Don't you know that you yourselves are God's temple and that God's Spirit dwells in your midst? If anyone destroys God's temple, God will

destroy that person; for God's temple is sacred, and you together are that temple.

Do not deceive yourselves. If any of you think you are wise by the standards of this age, you should become "fools" so that you may become wise. For the wisdom of this world is foolishness in God's sight. As it is written: "He catches the wise in their craftiness"; and again, "The Lord knows that the thoughts of the wise are futile." So then, no more boasting about human leaders! All things are yours, whether Paul or Apollos or Cephas or the world or life or death or the present or the future—all are yours, and you are of Christ, and Christ is of God. (1 Corinthians 3:16–22) (emphasis added)

Now look at what Paul had to say earlier in 1 Corinthians 1:10–12 (emphasis added):

I appeal to you, brothers and sisters, in the name of our Lord Jesus Christ, *that all of you agree with one another in what you say and that there be no divisions among you, but that you be perfectly united in mind and thought.* My brothers and sisters, some from Chloe's household have informed me that there are quarrels among you. What I mean is this: One of you says, "I follow Paul"; another, "I follow Apollos"; another, "I follow Cephas"; still another, "I follow Christ."

Here we are again. "I'm Protestant," "I'm Pentecostal," "I'm nondenominational."

"Is Christ divided?" (1 Corinthians 1:13). Wow! Now how should we answer that? I know that we shouldn't be, but if you look at the way that the body of Christ is acting today, I am afraid of the truth. "Was Paul crucified for you? Or were you baptized in the name of Paul?"

Or what about the Pope or Martin Luther or John Wesley?

> I thank God that I did not baptize any of you except Crispus and Gaius, so no one can say that you were baptized in my name. (Yes, I also baptized the household of Stephanas; beyond that, I don't remember if I baptized anyone else.) For Christ did not send me to baptize, but to preach the gospel—not with wisdom and eloquence, lest the cross of Christ be emptied of its power. (1 Corinthians 1:14–17).

Did you ever think about this: If sin is the loving of self and we are living in sin when we are not loving others, can a whole church or the congregation of a church all be living together in sin?

I think if you were to study the letters to the seven churches in the book of Revelations, you would see that he was writing to the congregations of the churches and not any individual. It can also be seen throughout church history, if one was to study it.

Not only did Paul teach this, but so did Peter. He says in 1 Peter 3:8–12 (AMP) (emphasis added):

> Finally, *all [of you] should be of one and the same mind (united in spirit),* sympathizing [with one another], loving [each other] as brethren [of one household], compassionate and courteous [tenderhearted and humble].
>
> Never return evil for evil or insult for insult [scolding, tongue-lashing, berating], but on the contrary blessing [praying for their welfare, happiness, and protection, and truly pitying and loving them]. For know that to this you have been called, that you may yourselves inherit a blessing [from God—that you may obtain a bless-

ing as heirs, bringing welfare and happiness and protection].

For let him who wants to enjoy life and see good days [good—whether apparent or not] keep his tongue free from evil and his lips from guile [treachery, deceit].

Let him turn away from wickedness and shun it, and let him do right. Let him search for peace [harmony; undisturbedness from fears, agitating passions, and moral conflicts] and seek it eagerly. [Do not merely desire peaceful relations with God, with your fellowmen, and with yourself, but pursue, go after them!]

For the eyes of the Lord are upon the righteous [those who are upright and in right standing with God], and His ears are attentive to their prayer. But the face of the Lord is against those who practice evil [to oppose them, to frustrate, and defeat them].

So if we are loving others, then we will inherit a blessing? Now I don't know about you, but when I see that I am entitled to a blessing, then I get excited. But I also have to wonder. Are we missing the blessings?

I know that there are a lot of debates about the healing power of Jesus. Some believe that it doesn't exist in this day and age. Others believe that God is sovereign and that he chooses to heal at his will. And then others believe it is an act of faith.

What if it is a condition of the heart of living in sin? We could be missing a blessing for not being unified, for speaking evil against another, or it could even be from unforgiveness. The point I am trying to make is this: Are we blocking God from the miracles? Could it be that God could do more if we were operating in love and peace with one another?

For he himself is our peace, who has made the two one and has destroyed the barrier, the dividing wall of hostility, by abolishing in his flesh the law with its commandments and regulations. *His purpose was to create in himself one new man out of the two, thus making peace,* and in this one body to reconcile both of them to God through the cross, by which he put to death their hostility. He came and preached peace to you who were far away and peace to those who were near. For through him we both have access to the Father by one Spirit. (Ephesians 2:14–18) (emphasis added)

I realize that this is talking about the joining of the Jews and the Gentiles by the blood of Jesus. But it does point out that Jesus is our peace. And his purpose was to unite the two to become one, that there may be peace. Now if Jesus our Lord and Savior and is the perfect example of how we are supposed to live, we are supposed to follow his commands. If his purpose is to unite the two to create "one new man" so that there is peace, then isn't it a reason that we are not supposed to be divided but to strive to make peace by being of one accord?

Isn't that what Paul was telling us in Ephesians 4:1–6 (NIV) (emphasis added):

As a prisoner for the Lord, then, I urge you to live a life worthy of the calling you have received. Be completely humble and gentle; be patient, *bearing with one another in love. Make every effort to keep the unity of the Spirit through the bond of peace. There is one body and one Spirit—* just as you were called to one hope when you were called—one Lord, one faith, one baptism; one God and Father of all, who is over all and through all and in all.

Seriously, let's think about this. When you are criticizing someone about their beliefs or the way that they are handling their ministry, are you having peace in doing so? Or are you uptight, maybe worried that they may get wind of it or all tensed up or even angry because of what is happening and because "it's not right"?

Well, how can you be in one accord, if you don't believe the same thing?

Let me try it this way. I have a friend who is a Christian. She belongs to a denomination that believes that there is no such thing as talking in tongues. I happen to pray in tongues myself, so naturally, there is a difference of beliefs here. We are discussing the fact that she has been taught that speaking in tongues was when Peter and the other disciples came out speaking in their own language, yet the people heard them in their language.

I will show you the scripture here in Acts 2:4–11:

> All of them were filled with the Holy Spirit and began to speak in other tongues as the Spirit enabled them.
>
> Now there were staying in Jerusalem God-fearing Jews from every nation under heaven. When they heard this sound, a crowd came together in bewilderment, because each one heard them speaking in his own language. Utterly amazed, they asked: "Are not all these men who are speaking Galileans? Then how is it that each of us hears them in his own native language? Parthians, Medes and Elamites; residents of Mesopotamia, Judea and Cappadocia, Pontus and Asia, Phrygia and Pamphylia, Egypt and the parts of Libya near Cyrene; visitors from Rome (both Jews and converts to Judaism Cretans and Arabs)—we hear them declaring the wonders of God in our own tongues!"

As you can see, the use of the word *tongues* as in verse 11 means language. So it is easy to see where you could draw this conclusion. So what is the problem?

Again you must always remember that I am not a walking concordance, and I don't know the Bible by heart. We had been talking about another subject in 1 Corinthians 13, and the Bible just happened to be laying open to chapter 14.

I go, "Okay, what does this mean in 1 Corinthians 14:2 (emphasis added)? 'For anyone who speaks in a tongue does not speak to people but to God. Indeed, *no one understands them*; they utter mysteries by the Spirit.'"

First off, it says, "does not speak to people" and that "no one understands him," so that tells me that it is not a known language. When Peter talked to everyone in Acts, everyone understood him, regardless of what the language of the person that was listening was. What's more is, Paul was saying that no man could understand it; then, that means that there is no person on this earth who will understand it. He speaks mysteries out of his spirit.

So now if we don't agree on whether or not praying in tongues is scriptural or not, does that mean that we can't come together in unity? How? Well, we could start by focusing on our similarities rather than our differences. We both believe that Jesus died to save us by the shedding of his blood. We believe that when we accepted him as Lord and Savior, we are both going to heaven. That's at least something to build on. Just because we don't agree on everything doesn't make one or the other any less of a Christian or that we cannot come together in unity.

Aren't we acting in pride, which is based on the love of ourselves, when we go around assuming that we have all knowledge of the Bible and God's Word? Could it be possible that we don't have all the answers, just the ones that we need to accomplish what it is we are put on this earth to do? I have to believe that the reason that there are so many different beliefs is that we don't have all the answers.

Another question is this: Could it be that God is using other people in a way that we may not understand? Since we don't understand why, we resort to the human trait of criticism. Think about it:

Isn't that the first thing that we mere mortal men do? We criticize that which we don't understand. We are supposed to focus on the calling that "we received" and then make every effort to keep the unity through peace. How do you do that? Let's start with humility. Philippians 2:1–4 (NKJV) (emphasis added) says,

> Therefore if there is any consolation in Christ, if any comfort of love, if any fellowship of the Spirit, if any affection and mercy, *fulfill my joy by being like-minded, having the same love, being of one accord, of one mind.* Let nothing be done through selfish ambition or conceit, but in lowliness of mind let each esteem others better than himself. Let each of you look out not only for his own interests, but also for the interests of others.

So why are we operating out of sense of pride? Paul said we are of many parts but only one body in 1 Corinthians 12.

> Now about the gifts of the Spirit, brothers and sisters, I do not want you to be uninformed. You know that when you were pagans, somehow or other you were influenced and led astray to mute idols. Therefore I want you to know that no one who is speaking by the Spirit of God says, "Jesus be cursed," and no one can say, "Jesus is Lord," except by the Holy Spirit.
>
> There are different kinds of gifts, but the same Spirit distributes them. There are different kinds of service, but the same Lord. There are different kinds of working, but in all of them and in everyone it is the same God at work.
>
> Now to each one the manifestation of the Spirit is given for the common good. To one there is given through the Spirit a message of

wisdom, to another a message of knowledge by means of the same Spirit, to another faith by the same Spirit, to another gifts of healing by that one Spirit, to another miraculous powers, to another prophecy, to another distinguishing between spirits, to another speaking in different kinds of tongues, and to still another the interpretation of tongues. All these are the work of one and the same Spirit, and he distributes them to each one, just as he determines.

Just as a body, though one, has many parts, but all its many parts form one body, so it is with Christ. For we were all baptized by one Spirit so as to form one body—whether Jews or Gentiles, slave or free—and we were all given the one Spirit to drink. Even so the body is not made up of one part but of many.

Now if the foot should say, "Because I am not a hand, I do not belong to the body," it would not for that reason stop being part of the body. And if the ear should say, "Because I am not an eye, I do not belong to the body," it would not for that reason stop being part of the body. If the whole body were an eye, where would the sense of hearing be? If the whole body were an ear, where would the sense of smell be? But in fact God has placed the parts in the body, every one of them, just as he wanted them to be. If they were all one part, where would the body be? As it is, there are many parts, but one body.

The eye cannot say to the hand, "I don't need you!" And the head cannot say to the feet, "I don't need you!" On the contrary, those parts of the body that seem to be weaker are indispensable, and the parts that we think are less honorable we treat with special honor. And the parts that are unpresentable are treated with special modesty, while our presentable parts need no special treatment. But God has put the body together, giving greater honor to the parts that lacked it, so that there should be no division in the body, but that its parts should have equal concern for each other. If one part suffers, every part suffers with it; if one part is honored, every part rejoices with it.

Now you are the body of Christ, and each one of you is a part of it. And God has placed in the church first of all apostles, second prophets, third teachers, then miracles, then gifts of healing, of helping, of guidance, and of different kinds of tongues. Are all apostles? Are all prophets? Are all teachers? Do all work miracles? Do all have gifts of healing? Do all speak in tongues? Do all interpret? Now eagerly desire the greater gifts. (1 Corinthians 12:1–31)

When are we going to realize that we are all created to do different jobs in the body and that we are not all going to do them the same way? We need to appreciate each other for their gifts and not compare them to our gift; otherwise, we become jealous and envious, creating strife and losing our peace. This is living in sin.

OUR RESPONSIBILITY

I am going to go back to Matthew 7 to address another issue.

> Enter by the narrow gate; for wide is the gate and broad is the way that leads to destruction, and there are many who go in by it. Because narrow is the gate and difficult is the way which leads to life, and there are few who find it.
>
> "Beware of false prophets, who come to you in sheep's clothing, but inwardly they are ravenous wolves. You will know them by their fruits. Do men gather grapes from thorn bushes or figs from thistles? Even so, every good tree bears good fruit, but a bad tree bears bad fruit. A good tree cannot bear bad fruit, nor can a bad tree bear good fruit. Every tree that does not bear good fruit is cut down and thrown into the fire. Therefore by their fruits you will know them.
>
> "Not everyone who says to Me, 'Lord, Lord,' shall enter the kingdom of heaven, but he who does the will of My Father in heaven. Many will say to Me in that day, 'Lord, Lord, have we not prophesied in Your name, cast out demons in Your name, and done many wonders in Your name?' And then I will declare to them, 'I never knew you; depart from Me, you who practice lawlessness!'
>
> "Therefore whoever hears these sayings of Mine, and does them, I will liken him to a wise

man who built his house on the rock: and the rain descended, the floods came, and the winds blew and beat on that house; and it did not fall, for it was founded on the rock.

"But everyone who hears these sayings of Mine, and does not do them, will be like a foolish man who built his house on the sand: and the rain descended, the floods came, and the winds blew and beat on that house; and it fell. And great was its fall." And so it was, when Jesus had ended these sayings, that the people were astonished at His teaching, for He taught them as one having authority, and not as the scribes. (Matthew 7:13–29)

But I *have* to put in here the same verses from *The Message* Bible.

"Don't look for shortcuts to God. The market is flooded with surefire, easygoing formulas for a successful life that can be practiced in your spare time. Don't fall for that stuff, even though crowds of people do. The way to life—to God!—is vigorous and requires total attention.

"Be wary of false preachers who smile a lot, dripping with practiced sincerity. Chances are they are out to rip you off some way or other. Don't be impressed with charisma; look for character. Knowing the correct password—saying 'Master, Master,' for instance—isn't going to get you anywhere with me. What is required is serious obedience—doing what my Father wills. I can see it now—at the Final Judgment thousands strutting up to me and saying, 'Master, we preached the Message, we bashed the demons, our God-sponsored projects had everyone talking.' And do you know what I am going to say? 'You missed the boat. All you did was use me to make yourselves important. You don't impress me one bit. You're out of here.'

"These words I speak to you are not incidental additions to your life, homeowner improvements to your standard of living. They are foundational words, words to build a life on. If you work these words into your life, you are like a smart carpenter who built his house on solid rock. Rain poured down, the river flooded, a tornado hit—but nothing moved that house. It was fixed to the rock.

"But if you just use my words in Bible studies and don't work them into your life, you are like a stupid carpenter who built his house on the sandy beach. When a storm rolled in and the waves came up, it collapsed like a house of cards."

When Jesus concluded his address, the crowd burst into applause. They had never heard teaching like this. It was apparent that he was living everything he was saying—quite a contrast to their religion teachers! This was the best teaching they had ever heard.

Do you remember the movie *Left Behind*? Everyone was missing, and no one knew what was going on. Then came the scene when Pastor Bruce Barnes was kneeling at the altar because he realized that he basically missed the boat and was left behind. Then he stood up at the pulpit and said something like this: "I know the Word. I used to stand right here and preach the Word. I used to preach some of the best sermons right here. But now you are all up there, and I am still here." As he was walking away from the pulpit, he said, "But I guess now I know, there is a difference in knowing the Word, believing the Word, and doing the Word." I do not want to be that preacher.

Now there is an argument that rapture is not biblical. But hey, I don't want to be the person Jesus told us about either—the person who is standing outside the door trying to get in. Jesus would look me in the eye and say, "Who are you?" That to me would be hell itself. The shock that would come over you when you realize that Jesus doesn't know who you are would be devastating. Talk about having a major meltdown.

"So are you saying that we won't be saved if we are not living according to his commands?" No, but what I am saying is pay attention to what Paul told the Corinthians.

Brothers, I could not address you as spiritual but as worldly—mere infants in Christ. I gave you milk, not solid food, for you were not yet ready for it. Indeed, you are still not ready. You are still worldly. For since there is jealousy and quarreling among you, are you not worldly? Are you not acting like mere men? For when one says, "I follow Paul," and another, "I follow Apollos," are you not mere men?

What, after all, is Apollos? And what is Paul? Only servants, through whom you came to believe—as the Lord has assigned to each his task. I planted the seed, Apollos watered it, but God made it grow. So neither he who plants nor he who waters is anything, but only God, who makes things grow. The man who plants and the man who waters have one purpose, and each will be rewarded according to his own labor. For we are God's fellow workers; you are God's field, God's building.

By the grace God has given me, I laid a foundation as an expert builder, and someone else is building on it. But each one should be careful how he builds. For no one can lay any foundation other than the one already laid, which is Jesus Christ. If any man builds on this foundation using gold, silver, costly stones, wood, hay or straw, his work will be shown for what it is, because the Day will bring it to light. It will be revealed with fire, and the fire will test the quality of each man's work. *If what he has built survives, he will receive his reward. If it is burned up, he will suffer loss; he himself will be saved, but only as one escaping through the flames.*

Don't you know that you yourselves are God's temple and that God's Spirit lives in you? If anyone destroys God's temple, God will destroy him; for God's temple is sacred, and you are that temple. (1 Corinthians 3:1–17 NIV) (emphasis added)

So we are saved by the fact that Jesus died on the cross for us, but we are responsible to build upon the life that Jesus gave us. It is our responsibility to use his gift of life that was given to us, in order to honor God the Father with. We are to live this life as if we were created out of the mold of Jesus himself, for everything he did was to bring honor to the Father.

Remember, when we claimed Christ as our Lord, then we were placing ourselves in a position of servants to the Lord. So as servants, we have responsibilities to fulfill.

Look at what Jesus told us in Luke 12:35–48 (AMP):

Keep your loins girded and your lamps burning,

And be like men who are waiting for their master to return home from the marriage feast, so that when he returns from the wedding and comes and knocks, they may open to him immediately.

Blessed [happy, fortunate, and to be envied] are those servants whom the master finds awake and alert and watching when he comes. Truly I say to you, he will gird himself and have them recline at table and will come and serve them!

If he comes in the second watch [before midnight] or the third watch [after midnight], and finds them so, blessed [happy, fortunate, and to be envied] are those servants!

But of this be assured: if the householder had known at what time the burglar was coming, he would have been awake and alert and watching and would not have permitted his house to be dug through and broken into.

You also must be ready, for the Son of Man is coming at an hour and a moment when you do not anticipate it.

Peter said, "Lord, are You telling this parable for us, or for all alike?"

And the Lord said, "Who then is that faithful steward, the wise man whom his master will set over those in his household service to supply them their allowance of food at the appointed time?"

Blessed [happy and to be envied] is that servant whom his master finds so doing when he arrives.

Truly I tell you, he will set him in charge over all his possessions.

But if that servant says in his heart, My master is late in coming, and begins to strike the menservants and the maids and to eat and drink and get drunk,

The master of that servant will come on a day when he does not expect him and at an hour of which he does not know, and will punish him and cut him off and assign his lot with the unfaithful.

And that servant who knew his master's will but did not get ready or act as he would wish him to act shall be beaten with many [lashes].

But he who did not know and did things worthy of a beating shall be beaten with few [lashes].

> For everyone to whom much is given, of him shall
> much be required; and of him to whom men entrust
> much, they will require and demand all the more.

You may think, "Well, that was said to all those who have been given a position of leadership or mentorship." I beg to differ with you. It seems to me that you have the position of mentorship with the unsaved. You received the *gift* of salvation, eternal life, and freedom of being a slave to sin or the love of self. He then expects you to mentor the world in the same way you were mentored. Remember you are now called to be the Lord's servant.

There is a saying that says, "What you do speaks so loud, I can't hear what you are saying." What you need to consider is your actions are the message that you are sending to those around you who are looking to you as the example? What example are you showing your children? What example are you showing God's children?

Remember what Jesus said in Matthew 23:15 (NIV), "Woe to you, teachers of the law and Pharisees, you hypocrites! You travel over land and sea to win a single convert, and when he becomes one, you make him twice as much a son of hell as you are." Great you got him or her to the Lord; now you are going to teach him or her to be a Christian like you? A Christian who goes around with a holy mackerel pasted on their car and a crucifix hanging with a picture of Jesus on the wall. Going to church twice on Sunday and Bible study on Wednesday night and every other social event there is. Yet at all these events, they gossip about brother Nick Nack did this, or sister Patty Wack did that, or they gossip about the preacher. They are irresponsible, never good for their word, give the minimum amount possible, etc. What example are you setting to the new person you are bringing into the body of Christ? That it is all about going to church?

Are we not showing them how to live in sin and creating hard hearts even more so than we have? Remember everything that comes from the mold loses detail, so that means if they are molded after us, then they will even be less a follower of Jesus than we are.

Look at what Jesus said in Mark 9:42, "But whoever causes one of these little ones who believe in Me to stumble, it would be better for him if a millstone were hung around his neck, and he were thrown into the sea." It seems that he was talking about little children. Was that all he was talking about?

When a new person first receives Christ as his personal Lord and Savior, we refer to them as "baby Christians." After they have been around a little while, then we refer to them as "young Christian." I still consider myself a young Christian.

Didn't Jesus continue to refer to us as children of God? So if you are bringing people to the Lord and you are instilling in them hard hearts by your bad examples, then you would be one of them he was referring to in Mark 9:42.

Jesus told us in John 13:34–35 (emphasis added), "A new command I give you: Love one another. As I have loved you, so you must love one another. *By this everyone will know that you are my disciples, if you love one another.*"

So if we are the examples to the children in the church, then it would also makes sense that we are the examples to those outside the church. Think about it: What good does it do to be telling the whole world that we have the love of Jesus in our heart and yet we act no different than they do? If we are not showing "agape" love to those who are supposed to be our brothers and sisters in Christ, then we are probably not showing it to them out there as well. Even if we are showing it out there, when they see us acting out of love in the body, they are going to peg us with being a hypocrite. Worse yet, they not only peg us with being a hypocrite, but they will do the same to all Christians. That is the way people are. They judge others by the ones that they are associated with. So the example that we are setting isn't giving just one person a bad name; it is giving the whole body a bad name.

If we want to go around acting like a hard-hearted fool, that is fine; we have the freedom to do it. Let's just not tell anyone that we are a Christian. Because we are dragging the rest of the body through the mud with us, and we have no right to do so. Worse than that, you are doing damage to the name of Jesus Christ and to the kingdom of God. And he may not deal with us here on this earth, but he will be dealing with us. This we can count on.

What about where it says in Matthew 10:33, "But whoever disowns me before others, I will disown before my Father in heaven." That's true. But he says this once. He tells us over and over throughout the Gospels to love our neighbor as ourselves. Besides, if we are loving our neighbor, then we will be doing more than telling men that we love Jesus; we will be showing the world that we love him. Again I give you John 13:34–35: "A new command I give you: Love one another. As I have loved you, so you must love one another. By this everyone will know that you are my disciples, if you love one another." So then we don't have to worry about denying him, because they will be able to see that we love him from our actions and not empty words.

If you flip that around, then if we are not *following his commandment* of "Love one another as I have loved you," we are not showing others that we are his disciple, which in turn means that we are in effect denying him by being disobedient to his Word.

Which only makes common sense. If you love someone that has authority over you, then you are going to obey that authority because you want to show your love. If there is a king in the land and that king makes a royal decree that everyone in the kingdom who loves the king shall greet everyone that they meet with "Praise the Lord," then you could go through the land and see how much loyalty there was by how the people greeted you.

Or take children for example. You can tell the children who truly love their parents by the way they act to the parents. Now I am not saying that they don't rebel against their parents sometimes. But when I was growing up, you could tell the difference between the kids who truly love their parents and the kids who loved them but didn't respect them or took them for granted. You don't think the Father in heaven, who knows our hearts, knows if we love him? John told us the same thing in 2 John that if we loved him, we would obey Jesus's commands. Second John 1:4–6 (NIV) (emphasis added) says,

> It has given me great joy to find some of
> your children walking in the truth, just as the
> Father commanded us. And now, dear lady, I am
> not writing you a new command but one we have

had from the beginning. I ask that we love one another. *And this is love: that we walk in obedience to his commands.* As you have heard from the beginning, his command is that you walk in love.

So just as you would show your natural parents that you love them by obedience, you show your heavenly Father that you love him by your obedience to his commands. As what I said earlier, "Obedience comes from love, not love from obedience." This is reverential fear of God. If you ask me, I see reverential fear of God comes in different phases.

Before you are saved, there is the fear of God's judgment or his wrath. You are not going to heaven if you do not accept his son as your savior. After you are saved, you should have another type of fear. That is the fear of God's disapproval to the way you are living on this earth. To me, the fear of God would come from the fact that I love God so much that I would not want him to look at me with any type of disapproval. I want him to think when he sees me, "That's my boy. I sure am proud of him." It would be the biggest shame not to hear the words, "Well done, good and faithful servant." The other phase of fearing God would be the judgment that would come against me if I was to continue to live in sin. Yes, you still will not get thrown in the lake of fire, but you barely escaped the flames. I would rather live in a cave in heaven than in hell, but I would rather stay in the mansions that Jesus promised us that were there.

The lack of reverential fear in the land is the cause of many of the problems that we have in and outside of the church. Outside of the church, people are not responsible for obeying Jesus's command, even though they do have a law written on their heart. They haven't committed to Jesus as being their Lord, so they don't have God's grace. Their biggest problem concerning themselves is accepting Jesus as their savior. But inside the church, they have made the commitment, and they do have his grace. So why is there so many transgressions going on in the body of Christ?

We must think that God is a fool if we think that we can be on this earth with hard hearts, living like the unsaved do, and not think God knows what is going on or that he doesn't care. Yet we continue to live in our sin or not be conscious of this sin, but now we are also transgressing deliberately without any fear of the consequences of our actions.

Not "loving our neighbor as ourselves" is a transgression that a lot of people are not consciously doing. But there are the transgressions that are being committed in the body of Christ that Christians are obviously doing, but today they are trying to justify that it is okay. This way, they don't have to live their lives in fear of condemnation. These are the same transgressions that are in the world, and the world is trying to get everyone to accept also. It really doesn't matter if the world accepts them as a transgression or not. If God calls it a transgression, then it is a transgression. Besides, for the Christian, we are to "be in the world, not of the world."

Paul wrote this to the Romans.

> Besides this you know what [a critical] hour this is, how it is high time now for you to wake up out of your sleep [rouse to reality]. For salvation [final deliverance] is nearer to us now than when we first believed [adhered to, trusted in, and relied on Christ, the Messiah].
>
> The night is far gone and the day is almost here. Let us then drop [fling away] the works and deeds of darkness and put on the [full] armor of light.
>
> Let us live and conduct ourselves honorably and becomingly as in the [open light of] day, not in reveling [carousing] and drunkenness, not in immorality and debauchery [sensuality and licentiousness], not in quarreling and jealousy.
>
> But clothe yourself with the Lord Jesus Christ [the Messiah], and make no provision for [indulging] the flesh [put a stop to thinking about the evil cravings of your physical nature] to [gratify its] desires [lusts]. (Romans 13:11–14 AMP)

We are supposed to set the standard for the world to see, not live by the standard that the world has set. Jesus tells us in Matthew 5:13–16,

> You are the salt of the earth. But if the salt loses its saltiness, how can it be made salty again? It is no longer good for anything, except to be thrown out and trampled underfoot. You are the light of the world. A town built on a hill cannot be hidden. Neither do people light a lamp and put it under a bowl. Instead they put it on its stand, and it gives light to everyone in the house. In the same way, let your light shine before others, that they may see your good deeds and glorify your Father in heaven.

Jesus didn't say, "I want you to be the salt and light." He said, "You are the salt and light of the world." Now what you do with that is up to you. But if you choose to lose your saltiness or hide your light from the world, then are you not like the nine lepers who didn't consider anyone else but themselves?

So if we are not setting the standard, then we are again being disobedient to the command that God expects from us. How can we be the salt and light of the world when we are living no different than the world does?

Paul told us in 2 Corinthians 10:3–6 (AMP) (emphasis added):

> For though we walk [live] in the flesh, we are not carrying on our warfare according to the flesh and using mere human weapons.
>
> For the weapons of our warfare are not physical [weapons of flesh and blood], but they are mighty before God for the overthrow and destruction of strongholds,
>
> *[Inasmuch as we] refute arguments and theories and reasonings and every proud and lofty thing*

that sets itself up against the [true] knowledge of God; and we lead every thought and purpose away captive into the obedience of Christ [the Messiah, the Anointed One],

Being in readiness to punish every [insubordinate for his] disobedience, when your own submission and obedience [as a church] are fully secured and complete. (2 Corinthians 10:3–6 AMP)

So I tell you this, and insist on it in the Lord, that you must no longer live as the Gentiles do, in the futility of their thinking. They are darkened in their understanding and separated from the life of God because of the ignorance that is in them due to the hardening of their hearts. Having lost all sensitivity, they have given themselves over to sensuality so as to indulge in every kind of impurity, with a continual lust for more.

You, however, did not come to know Christ that way. Surely you heard of him and were taught in him in accordance with the truth that is in Jesus. You were taught, with regard to your former way of life, to put off your old self, which is being corrupted by its deceitful desires; to be made new in the attitude of your minds; and to put on the new self, created to be like God in true righteousness and holiness.

Therefore each of you must put off falsehood and speak truthfully to his neighbor, *for we are all members of one body.* "In your anger do not sin": Do not let the sun go down while you are still angry, and do not give the devil a foothold. He who has been stealing must steal no longer, but must work, doing something useful with his own hands, that he may have something to share with those in need.

> Do not let any unwholesome talk come out of your mouths, but only what is helpful for building others up according to their needs, that it may benefit those who listen. And do not grieve the Holy Spirit of God, with whom you were sealed for the day of redemption. Get rid of all bitterness, rage and anger, brawling and slander, along with every form of malice. Be kind and compassionate to one another, forgiving each other, just as in Christ God forgave you. (Ephesians 4:17–32 NIV) (emphasis added)

So what kind of transgression are we talking about? There are so many to choose from, and one is not worse than the other. Transgressions are born of sin (love of self), and God abhors sin. He cannot be associated with sin, so all transgressions are equally bad, and since there are so many different types of transgressions going on in the church, a book could be written on that alone. Stealing, pride, adultery, fornication, pornography, divorce, abortion, homosexuality, gospel for gain, and the list goes on and on of the different transgressions that can be found in the church.

Paul tells us in Colossians 3:5–11:

> Put to death, therefore, whatever belongs to your earthly nature: sexual immorality, impurity, lust, evil desires and greed, which is idolatry. Because of these, the wrath of God is coming. You used to walk in these ways, in the life you once lived. But now you must also rid yourselves of all such things as these: anger, rage, malice, slander, and filthy language from your lips. Do not lie to each other, since you have taken off your old self with its practices and have put on the new self, which is being renewed in knowledge in the image of its Creator. Here there is no Gentile or Jew, circumcised or uncircumcised,

barbarian, Scythian, slave or free, but Christ is all, and is in all.

I think it should be read again in *The Message* just to make sure that we understand it.

> And that means killing off everything connected with that way of death: sexual promiscuity, impurity, lust, doing whatever you feel like whenever you feel like it, and grabbing whatever attracts your fancy. That's a life shaped by things and feelings instead of by God. It's because of this kind of thing that God is about to explode in anger. It wasn't long ago that you were doing all that stuff and not knowing any better. But you know better now, so make sure it's all gone for good: bad temper, irritability, meanness, profanity, dirty talk.
>
> Don't lie to one another. You're done with that old life. It's like a filthy set of ill-fitting clothes you've stripped off and put in the fire. Now you're dressed in a new wardrobe. Every item of your new way of life is custom-made by the Creator, with his label on it. All the old fashions are now obsolete. Words like Jewish and non-Jewish, religious and irreligious, insider and outsider, uncivilized and uncouth, slave and free, mean nothing. From now on everyone is defined by Christ, everyone is included in Christ.

Again, how can we be "salt and light" to those in the world when we are living the same way that they are? We are supposed to have lives that are different than those who are in the world. We are supposed to be setting the standard, not letting their standard set us! We are not to live by their standard—the standard of "If it feels good, do it." Think about what the world thinks if they watch the life of Christians that are no different than them. "Why do I need God? Why should I get involved with the Christians, they don't live any differently than I do?" We set ourselves up for hypocrisy criticism when we are not living the life that we preach.

If you truly loved an organization that you were a member of, you wouldn't do anything to ruin the reputation or the image of that organization. It is the members of the organization that are there to meet their own personal needs who don't really care what happens to the organization's image. As long as they get what they want, then everything is okay.

The same thing happens in the church. I believe that the reason transgressions are continuously growing in the body of Christ is that they are not realizing that they are loving themselves or, as the Bible states, due to the hardness of people's heart. People get focused on always trying to take care of the almighty "self," and they lose the focus on what the Lord taught us to do, which is to be a servant to others. They get hard hearts, and they are more concerned about themselves than they are about other people. So this in turn hurts the image of the body of Christ to the nonbelievers, who are supposed to be attracted to us.

Now when you have good Christians trying to live a good life, they are judged as hypocrites based on the actions of what the Christians who are choosing to live in sin are doing. I believe that if you truly *loved* God, you would not be able to drag his image, as well as the image of his children through the mud.

RELATIONSHIP NOT RELIGION

There is "the new and up-and-coming thing" that states, "It's about relationship, not religion." I understand their theory that there are those in the church that has created an atmosphere and practice that makes the importance of doing certain rituals and deeds more important than the relationship based on God's grace. They create a Jesus-plus-works theology that can leave anyone with the uncertainty of knowing whether they are saved or not. Problem with this is it leaves people with the fear of never doing or being enough or with the feeling of failure that "I will never be good enough, so why try?" Unfortunately, even though the RNR have merit to their theology, this thinking also creates a problem of the proverbial "throwing the baby out with the bathwater." I believe that this is another topic that finds itself trying to be water without the wet. Could the two be inclusive of each other, where there is an "and" approach rather than an "either or"?

The definition of religion as described on Dictionary.com is as follows:

1. a set of beliefs concerning the cause, nature, and purpose of the universe, especially when considered as the creation of a superhuman agency or agencies, usually involving devotional and ritual observances, and often containing a moral code governing the conduct of human affairs

2. a specific fundamental set of beliefs and practices generally agreed upon by a number of persons or sects: *the Christian religion; the Buddhist religion;* the body of persons adhering to a particular set of beliefs and practices: *a world council of religions*

3. the life or state of a monk, nun, etc.: *to enter religion*
4. the practice of religious beliefs; ritual observance of faith
5. something one believes in and follows devotedly; a point or matter of ethics or conscience: *to make a religion of fighting prejudice*

Isn't that the definition which we who call ourselves Christians live by? Isn't the bases of our beliefs based on the virgin birth, death, and resurrection of our Lord and Savior Jesus Christ? Didn't he ask us to remember him in the partaking of the Eucharist? Haven't we been given a call to action to live in a way that we are to love one another as we love ourselves, or rather as Jesus loved us? This is our religion.

What is the basis of the relationship if you don't have the basis of the religion? Doesn't that mean we could have a so-called relationship that isn't based on any truth? If he wasn't born of a virgin, he couldn't have been the Messiah. If he wasn't raised from the dead, he wouldn't be around to have a relationship with any way. At best, he would only have been a good teacher who really turned out to be a crackpot who died because he claimed he was the Son of God.

I understand where they are coming from, because there are scores of people that go to church on Sunday and live like the world on every other day of the week. I would even say that their statement would be more valid if they were to say that it's "not about ceremony, it's about relationship." People do have a tendency to go to church out of obligation, go through the ceremonies in the church house, and feel that makes them good for the week. Not much difference than the Jews who used to bring their sacrifice to the temple. So in that manner, yes, it is more about relationship than religion, if you are referring to ceremony.

But Jesus didn't condemn ceremony either. He participated in Jewish tradition while on this earth. Matthew 23:1–4 says,

> Then Jesus said to the crowds and to his disciples: "The teachers of the law and the Pharisees sit in Moses' seat. So you must be careful to do everything they tell you. But do not do what they

do, for they do not practice what they preach. They tie up heavy, cumbersome loads and put them on other people's shoulders, but they themselves are not willing to lift a finger to move them."

He didn't say, "Don't participate in the ceremonies"; he said, "Do it, just don't do it the way they do it with their hard hearts." When it came to tithing, he said in Matthew 23:23–24,

Woe to you, teachers of the law and Pharisees, you hypocrites! You give a tenth of your spices— mint, dill and cumin. But you have neglected the more important matters of the law—justice, mercy and faithfulness. You should have practiced the latter, without neglecting the former. You blind guides! You strain out a gnat but swallow a camel.

What he didn't say was "Don't do it." He said you should have been doing it, but you did it without doing the more important things. Isn't justice, mercy, and faithfulness given out of love?

It becomes a very slippery slope when you tell people that they can have the relationship but don't stress the importance on the religion. Is their relationship based on truth? I hear scores of people tell me that they can have a relationship with Christ without the church. That is a half-truth at best.

The early church was about a community of people walking out their faith together. They supported each other, not only spiritually or emotionally but also financially and physically. The writer of Hebrews tells us in Hebrews 10:24–25,

And let us consider how we may spur one another on toward love and good deeds, not giving up meeting together, as some are in the habit of doing, but encouraging one another—and all the more as you see the day approaching.

So nowhere is it stated that we should have a relationship with Christ without the relationship of others in the church.

Besides, how are you learning the truth without the help of others? I get it in this day and age we can almost hear every type or literally every preacher or priest there is on the net. So you can literally be living in a Bible study all day long. But which preacher do we usually like to listen to? The one who gives us what we want to hear? Do we know that what they are teaching is truth or what we need to hear?

Besides, it is in the church that you will receive the encouragement to walk it out. I haven't found much encouragement to live as Christ taught us to out in the world. Being with other Christians should be a source of strength to help you in your difficult times when you are dealing in the world. If not, you might want to hang around a different group.

I remember a conversation that I had with a lady friend of mine, and I said something about being a Christian. She said, "I can't stand Christians because they are nothing but a bunch of do-gooders."

I said, "We are not about being good enough. It's all about being forgiven. We do good because it's just the right thing to do."

She said, "Oh wow, I could live with that." Today she is walking with the Lord. Do we have to change the truth or even water it down to attract the lost?

I understand that what is trying to be done is getting people who are shy of religion to find their relationship with Christ. But I think what happens is that you lose the importance of understanding Christian history and the truth of God's saving grace. This is all based on our religion. I fail to see where trying to eliminate the one will increase the other. I believe in giving them the truth and let the Holy Spirit work out the rest.

HOLY SPIRIT

So how do we turn this around? How can we live this life without living it in sin? We rely on the help of the Holy Spirit.

> We do, however, speak a message of wisdom among the mature, but not the wisdom of this age or of the rulers of this age, who are coming to nothing. No, we declare God's wisdom, a mystery that has been hidden and that God destined for our glory before time began. None of the rulers of this age understood it, for if they had, they would not have crucified the Lord of glory. However, as it is written:
> "What no eye has seen,
> what no ear has heard,
> and what no human mind has conceived"—
> the things God has prepared for those who love him—
> these are the things God has revealed to us by his Spirit.
> The Spirit searches all things, even the deep things of God. For who knows a person's thoughts except their own spirit within them? In the same way no one knows the thoughts of God except the Spirit of God. What we have received is not the spirit of the world, but the Spirit who is from God, so that we may understand what God has freely given us. This is what we speak, not in words taught us by human wisdom but in words

taught by the Spirit, explaining spiritual realities with Spirit-taught words. The person without the Spirit does not accept the things that come from the Spirit of God but considers them foolishness, and cannot understand them because they are discerned only through the Spirit. The person with the Spirit makes judgments about all things, but such a person is not subject to merely human judgments, for,

"Who has known the mind of the Lord so as to instruct him?"

But we have the mind of Christ. (1 Corinthians 2:6–16)

Outside of salvation through Christ, I believe one of the major differences between Christians and non-Christians is basically this: non-Christians have God's Spirit around them; Christians have God's Spirit in them. Here is what I mean.

Before we accept Christ as our Lord and Savior, the Holy Spirit is around us trying to reveal God to us. This is seen when we are sharing the Gospel with the unsaved and everything seems to click with them right then. There are many times that I have shared Christ with someone who didn't receive him with me but did at a later time because something that I said clicked with something someone else said, and they had that aha moment. I have seen this work vice versa also.

I would like to think that I was able to say something that was so compelling that I was able to get them to see the light. But that is so far from the truth that it makes this thought funny. What happens is the fact that the Holy Spirit is working through me because he is in me, and he is at the same time talking to that person's spirit so that the person connects with the message that they hear.

Do they always accept it? I wish they did, but the answer is no. I have never had a person not somehow click with what is going on, but I have seen many people refuse it, mainly because they didn't want to change what they liked about their lifestyle. I have heard from many people that they plan to someday, just not today. They want to continue the love relationship that they are having with themselves since this is their way to fulfillment.

But once we have accepted Christ as our Lord and Savior, then what is the purpose of the Holy Spirit? I think the answer is that he becomes our personal power source.

The results always seem to turn out the same when we are trying to stop living in sin all by ourselves. We don't have the ability to do so. The harder I try to live like Jesus did or by what he taught, the less I am able to. Look at Paul's description of it in Romans 7:15–25:

> I do not understand what I do. For what I want to do I do not do, but what I hate I do. And if I do what I do not want to do, I agree that the law is good. As it is, it is no longer I myself who do it, but it is sin living in me. For I know that good itself does not dwell in me, that is, in my sinful nature. For I have the desire to do what is good, but I cannot carry it out. For I do not do the good I want to do, but the evil I do not want to do—this I keep on doing. Now if I do what I do not want to do, it is no longer I who do it, but it is sin living in me that does it.
>
> So I find this law at work: Although I want to do good, evil is right there with me. For in my inner being I delight in God's law; but I see another law at work in me, waging war against the law of my mind and making me a prisoner of the law of sin at work within me. What a wretched man I am! Who will rescue me from this body that is subject to death? Thanks be to God, who delivers me through Jesus Christ our Lord!
>
> So then, I myself in my mind am a slave to God's law, but in my sinful nature a slave to the law of sin.

I really do love Paul! I have no way of explaining this feeling that I am schizophrenic. But I believe Paul does it as best as it can be said. What makes me feel even better is the fact that I am not alone. If there is no other person who has ever lived on this planet who had to deal with this, at least I am not alone, because Paul did too.

I can remember countless times that I have decided to change a negative aspect in my life. Let me emphasize that I really wanted to change whatever it was in my life that I felt I need to change or I was being led to change. It seems like the minute that I would make the decision to change it, all hell breaks loose.

It's like when you decide to do something. Let's say you decide you need a new car, so you start to investigate what you might like, or maybe it is that you are trying to decide on a certain color. The next thing you know, everywhere you go, that certain car or color is there. You hardly even noticed it before, but now it seems to be everywhere you look.

It seems to happen the same way with me every time that I am trying to change a behavioral pattern in my life. I make a decision to not do something or start to do something and then the thing that I decided not to do is *right there in your face*.

I learned the hard way that under no circumstance, no matter what the situation is, do you ever ask God for patience. He doesn't give you patience. What he does is give you circumstances where you have to choose if you are going to be patient or not. And you don't get just one situation either. They come at you like a rapid firing machine gun so fast that you don't know what else to do but hit the dirt.

That is where the Holy Spirit comes in. I don't have to do it anymore; he does it through me.

I grew up on a farm where we had cattle, and we farmed a couple hundred acres. Usually we had a dog in the place, and it technically was a haven for them. They had acres of farm ground, and in addition, they had several acres of woods to get lost in. They could go running for hours through the woods and fields.

Even though this seems like it was all fun, there was a price that had to be paid. You see, in all the running and having fun, they would get in their hair things like cockle burrs and beggar's lice. Also, they were attracting a nasty little critter that looks at anything that has blood in them as a meal, which we call ticks.

Now the cockle burrs, and beggar's lice would get into their hair, and if you didn't get them out, they would eventually cause the hair to matt. But the ticks, well, as we all know, they just sucked the life right out of them.

So we would have to take time and check the dogs for ticks and pull the burrs and lice out of their hair. Now you would think that this didn't bother them because the frequency of this occurrence was so high. But actually, the opposite was true—they hated it. While we were in the process of cleaning them, we would have to constantly tell them to lay down, sit still, and knock it off the whole time that we were actually doing them a favor.

But they were not looking at it as if it was a favor. They were squirming all over place while looking at us, as to say as best they could, "Why are you doing this to me?"

Well, it has finally dawned on me that I am just like one of those dogs. See the Holy Spirit had spoken to my spirit to receive the truth of the Bible, but now he had to pick the ticks, burrs, and lice off me, which I picked up when I was running wildly around in love with me. The difference is that what I was doing for the dogs was an outside job, but what the Holy Spirit is doing is an inside job.

Some of the things are like the burrs and the lice that get in and tangle things up. But there are other things in me that actually are sucking the life right out of me. So the Holy Spirit is actually doing me a favor, but I am not seeing it that way. It hurts, and it is irritating, so can't we just leave it alone? Oh, come on.

Here is the difference: The Holy Spirit is gentle, and he isn't demanding me to sit still, lie down, or anything else. He comes along and tries to pick out the ticks and burrs, and when I resist, he backs off until I am ready to have him work again.

Here is the thing: The longer he continues to work on me, the better I feel in the long run. So each time that he starts to work on another issue, I get a little more cooperative. Then together, we can accomplish more in a shorter period.

But if I resist him and will not cooperate with his work, then he will leave me alone, in which the burrs will continue to tangle and the ticks continue to suck the life out of me. He will continue to coax me to let him finish his work, but if I argue too much, then he will eventually leave me alone. This why I believe Paul tells us in Ephesians 4:30 (AMP),

> And do not grieve the Holy Spirit of God [do not offend or vex or sadden Him], by Whom you were sealed [marked, branded as God's own, secured] for the day of redemption [of final deliverance through Christ from evil and the consequences of sin].

So how do you grieve him?

Imagine that you are trying to train a child to do something, like potty training or staying seated while they eat. No matter what you do or say, they just refuse to cooperate. Now think of yourself being the child, and I believe you will get the picture. We grieve him when we constantly fight him while he is in the process of cleaning us up and molding us to be like Christ.

When we use to make molds of the rocks I spoke about earlier, when you pulled the mold off the rock, little pieces of the rocks would stay in the mold. We would have to go and pick out of the mold all the little pieces; otherwise, it would distort the mold.

The Holy Spirit is the mold-maker who works on molding us to be like Christ. He takes out our hard heart and gives us a heart of flesh. Ezekiel 36:26 says, "I will give you a new heart and put a new spirit in you; I will remove from you your heart of stone and give you a heart of flesh." Since we have this new heart, we can now love just like God loves—outwardly, instead of ourselves. But the Spirit continues to pick the little fragments out of us left behind from our stony heart so that our mold of Christ isn't distorted.

If when we died and the only thing that would happen is we were put into the ground, I would still be a Christian because of the relationship that I have with God through his Spirit. Paul tells us in

1 Corinthians 3:16, "Don't you know that you yourselves are God's temple and that God's Spirit dwells in your midst?" This is what I depend on the most just to get through the day every day, no matter what the circumstance. Even if I am doing something that I have done a million times before, then I still depend on the Spirit's help. Why?

Well, would you rather do something in God's power and might or on your own? Let me give you a small example in my life.

I grew up with the mouth of a sailor. (Sailors sure get a bad rap about their mouth when everyone uses the same words.) Now even after I had become a Christian, I was still using four-letter words, and they were not words like the word *love*. I was attacked of conscience of the fact that I was using them, which I believe was the prompting of the Holy Spirit. But no matter how hard I tried, I couldn't stop myself from doing so.

I realize that there are those that do not see a problem with this. Again, we don't live under a law, but Paul did say in Colossians 3:1–10 (emphasis added):

> Since, then, you have been raised with Christ, set your hearts on things above, where Christ is, seated at the right hand of God. Set your minds on things above, not on earthly things. For you died, and your life is now hidden with Christ in God. When Christ, who is your life, appears, then you also will appear with him in glory.
>
> Put to death, therefore, whatever belongs to your earthly nature: sexual immorality, impurity, lust, evil desires and greed, which is idolatry. Because of these, the wrath of God is coming. You used to walk in these ways, in the life you once lived. But now *you must also rid yourselves of all such things as these: anger, rage, malice, slander, and filthy language from your lips.* Do not lie to each other, since you have taken off your old self with its practices and have put on the new

self, which is being renewed in knowledge in the image of its Creator.

Now I'm not sure what was considered filthy in the Greek language, but I just feel that cuss words of today would probably qualify. So I figure if I was going to commit and error, I would do so on the side of not using them.

I then asked God for help in not using them. Nothing happened overnight. At first, I started to notice every time I used one. Then I would have the ability to stop myself from saying one before I did. Over a period, I realized that I was no longer using those words, and I didn't for many years.

But then, I found myself in a situation where I was involved with people who used them like it was their first language. They couldn't complete a sentence without at least one cuss word in it. If the sentence consisted of one word, it was the cuss word. Over a period, I found myself slipping every once in a while. Before long, I was using them more often, and before you know it, I was not able to stop using them again. I was like, how did I get here again? And no matter how hard I try, I haven't been able to stop.

Now I play a part in all of this. I have to be willing to be led by the Spirit in order to stop. The Spirit doesn't force me to participate, but he will lead if I will follow. If I try and fight the Holy Spirit's guidance, then eventually he will quit trying to lead me until I am willing to humble myself and ask him to lead again. I will stop using them.

Now you may think that this is not a big deal, but let me show you another time that I was being changed by the Spirit and seen it in two different ways.

When I use the restroom in public places, I always use the towel to open the door handle because there are men out there, and who knows maybe women too, who don't wash their hands when they finish using the restroom, which is disgusting for the rest of us. It bugs me that men think that they have no reason to wash their hands when they just got done handling their private parts. What's worse is then they want you to shake their hands when you see them outside of the restroom. If I see you leaving the restroom and you didn't wash your hands, I will not shake your hand, and I will tell you why. I don't care if you feel that your parts are clean, mine are always too, but I won't impose that on you. I will wash my hands so you don't need to worry about it.

Now that I am done with that soapbox, I said all that to explain this. Not all public places would leave the trash can close enough to be able to open the door and throw it away. So I would either throw it at the trash can or toss it on the floor. It was not my fault that they were so ignorant that they didn't have a trash can close enough by.

Well, the Holy Spirit started to convict me to pick up the towel when I missed the trash can or tossed it on the floor. It used to drive me crazy to have to go to the trash can and do it again or pick it off the floor. So I got better at making it in the can, or I go over to the door, open it, run to the trash can, and throw it away and then run back to the door before it closed, or whatever I could not to get it on the floor. Actually later, I got smarter, and I would carry it out the door and look for a trash can outside. Luckily everyone is getting smarter and leaving the trash cans by the door, so I don't have to work so hard at it.

Now you may wonder why the Spirit would even care about such a trivial thing as this. But think of the mind-set behind it. I wouldn't care that the towel would hit the floor since they paid other people to pick it up. So wasn't I making that person's job harder for them? Don't I get upset when people make my job unnecessarily harder than it has to be? Is that the way that you love your neighbor? Isn't all my actions supposed to be Christlike? Remember, Christ lived his whole life for the benefits of mankind. Where does that give me any room to decide that I can pick and choose where I want to and where I don't want to do the same?

There might be the argument that this is just my own mind or conscience that is making me do this. I am sure that there are people out there who do the same thing without the so-called guidance of the Holy Spirit. I mean let's face it, they don't believe in Jesus, yet they are doing the same thing, so where do I get off in saying this is from the Spirit?

Well, I can't do justice by trying to explain how it is that the Spirit leads you other than by my own experiences and to say that once you recognize him leading you, it becomes easier for you to see. But I have an example that I believe will show his moving on a larger scale.

I used to attend several rock concerts BC (before Christ) since I enjoyed the music and the party that went with it. If you have ever been to one, or even to something like a county fair, you know that there is always a sea of trash that covers the ground left behind. It's like with the event, comes the trash.

Well, in St. Louis, they held a huge Christian rock concert for a whole day consisting of several bands, and the whole event was free. It was a great time, and there were several tens of thousands of people there attending. Naturally when it was over, there was a massive rush to leave, so my friends and I decided that there was no point in rushing. We would wait, and when the majority of the crowd left, we would leave also, but without the hassle.

When we finally decided to leave, I saw something astonishing. I mentioned to my friends to look and tell me what they saw. They didn't see anything. I told them to pay attention to the ground, yet they still didn't see it. Finally I said, "Look, there is little to no trash on the ground." Everywhere we looked, it was all picked up. Everyone had taken their trash to the trash cans, and since they were full, they neatly stacked all their trash around the cans.

There may be a chance that my picking up the trash on the bathroom floor was just me, but how can you give it to chance that tens of thousands of people did it at a type of event that no one ever does it at? There was nothing said from stage such as "Okay, everyone, clean up after yourself," or "We are Christians, let's not leave a mess." Nothing was said at all. Also, there is no way that one person did it and then another followed, which started a chain reaction, because there are people at secular concerts that are responsible and pick up behind them too. There had to be something greater than mankind to create that big of a reaction; I would find it hard that anyone could assume it to chance.

That is how the Spirit works to bring glory to God. He changes us from the inside out and stops the love relationship with ourselves. When we follow his lead, and we now are loving others; then, it brings glory to God and shows the world how he created us to live.

Jesus tells us in John 14:15–20,

> If you love me, keep my commands. And I will ask the Father, and he will give you another advocate to help you and be with you forever—the Spirit of truth. *The world cannot accept him, because it neither sees him nor knows him.* But you know him, for he lives with you and will be in you. I will not leave you as orphans; I will come to you. Before long, the world will not see me anymore, but you will see me. Because I live, you also will live. On that day you will realize that I am in my Father, and you are in me, and I am in you.

LOVE IS THE ANSWER

The world also believes that love is the answer. The reason they believe this is because it is written on their heart. Think about all the things that are of this world that actually proclaim this answer.

Here is a couple of verses of The Beatles's song written by John Lennon and Paul McCartney "All You Need Is Love":

All you need is love, all you need is love,
All you need is love, love, love is all you need.
All you need is love (all together now)
All you need is love (everybody)
All you need is love, love, love is all you need.

Here is the thing: They just can't seem to live a life of love or not for a very long or continuous time. Why? For the same reason that Paul, me, and you can't when we are trying to do it in our own power. They will not accept Jesus for who he is, so then they are not able to have the power of the Holy Spirit to change their hearts. Yet you can tell that unsaved people still have the answer written in their heart. Why do people who know that they are going to die want to make things right before they die?

What I mean is this: There are people who live their whole life selfishly and self-serving, but when they realize that they are on death's doorstep, they try to do an about-face. Why don't they just die the same way they lived? They had to know that the way they were living wasn't right, or why the sudden revelation?

The way that the world tries to change itself is to get more education, thinking the smarter they become, the more they will be able to overcome the problems of the world. Yet the solutions that they continue to come up with are not new solutions at all. They are solutions that create more problems than the solutions fixed or they are solutions that have been regurgitated from the past that didn't work then either. But what is more amazing is that now Christians seem to be following their suit.

Paul tells us in Romans 2:28–29,

> A person is not a Jew who is one only outwardly, nor is circumcision merely outward and physical. No, a person is a Jew who is one inwardly; and circumcision is circumcision of the heart, by the Spirit, not by the written code. Such a person's praise is not from other people, but from God.

So the better question then would be, if Christians have a circumcised heart or a new fleshly heart, why are they living like the world who still has a heart of stone? Is it because they are continuously grieving or ignoring the Spirit, because they are determined not to give up their love relationship with their self?

I don't look for the world to change. We have the power of God living in us to do it, not them. Besides, we are not supposed to be changing for the world. We are supposed to be changing for the glory of God. His glory will change the world.

Look at what Jesus prayed right before he gave up his life.

> After Jesus said this, he looked toward heaven and prayed:
>
> "Father, the hour has come. Glorify your Son, that your Son may glorify you. For you granted him authority over all people that he might give eternal life to all those you have given him. Now this is eternal life: that they know you, the only true God, and Jesus Christ, whom you have sent. *I have brought you glory on earth by finishing the work you gave me to do.* And now,

Father, glorify me in your presence with the glory I had with you before the world began.

"I have revealed you to those whom you gave me out of the world. They were yours; you gave them to me and they have obeyed your word. Now they know that everything you have given me comes from you. For I gave them the words you gave me and they accepted them. They knew with certainty that I came from you, and they believed that you sent me. I pray for them. *I am not praying for the world, but for those you have given me, for they are yours.* All I have is yours, and all you have is mine. And glory has come to me through them. I will remain in the world no longer, but they are still in the world, and I am coming to you. Holy Father, protect them by the power of your name, the name you gave me, so that they may be one as we are one. While I was with them, I protected them and kept them safe by that name you gave me. None has been lost except the one doomed to destruction so that Scripture would be fulfilled.

"I am coming to you now, but I say these things while I am still in the world, so that they may have the full measure of my joy within them. I have given them your word and the world has hated them, for they are not of the world any more than I am of the world. My prayer is not that you take them out of the world but that you protect them from the evil one. They are not of the world, even as I am not of it. Sanctify them by the truth; your word is truth. As you sent me into the world, I have sent them into the world. For them I sanctify myself, that they too may be truly sanctified.

"My prayer is not for them alone. I pray also for those who will believe in me through their message, that all of them may be one, Father, just as you are in me and I am in you. May they also be in us so that the world may believe that you have sent me. I have given them the glory that you gave me, that they may be one as we are one—I in them and you in me—so that they may be brought to complete unity. Then the world will know that you sent me and have loved them even as you have loved me.

"Father, I want those you have given me to be with me where I am, and to see my glory, the glory you have given me because you loved me before the creation of the world.

"Righteous Father, though the world does not know you, I know you, and they know that you have sent me. I have made you known to them, and will continue to make you known in order that the love you have for me may be in them and that I myself may be in them." (John 17:1–26) (emphasis added)

So when we have circumcised hearts, live Spirit-led lives, and are living in unity acting as one, then we let the world know that Jesus was sent and that the Father loves them. Why? Verse 23 said it, "May they be brought to complete unity to let the world know that you sent me and have loved them even as you have loved me."

Matthew Henry says this about verse 23:

He pleads the happy influence their oneness would have upon others, and the furtherance it would give to the public good. This is twice urged (John 17:21): That the world may believe that thou hast sent me. And again (John 17:23): That the world may know it, for without knowledge there can be no true faith. Believers must

know what they believe, and why and wherefore
they believe it. Those who believe at a venture,
venture too far. Now Christ here shows,

1.) His goodwill to the world of mankind
in general. Herein he is of his Father's
mind, as we are sure he is in every
thing, that he would have all men to be
saved, and to come to the knowledge
of the truth, 1 Tim. 2:4; 2 Pet. 3:9.
Therefore it is his will that all means
possible should be used, and no stone
left unturned, for the conviction and
conversion of the world. We know not
who are chosen, but we must in our
places do our utmost to further men's
salvation, and take heed of doing any
thing to hinder it.

2.) The good fruit of the church's oneness;
it will be an evidence of the truth of
Christianity, and a means of bringing
many to embrace it.

[1.] In general, it will recommend
Christianity to the world, and to
the good opinion of those that are
without. First, the embodying of
Christians in one society by the
gospel charter will greatly promote
Christianity. When the world shall
see so many of those that were
its children called out of its family, distinguished from others, and
changed from what they themselves
sometimes were—when they shall
see this society raised by the foolishness of preaching, and kept up
by miracles of divine providence

and grace, and how admirably well
it is modelled and constituted, they
will be ready to say, We will go with
you, for we see that God is with you.
Secondly, the uniting of Christians
in love and charity is the beauty of
their profession, and invites others
to join with them, as the love that
was among those primo-primitive
Christians, Acts 2:42, 43; 4:32, 33.
When Christianity, instead of caus-
ing quarrels about itself, makes all
other strifes to cease,—when it cools
the fiery, smoothens the rugged, and
disposes men to be kind and loving, courteous and beneficent, to all
men, studious to preserve and promote peace in all relations and soci-
eties, this will recommend it to all
that have any thing either of natural
religion or natural affection in them.

[2.] In particular, it will beget in men
good thoughts, First, Of Christ:
They will know and believe that
thou hast sent me, By this it will
appear that Christ was sent of God,
and that his doctrine was divine, in
that his religion prevails to join so
many of different capacities, tempers, and interests in other things,
in one body by faith, with one heart
by love. Certainly he was sent by the
God of power, who fashions men's
hearts alike, and the God of love
and peace; when the worshippers
of God are one, he is one, and his

name one. Secondly, Of Christians: They will know that thou hast loved them as thou hast loved me. Here is,

1. The privilege of believers: the Father himself loveth them with a love resembling his love to his Son, for they are loved in him with an everlasting love.

2. The evidence of their interest in this privilege, and that is their being one. By this it will appear that God loves us, if we love one another with a pure heart; for wherever the love of God is shed abroad in the heart it will change it into the same image. See how much good it would do to the world to know better how dear to God all good Christians are. The Jews had a saying, "If the world did but know the worth of good men, they would hedge them about with pearls." Those that have so much of God's love should have more of ours.

There is constant talk about how do we reach the unsaved. I have a noble idea. Why don't we go back to the throne, give up our sin, and live our life as we were created to? Then we can be the living example of Christ.

There is a story about someone looking at heaven and hell. He opens the door to hell and see a huge table with every kind of food you could imagine on it. But when he looked at the people around the table, they were sad and miserable, and they looked like they were starving to death. What he noticed was that their arms had no elbows, so they had no way to get the food into their mouth.

Then he opened the door to heaven. They had the same table with the same food and no elbows. Yet they were all having a blast, because they were all feeding each other.

What if the people in hell would be able to crack the door open far enough that they could see into the door of heaven and see how they were getting along? Would it not possibly give them an idea that they had the wrong heart in the matter and that they might need to change?

Look at the national impact the Amish school shootings had on the country at the West Nickel Mines School. The same day of the shootings, members of the community were comforting the members of the shooter's family, and they attended the funeral of the shooter for additional support. Then they collected donations to support the shooter's family.

The sad fact is that even though this kind of forgiveness had an impact on the world, it didn't have a lasting one, and I believe that it was in part that the Amish have such a different lifestyle that it didn't seem real to the rest of the nation. If this same type of thing happened to a Christian monastery and the monks were to act the same way, the average person would not be so affected by it because their life is so structured, they expect the monks to forgive. But what would happen if all the Christians in the nation were like this? Would this not make a serious impact on everyone else?

Right now, the Christians that the world is exposed to say prayers, go to church, give some of their money, and are possibly a little more honest than they are. But think about it, doesn't the world give some of their money to help others in need? Aren't they honest in some of their dealings? What are we doing that is so much different than they are, especially in this country?

Maybe that is all the world needs to see in us is the fact that we have a new heart and we are living in the power of the Creator and not in the power of our education, employment, wealth, or anything else. Wouldn't this give God the glory?

Now I am not discounting all the good and holy things that are done because of the body of Christ. They are all wonderful things, but what we are dealing here with is the condition of the heart of all of the body of Christ. You can't just look at certain parts and not look at the rest of the body.

When a man is in the hospital for a heart attack, the doctors don't say, "Well, his heart is bad, but he still has good hands and feet." No, without a healthy heart, the whole body is in danger. This is to address the unhealthy heart that the body of Christ has. It is not beyond repair any more than a man that has had a heart attack is beyond repair. With the right type of diet and the right amount of exercise, that man can live a long, productive life.

The same goes for the body of Christ. If we will remember that we are made in the image of God, whose character is love, and that we were created to give it the way that God gives it, which is outwardly to God through others, and when we use our love for ourselves, we have separated ourselves from God, and we are now living in sin, then we can change the condition of the body's heart. When we change the condition of the body's heart, then we will be obedient to the way that God wants us to live, and the whole world will know the God that we love and will be able to see him as he is through us.

The way that we do this is by repenting of loving ourselves, which is sin. We accept the sacrifice for that sin that the Father has freely given us, which is through the death of his son Jesus Christ. We then surrender our life to Jesus and ask him to be Lord of our life. We then make a commitment to follow the guidance of the helper given to us who is the Holy Spirit. When we live in the guidance of the Holy Spirit, we will no longer be in bondage to ourselves, but we will be under the easy yoke of our Lord and Savior Jesus Christ. Under this new life, with the new heart, we will learn how to love the way God loves—loving outwardly to him through others, which is the way that he created us. Then we will find a life that we have never imagined and could never attain on our own, and it will all bring glory to the only one that is worthy to receive it.

I believe this is the Gospel that the early church preached and somehow got lost over time.

ABOUT THE AUTHOR

Steve Stellhorn is a brother in Christ from southern Illinois who is learning to live life as Christ instructed us to one day at a time. He also enjoys riding, traveling, building, and working on his Harleys and other vehicles.

CPSIA information can be obtained
at www.ICGtesting.com
Printed in the USA
FSHW022206090221
78343FS

9 781636 303260